Praise for the *Best Food Writing* series

"An exceptional collection worth revisiting, this will be a surefire hit with epicureans and cooks."—*Publishers Weekly*, starred review

"If you're looking to find new authors and voices about food, there's an abundance to chew on here."—*Tampa Tribune*

"Fascinating to read now, this book will also be interesting to pick up a year from now, or ten years from now."—Popmatters.com

"Some of these stories can make you burn with a need to taste what they're writing about."—*Los Angeles Times*

"Reflects not only a well-developed esthetic but also increasingly a perceptive politics that demands attention to agricultural and nutritional policies by both individuals and governments."—*Booklist*

"This is a book worth devouring."—*Sacramento Bee*

"The cream of the crop of food writing compilations."
—*Milwaukee Journal Sentinel*

"The book captures the gastronomic zeitgeist in a broad range of essays."—*San Jose Mercury News*

"There are a few recipes among the stories, but mostly its just delicious tales about eating out, cooking at home and even the politics surrounding the food on our plates."—*Spokesman-Review*

"The next best thing to eating there is."—*New York Metro*

"Stories for connoisseurs, celebrations of the specialized, the odd, or simply the excellent."—*Entertainment Weekly*

"Spans the globe and palate."-

"The perfect gift for the liter
—*Pittsburgh Post-Gazette*

best *Food* WRITING 2010

best Food WRITING 2010

Edited by

HOLLY HUGHES

Da Capo
LIFE
LONG

A Member of the Perseus Books Group

Set in 11 point Bembo by the Perseus Books Group

Cataloging-in-Publication data for this book is available from the Library of Congress.

First Da Capo Press edition 2010
ISBN 978-0-7382-1381-1

Published by Da Capo Press
A Member of the Perseus Books Group
www.dacapopress.com

Da Capo Press books are available at special discounts for bulk purchases in the United States by corporations, institutions, and other organizations. For more information, please contact the Special Markets Department at the Perseus Books Group, 2300 Chestnut Street, Suite 200, Philadelphia, PA 19103, or call (800) 255-1514, or e-mail special.markets@perseusbooks.com.

10 9 8 7 6 5 4 3 2 1

CONTENTS

SOMEONE'S IN THE KITCHEN

STOCKING THE PANTRY

HOME COOKING

THE RECIPE FILE

PERSONAL TASTES

INTRODUCTION

by Holly Hughes

"But I'm *already* a *Bon Appétit* subscriber!" I protest to the faceless woman at the other end of the phone line. "I have *years* left on that subscription."

"Then we'd be happy to extend your *Bon Appetit* subscription to . . . [she checks her records] . . . the year 2025." A drecky 1970s pop single flashes into my mind: *In the year twenty-five twenty-five, if man is still alive. . . .* At that moment, I feel a desperate impulse to reach my arm through the telephone and inflict grievous bodily harm on that poor innocent customer service operator.

"Look, I've got nothing against *Bon Appetit*," I plead. "It's a perfectly lovely magazine; that's why I already subscribe to it. That's not the point. *I want my Gourmet back.*"

A moment of silence at the other end, then a weary sigh. "Yes, ma'am. I understand. We're hearing that from a lot of our customers."

I have the feeling that if Condé Nast had listened to its readers instead of high-priced business consultants, that landmark culinary magazine—founded in 1949—would still be with us. (It still *is* alive, in fact—at least online.) I reckon that once management has paid top dollar for consultants, they're pretty much obligated to follow that expensive advice, no matter how drastic. But still— terminate *Gourmet*? It just doesn't make sense.

THE DEATH KNELL of *Gourmet* hung gloomily over my head as I began reading for this 2010 collection. Was food writing a dying art, I wondered?

Yet the more I read, the more baffled I became. Maybe I'm not one-hundred-percent subjective—after all, I spend a goodly amount of time every year trying to read all the food writing that is produced, in books, magazines, newspapers, and Web sites. (Best job *ever.)* Still, I've been doing this for eleven years now, and from where I sit, food writing seems more robust than ever.

Reading the flurry of articles that came out right after the announcement, I saw that the Condé Nast executives who shuttered *Gourmet* were quick to blame the new media. The market for a culinary magazine has been steadily dwindling, they claimed, because readers nowadays generally pick up all their recipes on the internet. The very thought of this depressed me. And yet lo and behold, a few days later, I found my own teenage daughter sauntering into our kitchen, cradling her laptop, declaring that she'd found a recipe for blondies to bake for her basketball team. Could the Condé Nast suits be onto something, I wondered?

Over the new few months, as her baking hobby flowered (or should I say floured?), the long row of cookbooks on our counter went untouched while she downloaded recipe after recipe—cupcakes, s'more bars, snickerdoodles. But then her birthday came around, and lo and behold, she came home from a surprise birthday dinner loaded down with cute pastel-colored cookbooks, courtesy of her girlfriends (smart girls, to keep the stream of baked goods flowing). She's been happily discovering new recipes out of them ever since.

The reality? Those quick-and-easy recipe sites could never be a satisfying replacement for *Gourmet,* not by a long shot. Sometimes we need the gorgeous photographs, the colorful writing—and yes, the glossy ads to flip through. And the more I read, the more I sensed that serious foodies demand more than ever that a recipe be meticulously tested, as the *Gourmet* test kitchen did so superbly; they want at least a little write-up, to give the recipe context, to explain the food's history. I realized that it was time to add a new section to the book, **The Recipe File**, to compare and contrast different takes on this question, from Adam Gopnik's essay on browsing through cookbooks (page 264), to Monica Bhide's reflections on the value of simplicity in a recipe (page 294).

It's so easy to blame the internet for everything—the death of good writing, the death of measured thought, the death of the printed word, blah blah blah. The truth is, a great deal of today's best food writing is being published online, on a proliferating number of serious food Web sites. With production costs eliminated (no paper, no printing press, no trucks hauling physical copies across the country), these sites can devote themselves to smart writing. With readers posting comments online, articles launch conversations; on timely topics, stories can be published immediately. My must-read list now includes chow.com, egullet.com, culinate.com, leitesculinaria.com, seriouseats.com, zesterdaily.com, among others. Nearly a dozen of the pieces selected for this year's edition were published first on Web sites—and that doesn't even begin to dip into the crazy number of independent blogs out there, or the many online components posted by traditional print media.

Food writing has moved out of its "ghetto," no longer confined to food magazines or the dining sections of newspapers (once referred to as "the women's pages"). Such general interest magazines as *The New Yorker, The Oxford American, The New York Times* magazine, and salon.com have all gone so far as to set up annual food issues. Even the esteemed Atlantic Monthly magazine has added an entire section for food issues (dubbed the Atlantic Food Channel) on atlantic.com. A well-established core of professional food writers is thriving nowadays, getting more mainstream respect than ever. Jonathan Gold, page 68, broke the barrier first by winning a Pulitzer Prize—and I'll bet he will soon be followed by others.

Indeed, provocative food journalism has never been more widely read, with food matters increasingly on the public's mind—thanks not only to Michael Pollan's bestsellers, but to solid reporting by journalists such as Jane Black (page 175), Kim Severson (page 329), and former *Gourmet* contributor Barry Estabrook (page 34). That may be a chicken-and-egg situation—reporting whips up concern, which in turn creates more of an audience for more reporting, and on and on in an upwards spiral. Whatever the cause, the section that leads off this book, **Food Fights**, seems to overflow every year. This year, I found the carnivores and vegetarians still duking it out (as if that issue could ever be settled), but several other stories reveal an interesting backlash against the locavore trend (check out Jonathan Kauffman's comparison of locavores to indie rockers, page 16, or Brett Martin's lunatic plan to become a "global-vore," page 2) and a pushback against restaurant ratings—whether compiled by critics, chef judges, or "ordinary" diners.

These days, fluff is out and substance is in. Just look at The Food Network, which had long been trending toward puffy entertainment programs. This year, however, its executives launched a second channel, the Cooking Channel, that puts the focus back on hands-on cooking and kitchen technique (which is where food television began, after all—remember Julia Child?).

When you get right down to it, food writing can't be a dying art when there are so many talented practitioners of the art working at the top of their game. While no one writer has made it into all eleven editions of *Best Food Writing*, this year's edition features 11 writers whose work merited inclusion five or more times in that 11-year span. That's a broad range of writers, from New Englander John Thorne (page 251, nine times) and quintessential Southerner John T. Edge (page 163, also nine times) to the humor of David Leite (page 290, eight times) and the gonzo restaurant reviews of Jason Sheehan (page 149, eight times). But to really judge the state of food writing today, just look at how many new voices are in this year's book. A handful of these, of course, are topnotch writers known for fiction or other nonfiction subjects, who only occasionally turn their attention to food—writers like Adam Gopnik (page 264), Charlotte Freeman (page 276), Wright Thompson (page 286), and Jonathan Safran Foer (page 38). Yet with 22 of the writers in this year's *Best Food Writing*—nearly half of the contributors—being first-time entrants, that's a lot of dynamic new food writers. They include J. Kenji Lopez-Alt (page 241), Oliver Strand (page 227), Mike Sula (page 192), Rowan Jacobsen (page 170), Kevin Pang (page 81), and Rachel Wharton (page 157), not to mention guys with a wholly different day job, such as William Alexander (page 232) and Robert Dickinson (page 203).

My conclusion? We may still have to mourn *Gourmet*'s demise, but the rumors of food writing's death have been greatly exaggerated. I'd go even farther—I think food writing is enjoying a spectacular moment in the spotlight. May it last forever!

Food Fights

The FedEx Meal Plan

By Brett Martin

From *GQ*

Throwing locavore virtue and carbon footprint caution to the winds, Brett Martin embarked on a quixotic—and very funny—project: To feed himself exclusively with delicacies overnighted from around the globe.

One should never underestimate the value of having friends whose first reaction, when you tell them you need two In-N-Out burgers FedExed from Los Angeles to New York by the next morning, is to ask, "Regular or Double-Double?" These are the kind of people with whom you'd be happy to share either a foxhole or a beer, the kind you know would be willing to follow you into any drunkenly conceived, willfully contrary, possibly wrongheaded, and certainly obnoxious scheme you'd manage to dream up. I happen to have such friends (their names are Oliver and Sarah), and I happened to have had such a scheme. It was this: To get as many foods as possible, from all over the world, sent overnight via FedEx to my home in Brooklyn.

The idea came to me in the midst of one of those morose funks that occur after coming home from a long trip. In this case, I had just returned from Kuala Lumpur, Malaysia. I was moping about the house, dreaming of days spent stuffing myself with a mix of Chinese, Indian, and Malay delicacies unavailable anywhere else in the world.

Or were they? I suddenly thought, snapping awake. Unavailable? What did that even mean in these modern times? After all, there is a network of couriers crisscrossing the globe twenty-four hours a day and promising that anything can be anywhere within a matter of hours. So if I craved a bowl of pork noodles of the sort sold on the streets of Kuala Lumpur, why would I need to do something as old-fashioned as actually *visiting* Kuala Lumpur? International shipping may be pricey, but as a way to stay connected to the tastes of the planet during lean times, it seems downright affordable.

But hold on, I hear you say, doesn't this fly in the face of every single thing going on in the food world? Aren't all right-minded eaters supposed to be eating locally, seasonally, and sustainably, with exquisite sensitivity to each ingredient's provenance, genetic heritage, and carbon footprint?

Well, yes. And the truth is that this made the prospect all the sweeter. It's not that I don't believe in local and seasonal eating. Clearly, the food revolution of the past two decades has made eating in America a better experience for mouth, belly, and conscience alike. The thing is, the revolutionaries have won. Ask any young chef for his or her culinary philosophy and you'll hear *localandseasonal* rattled off so fast the actual words lose all meaning. Even behemoths like McDonald's and Walmart have made concessions to the values of Alice Waters and Michael Pollan.

Obviously, the local eating orthodoxy can produce some astonishing food. At Blue Hill at Stone Barns, Dan Barber's restaurant-cum-farm in Westchester County, New York, I had a midwinter dinner that, as far as I could tell, eschewed even such alien ingredients as lemon and black pepper. The meal was very beige and utterly transcendent. But like any other true belief that morphs into a tired buzzword, it's worth taking a step back to note how, in the hands of lesser talents, this one may be abused: by the restaurateurs who believe that having a chalkboard menu crammed with farm names is more important than such incidentals as serving well-prepared, delicious food. By the chefs who equate the word *local* with a chance to up a dish's price by $10. By those who would deny us the joy of acknowledging that we live in a gastronomic Age of Miracles. (Tomatoes in January? In biblical times, you could get five or six apostles for less.) And by the just plain silly; it was about the time that my local bar started listing Blue Diamond Almonds on its snack menu with the added parenthetical "(Sacramento)" that it became clear that local, seasonal, and their attendant food pieties had jumped the line-caught, fair-trade, National Marine Fisheries Service-approved mako shark.

And the fact remains that, at Blue Hill, I had paid hundreds of dollars for the privilege of enacting a massive historical reversal. For the rest of human existence, as Felipe Fernández-Armesto points out in *Near a Thousand Tables: A History of Food*, one mark of a great empire has been the diversity of its ingredients and the distances they traveled to get to the elite. The Greeks and Romans filled their tables with spices, fruits, and fish from the farthest reaches of their dominions. Peter the Great had oysters brought to then landlocked Russia from thousands of miles away, packed in sawdust and hay. The British once cooled their gin-and-tonics in Calcutta with ice cut from Massachusetts ponds.

Moreover, the movement of food across vast distances is literally the story of civilization: Science, mathematics, religion, language— all were carried around the world in ships' holds filled with bread-fruit, amid camel caravans carrying spices, even (or especially) in shipping containers crammed with frozen McDonald's beef. *Loca-vore* may have been the 2007 *New Oxford American Dictionary* Word of the Year, but there's already been a word for those whose diets are restricted to seasonal items grown in their immediate area: That word is *peasant*.

Which, anyway, is what I told myself at 8:30 A.M. when the doorbell rang and I signed for a miraculous purple-white-and-orange package containing two slightly wilted but—or was it my imagination?—still warm In-N-Out Double-Doubles.

HERE WERE MY CRITERIA: I would only order foods that were distinctly of their place. They would have to be *meals*—prepared dishes that, in the past, I would have been obliged to travel to distant lands to taste, or taste again. My dream list included *bollito misto* from Ristorante Diana in Bologna, Italy—dripping cuts of meat boiled together in a rich stock and served with spicy fruit mustards; muffuletta sandwiches from New Orleans's Central Grocery Co.; Allen & Son Barbeque's North Carolina pulled pork; parsley-and-marrow salad from St. John Restaurant in London; *tonkatsu* from Tokyo; the Malaysian noodles.

I suppose I expected the food purveyors of the world to hear my plan, join hands, sing a round of "It's a Small World," and make haste for the nearest FedEx drop box. This may have been a touch naive. For one thing, I do not know the words for "obnoxious scheme" in Italian or Japanese. Even in English, the mission proved a hard sell. "That is not something we could possibly do," the general manager of St. John politely told me. A Bolognese friend living in Brazil burned up his Skype account trying to find a willing partner for me in Italy. "How to FedEx a *bollito misto* . . . this is a very difficult thing to explain," he reported sorrowfully. My contact in Toulouse, France, from whom I'd hoped to procure some cassoulet, had only this to say: "Clearly you are not familiar with the French."

Old Europe, though, was nothing compared with the legal issues here at home. The great traders of old dealt with sandstorms and tsunamis; they crossed mountain ranges and dodged pirates. My challenge was to navigate something called the *Animal Product Manual*, a publication of the United States Department of Agriculture. I would have rather had pirates.

At 931 pages, filled with more acronyms than a Tom Clancy novel and more appendixes than a hospital Dumpster, the *APM* suggests a national strategy of protectionism through sheer confusion. The regulations on receiving gifts of food from foreign countries are buried somewhere among categories like "Powdered Bird Guano That Lacks Certification" and "Commercial Importations of Cooked Meat or Meat Products of Poultry and Fowl from a Country or Region of Origin Known to Be Free from HPAI (H5N1) but Affected with END." What little I could decipher was not promising: Malaysia, it seemed, was, by USDA standards, a veritable pit of disease, home to "Classical Swine Fever, Exotic Newcastle Disease, Foot and Mouth Disease, Highly Contagious Avian Influenza and Swine Vesicular Disease." It was amazing I'd even gotten out alive. Sweden was hardly better. That meant that, even for those dishes allowed into the United States, each ingredient would need to be accompanied by reams of paperwork. When I got USDA senior staff veterinarian Christopher Robinson on the phone to assess my plan, he cut handily through the bureaucratspeak: "I'd say it was pretty much impossible," he said.

Indeed, while I can't vouch for dirty bombs, bales of heroin, or hordes of illegal aliens, I can report that our nation is perfectly safe from rogue shipments of suckling pig. That's what I had coming in from the restaurant Ibu Oka in Ubud, Bali, where the pigs are stuffed to bursting with shallots, garlic, lemongrass, and chilies, bathed in coconut oil, and then hand-turned before a blazing pyre of coffee branches. The beauty of that description left customs agents at JFK unmoved: The shipment was destroyed. Likewise the noodles from KL. And a shipment of *cotechino* and tortellini from Italy. I began picturing my house as one of those little bases in Missile Command: Packages of delicious food came arcing toward my door from around the world, only to get zapped at the last moment by authorities at various ports of entry.

CLEARLY, ANOTHER APPROACH was needed. But while I plotted, I contented myself with domestic goodies.

I am convinced that we are evolutionarily equipped with a gene that makes us forget the taste of North Carolina barbecue, just so we continue to eat lesser foods in between pulled-pork sand-wiches. The tub of Allen & Son pulled pork that showed up at my door was every bit as good in Brooklyn as it had been the last time I'd gorged on it at the restaurant's vinyl-covered tables in Chapel Hill. In college my friends and I had stonedly fantasized about be-ing able to be faxed a pizza. This wasn't quite that level of instant gratification, but it was damned close. Even the hush puppies worked well when reheated, though owner and eponymous "Son" Keith Allen had categorically refused to send coleslaw, saying it wouldn't survive the trip in a condition up to Allen & Son stan-dards. "Sometimes I worry about you northern boys," he told me.

From New Orleans came the muffuletta, a stacked sheaf of sliced Italian meats and sharp provolone stuck between enormous rounds of bread and topped with olive relish. Central Grocery would only send frozen batches of three, but they arrived in sur-prisingly perfect shape. From New Mexico came a Tupperware container of green-chili enchiladas from a legendary shack of a diner called El Farolito; from Kansas City, Missouri, an order of Arthur Bryant's "burnt ends," the most grizzled, succulent parts of a smoked brisket.

When a friend said, "You're pretty much obliged to get something from Chez Panisse," a shiver went up my spine. Alice Waters's Berkeley restaurant is considered the very cradle of the *localandseasonal* movement. When I asked them to FedEx me a dinner, I was told, with just a hint of Northern California frost, "We don't do takeout." Undeterred, I dragooned a friend who happened to be visiting the Bay Area into visiting for dinner, ordering an extra entrée, and then shipping me the doggie bag. The short ribs with polenta were delicious but unmistakably tinged with guilt. I felt like I had just peed on Jacques Pépin.

Meanwhile I thought I'd solved my international-shipping issues. It occurred to me that the USDA doesn't police fish, so I switched to an all-seafood menu, carefully avoiding any knowledge of ingredients like chicken stock and butter to preserve deniability when it came to customs forms. From Stockholm's great fish emporium, Melanders Fisk, I ordered fatty Baltic herring—strömming—pickled, and then breaded and fried. Then I breathlessly watched the FedEx tracking page. Sure enough, after a short delay at JFK, the package was released. Emboldened, my Malaysian contact and I switched to a noodle dish that seemed to pass the USDA test—*prawn mee*, a deeply spicy, complex seafood soup. I watched as it was picked up in KL, cleared Malaysian customs, and took wing across the Pacific. The next morning, it reached Anchorage and then . . . stopped, held for inspection.

The herring, on the other hand, had arrived accompanied by tiny plastic containers of dill-laced mashed potatoes, lingonberry preserves, and drawn butter. (Oops.) It was delicious, but standing and eating in my kitchen, once the FedEx man had departed, I felt my vague misgivings begin to solidify. Was the strömming really as good as when I'd had it as a picnic on an island just north of Stockholm, drenched in sunshine and surrounded by happy, pink vacationing families? By the same token, the muffuletta had been a fantastic sandwich, but did it really measure up to the one I'd had in New Orleans years before—the time I'd snuck out of the hotel while my girlfriend napped to greedily down a sandwich between the second of two lunches and a dinner at Galatoire's? Cervantes may have said that hunger was the best sauce, but context runs a close second.

I was even more conflicted about the dishes from places I *hadn't been*. For years I'd planned on making the trip to Kansas City to visit Arthur Bryant's. Now, why would I ever go to Kansas City? Or to the lonely high-desert crossroads where El Farolito sits? Even the massive carbon footprint of the sourdough loaf I'd had sent from San Francisco wasn't quite enough to assuage my melancholy at having never been to San Francisco. I wondered if Peter the Great dreamt of standing knee-deep in the Atlantic, gathering his own oysters.

This, I realized, is the dark side of the miracle of everything, everywhere, all the time—something we experience in realms well beyond food. Once upon a time, I would wait for the chance to hear Bessie Banks's original version of "Go Now." Banks's version would come on the radio about once every two years. Each time I happened to catch it, I would all but have to pull the car over to let her stirring, wounded vocal wash over me. Now, of course, I own a digital copy of the song, but I have to keep it off my iTunes playlist for fear of it popping up on shuffle too often and losing all meaning.For that matter, there's the rush of emotion that occurs every time a long-lost friend suddenly pops up on Facebook, which is so frequently that I've been forced to either stop caring or lose whole days in a paralysis of nostalgic reverie. For all its legitimate political, environmental, and gastronomic rationales, it may be that the *localandseasonal* movement is more about this, ultimately conservative, impulse than anything else—a self-protective retrenchment in the face of too much available data.

I HAD ONE MORE free-floating bit of data out there, one more missile aimed at my front door. Day after day, I tracked the status of my *prawn mee*, greeted each time by the dread message: clearance delay. By the time it arrived, it had been a week since it was packed, some 10,000 miles away.

Unwilling to give up the dream, I called the Customs and Border Protection office in Anchorage. Had the package been refrigerated? I asked the woman who picked up the phone. No, she said, it had probably just sat in a fenced-in portion of the warehouse.

Hmm. What temperature would she say it was?

"Um, this is Alaska. It's pretty cold," she said. "I sometimes wear a sweater in there."

Dear reader, is it weird that I still thought long and hard about eating the soup? Even though the package was starting to smell downright funky? Well, consider this: The last time I'd smelled *prawn mee* had been at a sidewalk market filled with *all kinds* of smells—cooking meat, fermented fish paste, ripe-to-bursting melons, tropical flowers. Maybe the funky aroma had been just one perfectly healthy note in the symphony? More to the point, isn't that where it belonged?

I'd like to think that it was this, rather than fear of salmonella, that brought my experiment to an end. I took a deep breath and dumped the soup down the sink. I took care to bale up the FedEx box for recycling. Then I went out for a slice of pizza.

Forgotten Fruits

By Gary Paul Nabhan

From *Saveur*

In his 2001 book *Coming Home To Eat*, chronicling a year of eating only out of his own Arizona foodshed, Gary Nabhan established himself as a leader of the local-eating movement. Here he trumpets the virtues of heirloom fruits and vegetables.

The morning sun is just peeking over the ridges of the Great Smoky Mountains when my friend Jim Veteto and I spot a tall, old-looking apple tree arching over the side of the road. We swerve our rented PT Cruiser to the shoulder and get out. I'm hoping that these apples are Nickajacks, a rare variety that's native to the highlands of western North Carolina, so I climb onto the hood of the car and reach as high as I can, to no avail. Jim, who is quite a bit taller than I am, climbs up next to me and, with a little bounce, snatches a low-hanging fruit. He holds it up for inspection. I can tell from its color and irregular shape that it's not the apple we were searching for.

"It kind of looks like a Mudhole," I say, referring to a type once known in these parts for making excellent apple butter. I take a bite. Nope, this one is creamier, with whiter flesh. It's probably just one of the countless unnamed apple varieties you find in the wild around here.

"That's the dilemma," Jim says, as we get back in the car. "There are so many heirloom varieties that have adapted to the micro climates up here, it's hard to identify them." Jim, a lanky, bearded 35-year-old, knows a lot about heirloom fruits and vegetables. He works with the Southern Seed Legacy in Athens, Georgia, an organization devoted to preserving the seeds of heirloom plants in order to restore some of the genetic diversity that industrial agriculture has eroded over the years.

On this trip, though, we're looking for forgotten fruits, not seeds. We're on a late-summer apple search-and-rescue mission in the mountains of North Carolina for a program I started five years ago called Renewing America's Food Traditions (RAFT). With the help of Slow Food USA and six other national organizations, RAFT aims to restore foods and culinary customs that are at risk of disappearing. Apples are at the top of our list because hundreds of varieties have become extinct in recent decades, their unique physical attributes and tastes basically erased. For a food that is as iconic and as essential to the American culinary canon as the apple, it's tragic that only 11 varieties—out of the estimated 14,000 that evolved from the seeds English settlers brought to North America from Europe—constitute 90 percent of all apple consumption in the United States.

The remaining 10 percent includes heirloom apples of all shapes and sizes—some gnarly and spotted and downright ugly, others with graceful silhouettes and glossy skin. Some are honey sweet; others have a lip-puckering, tannic tartness; still others fall somewhere in between, offering subtle hints of flavors most people may never have tasted in an apple. They have names like Gloria Mundi, Seek-No-Further, Ohio Nonpareil, Brushy Mountains Limbertwig, and Shiawassee Beauty, to name just a few. The problem is that fewer and fewer of these fruits are commercially available, as one small orchard after another is let go to seed and the names of the old varieties are forgotten. The trees themselves may survive, in the wild or on private property, but the histories of their fruit are often a mystery.

That's one reason why I'm driving the country roads of North Carolina with Jim: I'm meeting up with locals who can help me identify and revive some of these old varieties. This part of Appalachia—particularly the region known as the Southern Highlands, which encompasses the Blue Ridge, Great Smoky, and parts of the Cumberland and Allegheny mountain ranges—is one of the richest apple habitats in the country. Today, somewhere between

800 and 1,000 distinct heirloom varieties still grow in the area's hills, coves, and hollers—more kinds, by some counts, than are found in all the other regions of North America combined.

Not surprisingly, the cooks of Appalachia have strong preferences for specific varieties—one kind for eating fresh, another kind for applesauce, another for pie, and so on—that are different from the tastes of their Northern neighbors. "In the North, they eat a tart and cook a sweet. Here in the South, it runs the other way," one North Carolina orchard owner tells us. "I love a tart Jonathan in a pie, but those Yankees might use an apple as sweet as a Golden Delicious." What's more, Appalachian cooks use apples in some altogether remarkable ways. Outside Appalachia, you just aren't going to find so many people inclined to make fried apple pies, cook sliced apples with chopped cabbage, spread applesauce between layers of molasses cake, stew sun-dried apples, or dip ringlike slices of apples in batter and fry them to make fritters.

To PEOPLE LIKE ME, the disappearance of old apple varieties—like the die-off of an animal species—represents a profound loss, in terms not just of botanical diversity or rural cultural history but also of the way we eat. The striking, unusual flavors and cooking properties possessed by these heirloom apples simply don't exist in supermarket varieties. And yet, Jim reminds me, most people in the region don't refer to the apples growing in their midst as heritage breeds. "Most people around here have never heard the term *heirloom* applied to plants," Jim says. "They just call them old-timey apples."

In the broadest sense, an heirloom apple is any distinct, named variety of the fruit that has been passed down in a family, community, or culture for generations. To preserve an heirloom variety, it's not enough simply to save the seeds, though. Growing a genetically identical apple requires a concerted, calculated effort: you have to graft cuttings from one tree onto the rootstock of another. The reason for this is that seedling apple trees—those that grow in the wild from seed—produce fruit that's essentially a hybrid of their parents and therefore a new kind of apple. This explains why countless varieties of the fruit, believed to have originated in Kazakhstan thousands of years ago, have propagated around the world.

My trip in North Carolina with Jim is just the latest in a series of travels I've made with RAFT collaborators over the past few years to seek out, recruit, and learn from other Southern heirloom apple preservationists. These journeys have led me to forge friendships with some remarkable people—orchard keepers, historians, cider makers, horticulturists, and others. Perhaps the most respected scholar among them is the North Carolina apple historian Creighton Lee Calhoun Jr., who spends the majority of his waking hours matching forgotten fruits to their names. Since he took up this pursuit, in 1982, he has discovered and identified a slew of apples formerly thought to be extinct, relying mostly on horticulture books, old nursery catalogues, and archival illustrations. Calhoun, a soft-spoken 75-year-old, has also brought 300 heirloom varieties into cultivation at nurseries he consults with across the South.

In 1995 Calhoun published *Old Southern Apples* (McDonald & Woodward Publishing Company), a lavishly illustrated tome that has become a bible for apple preservationists. Not only does the volume present detailed descriptions of some 1,600 varieties, but it also brings to life the people and histories wrapped up with this food. He describes the significance of the apple in the rural South, where, before the days of refrigeration, it was the only fruit that could be kept through the cold months "to provide a taste of freshness." Of the elderly Southerners who helped him reclaim knowledge about heirloom apples, Calhoun writes, "They remember storing boxes of apples through the winter in unheated rooms . . . how those apples perfumed the whole house. They recall drying apple slices on a tin roof, and they can tell you how to make cider and vinegar. But most of all, they remember the incomparable taste of a freshly picked southern apple . . . baked right on the tree by those long, hot southern summers."

Other apple preservationists I've met are more recent converts to the cause. One of them, Tom Brown, is a retired chemical engineer in his late 60s who lives in Clemmons, North Carolina. In 1998 he became obsessed with a juicy variety believed to be extinct called Harper's Seedling and has since tracked down at least seven locales near his home where those apples once grew; he took cuttings from a surviving tree in the area just before it died and grafted them onto trees on his property in hopes that, in a few years, he will have a steady supply of the delicious fruits. His hunt for Harper's Seedling has fueled a passion for finding other forgotten varieties. These days, Brown estimates, he racks up at least 20,000 miles a year on Southern back roads, traveling as far as Kentucky, Virginia, and Tennessee to chase down leads given to him by old-timers at regional festivals, people who grew up with these apples and can remember their names and characteristics.

"Time is running out," Brown told me when I ran into him at the Forgotten Fruits Summit, the first annual powwow for apple preservationists, held in Madison, Wisconsin, last March. "I recently picked up a picture I had taken of the six folks who had helped me the most in my search for apples, and I realized that five of them had died."

At that same summit, I met up with another dedicated preservationist: an orchard owner from Boone, North Carolina, named Bill Moretz. His orchard was started by his grandfather in the 1930s and is now home to one of the country's first community supported agriculture projects devoted to promoting apple diversity. Once a week, his customers receive a bag of several different kinds of heirloom apples.

One of their favorites is the Sweet Dixon, a dessert apple that has red-striped skin and crisp, sugary-sweet flesh. The story behind the Sweet Dixon, which was widely thought to have disappeared, goes like this: Seventeen years ago Calhoun got wind that an elderly North Carolina woman had a huge old Sweet Dixon tree on her property that still produced fruit. By the time he arrived at her home to take cuttings, however, the tree had been cut down. Sensing Calhoun's disappointment, the woman managed to find another tree growing nearby, one she remembered from her childhood; he took cuttings and has been growing Sweet Dixons ever since. What Calhoun didn't know until years later—when he was asked by Moretz to identify an old tree growing near his barn—was that the same kind of apple had been growing on Moretz's property all along.

Toward the end of our North Carolina trip, Jim Veteto and I decide to visit Moretz at his orchard. When we arrive, he hands us a couple of Sweet Dixons straight from the tree to sample. Then he picks one for himself and takes a bite. "It's still green yet," Moretz says, "but you can taste all the sugars and the flavors developing." It is clearly one of his favorites, but Moretz, like many other orchard keepers dedicated to bringing back as many old varieties as they can, is reluctant to proclaim the flavor of any single apple to be better than that of others.

Moretz's orchard, which is home to 100 different varieties of apple, is a supremely serene place, a grid of tidily pruned trees in evenly spaced rows that extend over rolling hills. The air is fragrant with fruit, and the grass underfoot is lush. Resisting the temptation to lie down right where I stand and soak up the scene, I follow Moretz as he makes his rounds, stopping before every other tree to examine its apples and the health of its bark, branches, and leaves.

Watching Moretz tend to his orchard of rare fruits, I come to the realization that it's more than nostalgia that drives people like him to keep such historic apple varieties alive. It's the sheer love of the food itself, in all its incarnations, and the joy of sharing them with friends and passing them on to a new generation. "I grow them to embrace the future," he says to Jim and me before we leave. "But it's not enough just to grow them. You have to eat them, too."

AND YOU WILL KNOW US BY THE TRAIL OF GERMAN BUTTERBALLS

By Jonathan Kauffman

From *Seattle Weekly*

Is the food world beginning to see a backlash against the buzzword "locavore"? Kauffman, former food editor for *Seattle Weekly* (he's now at *SF Weekly* in San Francisco), dares to question how a food trend proliferates.

Back in April 2004, Sage Van Wing, then a grass-fed-beef rancher and chicken farmer in northern California, read Gary Paul Nabhan's *Coming Home to Eat*, a chronicle of his experiment to eat only food produced within a 200-mile radius of his Arizona home. "I thought, this guy did this for a year in the middle of the Southwest," Van Wing says. "Surely it ought to be possible to do the same here. So I asked my friend Jessica [Prentice, a chef and cooking instructor] if she'd join in. We picked the easiest month of the year, August, and decided to stick to 100 miles." They got a few more friends to join in, and came up with a catchy word to describe their group: *locavores*.

"Then we wrote a press release for the hell of it," continues Van Wing, now off the ranch and living in Seattle. "We thought, why not invite other people to join us? Within the first couple of weeks, over 800 people had signed up for the challenge. We'd really tapped a vein." In 2007, *locavore* was added to the Oxford American Dictionary. Van Wing and company's 100-mile-diet challenge spawned best sellers like Barbara Kingsolver's *Animal, Vegetable, Miracle*, influenced thousands of menus, and pissed off more than a few people, most of whom didn't realize that the 100-mile diet was meant to be a short-term thought exercise, not a barbed-wire perimeter. The local-foods movement continues to be the largest, most influential food trend in the country.

Those of us who now favor the local over the certified organic certainly do it out of deeply felt beliefs about how to spend our dollars, support producers we trust, protect our bodies from pesticides and *E. coli*, and preserve the planet. But the local-foods movement has also been wildly successful because it taps into the way the indie-rock generation forms its ever-shifting musical allegiances.

When I walk down East Thomas Street to the Broadway Farmers Market every Sunday, fold-up tote in hand, I'm not there to revamp the food system—I'm out to see what's new in the crates this week. Take the Olsen Farms Potatoes stand, with its ever-rotating supply of purple, red, yellow, and white lumps. I remember when Yukon Golds became the darling of early-1990s bistros, but at Olsen's stand I pass them over in favor of varieties like German Butterball, Maris Piper, or Mountain Rose. Never heard of something before? It's going into the little red bag.

When I went seed shopping for the first time this year at City People's in Madison Valley, there were shelves and shelves of Sweet 1000s and Early Girls, which are proven to work in the Northwest climate. But of course City People's doesn't stock only the tried-and-true—there's also a set of rarities for foodie hipsters and the early adopters like me. I spotted a tag on a tomato start that two of *my* friends had just been raving about. There! That was going to be my tomato. Should the slugs not intervene, I foresee a day when I bring my friends fist-size, bright-red tomatoes. Oh, that? I'll say offhandedly. It's a Moskvits. Heard of it? I grew it myself.

Trumpeting a band you're devoted to—or a specific farm's lacinato kale—isn't just about love for the product. It's about making the product part of you. In his book *Buying In*, the *New York Times Magazine* columnist Rob Walker writes about the rise of micro-brands like Barking Irons, whose T-shirts have made it into *Barney's*, *GQ*, and *People*. If you're a Barking Irons consumer, Walker says, the important thing isn't to advertise your possession of the brand to the general public. It's to be recognized by other people who are clued in to the exclusive nature of Barking Irons. Even more important is that when you wear the T-shirt, *you* know you're a member of that elite. The effect reminds me of the tiny pins I affixed to my coats in high school, laying out the contours of my (social) identity as if I were drafting my own astrological chart.

In an age when we're trained from birth to acknowledge brands—and everything becomes a brand—my Moskvits tomato is yet another one. When I dice it up with a bunch of onions and herbs to make salsa fresca, who's going to know that it's a Moskvits? Only me and a few other people in the know. That's a huge part of its appeal.

A food's status has been defined by its rarity since the days when Marcus Gavius Apicius talked up the succulence of flamingo tongues. Black truffles are getting scarcer and more exorbitantly priced by the year, and thousands of people buy Opus One for two reasons: because Robert Parker gives the small-production Napa red great marks, and because everyone around the dinner table will know the bottle cost several hundred bucks.

But there's another kind of rarity valued by generations X and whatever-you-call-the-one-after-mine: specificity. In an age when I can walk into a Sam's Club near my parents' house in the Chicago suburbs and recognize three-fourths of the products from the Capitol Hill Safeway, a potato that I buy off Brent Olsen carries a special aura. It's not a 79-cents-a-pound-on-sale potato, a commodity potato, a shove-this-in-your-mouth potato, a just-a-potato potato. What am I hunting for, exactly? A new flavor, perhaps. A different texture. Something that will taste unique even when I boil it until tender and roll it in melted butter and fresh parsley like I have so many times before—if only because there's a story (farmer, market, name) wrapped around it.

Our generation is addicted to keeping up with the entire planet—in real time, no less—yet we nurse a deep romance for anything that helps us feel anchored in the here and now. And the seasonality of local foods is just as significant an element of their specificity. Asparagus in January used to be a luxury food precisely because it had to be flown in from across the world. Now when asparagus shows up at Whole Foods at least half the year, I prize the fact that I can only get fat Washington spears in April and May. Do my local asparagus taste that much better than November's Chilean asparagus when I toss them with olive oil and shallots and roast them for 20 minutes till they shrivel and brown? No. But I'm prizing something I won't be tasting in July.

Locavores like to believe that their focus on specificity—on *terroir*, on knowing the farmer who sells you your food, on heirloom varieties of vegetables that grow in odd shapes and colors—provides "a sense of connection to their food." Let's face it: Specificity also confers cachet.

It's the same branding magic that occurs in the indie-music scene. As Michael Jaworski—singer for the Cops, owner of Mt. Fuji Records (Maldives, Whore Moans), and Sunset Tavern booker—puts it: "[We're] people who love to find things, people who are attracted to something a little more interesting than cookie-cutter, top-40 mass-media pop. Not that I can't appreciate a well-written pop song, but I feel much better when I'm supporting something more honest and genuine, not huge marketing machines. It feels really satisfying to be part of something that is starting out, and not so huge—when you feel like there's a stronger connection between you and whoever's making the music."

THE SAME REACTION against universal familiarity—the longing for what's novel, direct, and specific—is permeating the early adopters of the wine world. As has been widely documented in films like *Mondovino*, regional varietals are being pushed out around the world in favor of the popular heavyweight grapes. "A lot of regions are being taken over by merlot, cabernet, and chardonnay. It's easier for winemakers to sell their wines abroad," says Shawn Mead, former wine director at Pike Place Market's Campagne, who now works for Louis/Dressner, a New York importer specializing in natural wines from small growers in France and Italy. "The use of modern winemaking techniques, combined with the [wine critics'] point systems," continues Mead, "have conspired to create a very homogeneous style of wine. These wines could be from anywhere. They may taste yummy or lush, but don't suggest, say, the Loire Valley."

In reaction to this trend, the new generation of wine importers, merchants, sommeliers, and wine lovers have become smitten with inexpensive, unique, obscure varietals—falanghina, mondeuse, xynomavro. (Just knowing how to pronounce the name confers a certain status on the drinker.) To achieve even a base level of respect among this crowd, a wine list can't just have chardonnay and syrah anymore, but must include grapes like Argentinian torrontés and Piedmontese arneis. While the phenomenon seems the very opposite of locavorism—pursuing obscure wines from the far reaches of Europe and South America—the passion for specificity is the same. And as with endangered local farmers, your purchase is meant to preserve a legacy and a lifestyle. Says Mead of her company's pineau d'Aunis and mondeuses: "For us, it's important to focus on the endangered species, the spotted owl of the grape world—we have to commit to these varieties now or they'll be lost."

The popularity of these little grapes tends to follow an arc that will be very familiar to observers of the indie-music scene. For example, five years ago, a dry Austrian white named grüner veltliner, whose unique flavor is often described as "licking a stone," started moving out of supergeek circles and into the consciousness of the general food cognoscenti. Articles in wine magazines led to articles in the food sections of newspapers; grüner veltliner went from being offered by the bottle to making by-the-glass lists. Now it's at Fleet Foxes popularity—not top-40, but readily acknowledged by the Pitchfork masses. Who knows: If American winegrowers start planting grüner, someday it may follow in the footsteps of viognier and reach Coldplay status. Meanwhile, the geeks who first embraced it have moved on to touting blaufränkisch and scheurebe.

I'm still a fan of both grüner veltliner and Fleet Foxes, whom I saw, dainty cough, at the Sunset before their EP dropped. I also use my (limited) knowledge of obscure grapes as a secret handshake to get me better service in restaurants. When I ask a waiter about smaller Italian whites or trendy little regions in France, he'll refer me to the restaurant's wine pro, who talks to me longer and more specifically about the food and wine pairing, and often gets enthusiastic about my final selection even if the bottle costs less than

$50. (On the flip side, during visits when I'd just as soon be left alone, I ask for sauvignon blanc. Conversation stops there.)

IT'S BEEN ALMOST FIVE YEARS since the first 100-mile-diet exercise, and quite a band of activists, writers, cooks, and consumers has united behind the belief that the industrialization of American agriculture has gone far too far. We're putting a lot of pressure on the family farms we're now desperate to save, believing that by re-building the local food system we'll do everything from rescuing the ecosystem to lowering our cholesterol counts. But the advocates are butting up against an emphatic objection: that organic and local foods are exclusionary and elitist.

Cost is always at the heart of the skeptics' charge. What's so great about Willie Green's broccoli that I'm supposed to pay $4 for a head of it? Who gives a whit about pasture-raised pork when it's on sale for $4 a pound at Safeway and I have to feed a family of four on $200 a month? The cost argument is the one that local-foods activists are scurrying to refute (at least the ones who aren't floating on the same cloud as Alice Waters). They argue, for example, that CAFO (confined animal feedlot operation) meats are so cheap because of government subsidies. They show evidence that farmers-market apples cost about the same as QFC apples, and that they're less expensive than the mushy, spotted apples at your local convenience stores. Nevertheless, the elitism charge seems impossible to shake off.

Price matters. Of course it does. So does time: Once you get around to subscribing to an affordable CSA box that fills your fridge with antioxidants and idealism every week, how are you supposed to finish up all the calls you need to make that day at work, pick up the kids from their aunt's house, get the dog walked, check your home e-mail, and then figure out what to do with five rutabagas and your fifth bunch of rainbow chard in three weeks before the kids crankily raid the freezer for Dinosaur Nuggets?

It's a legitimate concern for the partisans of locavorism. But food activists have been so focused on refuting it that they're not addressing the subtler ways the locavore movement shapes, markets, and promotes itself. Specificity has become the cornerstone of the appeal of local foods—driving out to Oxbow Farm in Carnation with the kids so you know exactly where your weekly produce box comes from, getting to ask Brent Olsen himself about his Maris Pipers at the market. But the specificity that carries so much cachet for the people who buy into locavorism is exactly the thing that makes it so suspicious to the people who don't. There are thousands of Seattleites who will drop $35 a person on dinner at Outback Steakhouse because they mistakenly think 35th St. Bistro is way too pricey. Even more will pass over the Charentais melons at one farmers-market stand in favor of plain old cantaloupes at another—if they're not already put off, of course, by the gelato carts and freshly made pasta vendors flanking the fruit. If you really want the movement to go mainstream, O locavore, you're going to have to give up the cachet.

The worry is that local foods will follow the same path as organics. Just as Nirvana's hipster cred plummeted the moment Sam Goody started papering its windows with *Nevermind* posters, the mass production of organic food has sullied the purity—and cachet—that we longtime believers relied on the label for. Fewer and fewer people would call certified organic food "elitist," but in exchange for this new populism we've been given corporate lobbying to relax certification standards, organic spinach *E. coli* scares, small-scale farmers dropping their organic certification once the bureaucracy becomes too knotty, organic corn dogs. To many of the people now backing local foods, the word *organic* has all but lost its connotation for being, as Jaworski might say, "honest and genuine."

Not surprisingly, corporate America has its eye on the locavore movement. Two weeks ago, the University Village Safeway mounted a poster in the produce section, part of an initiative that began in northern California a few months ago. The poster, titled "Locally Grown," displays a map of Washington state and lists the names and locations of the Washington farms—most of them large-scale commercial enterprises—that supply Seattle stores. Now, is this a success or a betrayal of the movement? The answer depends, perhaps, on the values you're investing local foods with.

If we're talking about reducing food miles and strengthening your personal 100-mile food system, then it's fantastic to see a major grocery chain prioritize Washington lettuce and carrots. But if "local foods" to you really means opting out of industrial farming, paying farm workers a living wage, buying fragile, deep-red shaksun strawberries instead of those pink monsters from California, and, above all, sustaining that oh-so-ambiguous sense of personal connection to our food—well, then, Safeway's campaign is a cheap stunt that flouts everything good and true.

Van Wing, for one, takes a sanguine stance regarding the future of the movement she helped publicize. "I don't think eating only local food is ever going to be a sensible option for most people," she says. Interregional trade has been important throughout human history, after all. She continues, "I think that there's going to be a large change in our food delivery systems, however, and that change is beginning to happen."

That hipster hunt for a new farmer from Carnation, a rare heirloom variety, or some unpronounceable wine from Austria may just be the new mechanism by which great tastes get discovered and publicized. Lacinato kale, which I first discovered on restaurant menus back in the early aughts, is on every grocery store shelf now, and it's still the kale I buy for sautéing. The heirloom tomato craze that began 15 years ago weaned me forever from February Flavr Savrs from Safeway—not because Green Zebras and Black Princes are the most interesting thing in the market, but because they made me so disgusted with mealy pink tomatoes that I've sworn off them throughout winter. And I take heart that the wine-geek passion for scheurebes and blaufränkisches means that more restaurants will serve wines that are less jammy, more distinctive, and under $40.

Perhaps if the locavore movement is looking for ways to expand without losing its core audience, they should look to the success of one of the world's largest rock bands. In 2007, Radiohead—a band that could prop up the Alaskan Way Viaduct with its platinum records—pulled off a stunt that savvily maneuvered between independent and corporate tactics to market a great product. The band split from longtime label EMI, produced *In Rainbows* themselves, and released the album online, charging customers whatever they wanted to pay. In a *Wired* interview published a couple of months later, Thom Yorke claimed the release made the band more money than all its previous albums together, but acknowledged that that wouldn't have been possible without the decade of corporate marketing that preceded it. Indie? Hardly. Pitchfork gave the album a 9.2 rating anyway.

Soul Food

By Amanda M. Faison
From *5280* Magazine

One new trend in the meat-eating debate: The "ethical"
carnivore, who gets a free pass by being willing to confront
where one's meat comes from. It's a natural angle for food
editor Faison to explore for this Denver monthly, in the heart
of ranch country.

One hundred miles east of Denver, a bison herd roams
the endless horizon. Silhouetted against the frozen January sky, the beasts' woolly humps and sheer size distinguish them
from grazing cattle. We bump along in a dirt-caked GMC truck,
following a crude trail of crescent-shape hoof prints. The herd
hears us coming from over the rise and scatters, thunderous bodies
kicking up dust and churning dried prairie grass into bits. As we
get closer, a curious few turn to face us, tossing their massive,
bearded heads and sputtering puffs of icy breath.

The truck slows to a crawl. We're close enough to see the thick,
tricolored hair tousled and matted by the wind, the black ring of
soft fur that encircles both eyes, the sharp horns, and the coffee-
brown eyes that look both wild and placid in the same stare. I can
read the handwritten numbers on the tags that hang from the bison's left ears.

"She's a beauty, ain't she?" says Larry Higgins, pointing to a cow
affectionately referred to as Pretty Woman for her stunning coat
and large, sculpted head. She doesn't know it, but she's lucky. As
just one of four bison among the 60-plus animals to receive a
name, she'll never be carted off to the packing plant. The Higgins

slaughter about 30 animals a year and sell the meat—jerky, quarters, halves, and whole animals—under the Heart Rock Bison label. "I just go by ear tags," Higgins says. "I don't like to name anything I'm going to eat." With one hand he adjusts his yellow and navy baseball cap. "Heart Rock Bison" is embroidered on the front; "Jesus is Lord" is stitched in blue on the left side.

We inch along, allowing Larry's wife, Jacki, and their third son, Josiah, a 13-year-old with a baby face and wise blue eyes, time to heave bales of hay from the truck bed. The family has raised bison on its fourth-generation ranch near Genoa since 2000. For most of the year, the herd subsists on nutrient-dense natural prairie grasses. In the winter, though, when food is in short supply, the Higgins supplement with hay from their own land and with protein-packed nuggets they call "cookies."

Larry puts the truck in park and digs a handful of the treats out of a bucket on the seat. He instructs me to keep my palm flat and thumb tucked, as if I'm feeding a horse. He also tells me to which bison I should direct my offerings—and to beware of the animal suddenly throwing its 150-pound head. I stick my arm out of the window, and within a couple of minutes a woolly face sizes me up, gives the cookies a sniff, and snatches them with teeth so white and square they remind me of dentures.

Each year, Larry sizes up the herd's calves and then separates the ones that show the most promise of health and vitality. Instead of roaming the ranch's 6,000 acres, the chosen 450-pound youngsters (all now wearing white ear tags) spend their remaining days in a corral. This high-fenced pen—bison can jump up to six feet—is located about 10 yards from the main ranch house in the shadow of a silvery windmill that never seems to stop spinning. Here, the bison freely graze on hay (about 1,800 pounds every five days), corn, and cookies, until they reach an optimal weight of about 1,100 pounds. This takes about a year—sometimes less, sometimes more. "You learn how to eye it," Larry says, directing my attention to his son's hulking yearlings, whose ear tags dangle with #7B and #142. These animals, plus two others, are due for slaughter shortly.

And that's why I'm here, riding around in Larry's truck and chasing the herd. I knew before I arrived this morning that time was short for four of these beasts. I'm here to follow the process, to track an animal from the ranch on which it grazes to the plate on which it ultimately lands.

Josiah, wearing a too-big Carhartt vest and oversize leather work gloves, helps dump a new load of hay into the corral, and he fills up the feeder with corn. "Everyone knows me at school as the person who has buffalo," he says, mentioning that he's the youngest member of the National Bison Association, and that he wants to be a rancher like his dad when he grows up. He also plays football, basketball, baseball, and runs track at Genoa-Hugo Middle School, which is 25 miles away. There are nine kids in his seventh-grade class. "I did have a pet buffalo one year; I loved it," he says, kicking at the dirt with his boot. "Now I don't name them because I don't want to get too attached."

In just a few days, father and son will load four bison—including Josiah's bull (#142) and heifer (#7B)—into a trailer and drive north 168 miles to Pierce. Their destination is the loading dock behind the town's slaughterhouse.

THE PACKING PLANT smells raw and clean, like blood and iron. The cooler's floor is wet with a wash of blood and water mixed with bits of cartilage, bone, and fat. In the middle of the chilled, gaping space, 18 humped bison carcasses—four of which are from the Higgins' ranch—dangle from meat hooks.

Every few minutes, another steaming carcass is thrust through huge swinging doors on the far side of the room. When the doors close, the whirring of saws and power washers abates. Metal rails crisscross the 18-foot-high ceiling so the bodies can be shimmied from one end of the room to the other quickly and easily. It takes about 10 minutes to kill, skin, and dismember an animal.

On a normal day, Double J Meat Packing processes 120 to 150 head of cattle. At 200 head a week, bison make up a third of Double J's annual business. And with the industry growing about 10 percent a year—thanks to more ranchers raising bison and more market demand from restaurants and home cooks—Double J is poised to accommodate the growth.

This morning, dressed in a borrowed cooler-jacket for warmth, a hard hat for protection, and a hairnet and white frock for protocol, I'm trailing Stephen Cave, a U.S. Department of Agriculture meat grader who's worked for the department for 32 years. He's a self-important 54-year-old with brassy blond hair and tan-in-a-bottle skin tone. Today's load, just 18 bison carcasses, is a small job for a guy who averages hundreds of beef cattle a day.

Cave is assessing these 18 specimens for an upcoming competition. After judging, the carcasses will go up for auction as part of the National Bison Association's Gold Trophy Show and Sale at the National Western Stock Show—at which point, they'll land in top bidders' freezers.

He pulls out his clipboard and begins to methodically evaluate each bison. With gloved hands he handles the meat. He pushes and pulls at the whittled-down, 650-pound carcasses, sometimes using all of his body weight to move the animal so he can inspect every angle. He measures the size of the rib-eye, a muscle that runs the length of the animal, with a clear plastic instrument that looks like a protractor. Afterward, he wipes the wet, pinkish residue on his white frock. Cave inspects sheared-off bones for ossification (cartilage hardening into bone indicates age and lowers the score). He pulls out his plastic ruler again and measures the thickness of fat encircling the rib-eye (four-tenths to six-tenths of an inch is ideal). He evaluates the fat and muscle color—the brighter the better. And then he looks for flaws: bruises, lacerations, abscesses, injection sites. He also looks for something called "dark cutter," an indication that an animal was unusually stressed in the moments before slaughter. When that happens, a build-up of lactic acid and insulin turns the meat dark and splotchy. It becomes ground meat.

When he's finished with his assessment, Cave waves me toward the exit; we'll leave the 32-degree Fahrenheit cooler to talk about his findings. He turns, but I hang back for one last look at the stripped-down bodies. Cave may see the carcasses as bits and pieces to be systematically inspected, measured, and judged, but to me the scene is humbling—and oddly beautiful. Only a few hours ago, these patchworks of raw muscle, fat, and bone were vigorous, curious, living creatures. And only a few days ago, I'd stood inside Larry Higgins' holding pen, just a few feet away from four of these animals. Now, their bodies are indistinguishable from the others, but I silently pay them my respects anyway.

YEARS AGO, MY FAMILY owned a sprawling ranch outside of Kirbyville, a town marked by a general store and a dozen houses, in southwestern Missouri. The wooded, smoke-colored landscape was cloaked in American history—the Civil War was fought on many of the 6,000 acres, and the homestead itself was originally owned by the family of author Samuel Clemens, better known by his pen name Mark Twain. To me, in typical childlike indifference, those details seemed weightless. What mattered, what made the long road trip from Colorado to Missouri worthwhile, were the wide-open spaces, the long horseback rides, and the bison that roamed the land. For as long as I can remember, we called them buffalo, although their proper Latin name is *Bison bison*.

Until I was 13, I spent every spring break and many autumns at the ranch. Some mornings, I would wake to find the herd grazing outside the fence that enclosed the homes, barn, and gardens. I'd pull on jeans and a fleece, run outside, and clamber to the top of the fence for the best vantage point. The animals were so close I could smell their muskiness, and from my perch I could look down and spot where the calves' humps were gradually pushing up under their rust-colored fur. I'd try and make eye contact, and I'd quietly talk, but I was never allowed to reach my hand out. They were, by all accounts, still wild.

When we ran into the herd on horseback, we kept our distance—sometimes even backtracking over difficult terrain. The buffalo never charged, but we kept our voices low and our eyes alert for a lifted tail, a sure sign of aggression. I recall my parents and the ranch hands instinctively edging their horses between my docile pony and the powerful beasts.

My deference for the bison was born of observations made in the saddle and at the top of the ranch's fence. That's where I studied the animal, where my American history lessons came to life, and where I tried to imagine our ranch without the animals' magnificent presence.

For such a celebrated symbol of the West, the bison has suffered a grim history. When the White Man arrived on the Great Plains, the herds were so robust that early explorers reported that the horizon appeared to be in constant motion. But, in the 1800s, the fur trade's unrelenting demand for buffalo hides and tongues, the railroad's cavalier slaughtering (bison were considered a nuisance), and the government's determination to starve and weaken the American Indians decimated the population. At the turn of the 20th century, fewer than 700 animals remained—down from some 60 million. Today, there are about 200,000 bison, few of which are truly wild, in the United States.

On my family's ranch, the herd's numbers were closely monitored—too many bison meant the land couldn't sustain their grazing. Too few, and noxious weeds would encroach upon the rich expanses of Savannah grass and alfalfa. Unlike cattle, bison are not stagnant; they tear at grass tufts and chew as they walk. They can easily roam 10 to 15 miles a day, eating along the way. Their hooves constantly till the soil, uprooting unwanted weeds and giving fallen grass seeds a new beginning. It's a symbiotic relationship: The land nurtures the herd as the herd nurtures the land.

Each fall the men would hunt. They'd suit up in leather boots and cold-weather gear, load their guns, and set out in the ranch clunker. I was never allowed to tag along: I was too young. But I remember the crack of gunshots cutting through the crisp, misty morning during our last trip to the ranch. The air smelled of wood smoke and soggy oak leaves.

Later that afternoon, a pickup truck carrying a massive, lifeless body trundled through the gates, and I ran across the wide lawn in pursuit. The truck came to a stop just outside of the meat locker, which sat adjacent to the big yellow barn. Using a pulley system looped around a tall white oak, the men suspended the bison, head down, until it dangled a dozen feet off the ground. After a long while, the animal's stomach lurched loudly and emptied its contents onto the dirt below. Chewed-up grass and acorns mingled with bright red blood. The real work was about to begin—the task of skinning and breaking down the body. The meat would age in the dark chill of the meat locker before finding a new home in the freezer—and then on the dinner table.

THE SUN WARMS THE CHILLY January morning when I meet up with Bob Dineen at the National Western Stock Show. I find him atop a concrete platform overlooking the stockyards, where scores of bison and cattle fidget in their pens. The scent of dust, hay, and dung mixes with the cold winter air. It smells of honest work. The lanky Dineen, who is the president of Rocky Mountain Natural Meats, is wearing a black cowboy hat, dark Wranglers, and a denim jacket. He has a turquoise bandana tied around his neck.

We hop down from the platform and join the throngs of people, many clad in dusty boots and crisp-brimmed hats, moving in the direction of the livestock auction arena. The Gold Trophy Show and Sale, the National Bison Association's annual auction of carcasses and live animals, starts in about 30 minutes. We find seats in plain view of the auctioneers, which is important because Dineen will likely be the day's biggest bidder.

Rocky Mountain Natural Meats buys 400 head of bison a week, with the prime cuts (about 11 percent of an animal) going to local outlets of Ted's Montana Grill and Whole Foods Market, and the ground meat destined for the grocery stores. "This is a handshake business, and we like that," Dineen says. "In 2008 we bought 19,470 head on a handshake."

The Higgins sit behind us: Larry, Jacki, and Josiah drove from their Genoa ranch this morning. Like everyone in the arena, they're poring over the auction program, which details how each of the 18 bison carcasses fared. Stephen Cave's USDA-assessed findings are outlined in chart form, with numbers adhering to each category, including the all-important rib-eye size, fat color, and percent yield (the carcass weight versus the live weight) for each animal. In a matter of minutes, four medals will be awarded—one gold and one silver for the top two bulls, and another gold and silver for the top two heifers.

I turn to greet the Higgins—and congratulate Josiah. Not even the shadow of his black cowboy hat can hide the boyish elation: His heifer took gold in her category, and his bull took fourth. While Larry and Jacki's animals didn't do nearly as well, Josiah's winning heifer is virtually guaranteed to bring the family a high price per pound.

Across the auditorium, a local contingent from Slow Food USA—a national organization championing the farm-to-table way of eating—fills a row of the plastic seats. They sit together, all wearing the same T-shirts emblazoned with "Slow Food." Their presence underscores their belief in knowing where one's food comes from. Today, they're bidding on five animals, the meat of which will be divvied up among interested members. Several weeks ago, I had contacted Krista Roberts, president of the Denver chapter, and asked if I could go in on one-sixteenth of an animal.

Just after 11 a.m. the auction begins with the announcement of the winning bull's measurements: He weighed 680 pounds after slaughter, showed no signs of ossification, had a 12.1-inch rib-eye, and excellent fat and muscle color. The gathered crowd nods in approval. Soon after, the head auctioneer begins his singsong and Dineen kicks off the bidding with a sharp nod. He's procuring meat for both Ted's Montana Grill and for Rocky Mountain Natural Meats. He plans to purchase five or six carcasses, depending on size and price.

The gold-medal bull goes for $3.20 a pound, despite Dineen expecting prices closer to $4. (Josiah's 586-pound bull, the lightest in its class, ultimately sells for $3.10 a pound.) But the final bid for Josiah's 583-pound, gold-winning heifer comes in at $3.60—a fair price.

After the auction concludes and the crowd filters to the exits, Roberts makes her way over to tell me the news: Along with four other carcasses, Slow Food Denver is the proud owner of Josiah's bull.

I'm standing in my basement, in front of a freezer with the door wide open. Inside, 40 pounds of Josiah's bull, long since cut and neatly packaged into steaks, short ribs, roasts, and ground meat, are stacked to the top. I pull out a brick of short ribs, close the door, and head upstairs to find a plate for defrosting.

It's been a week since I drove to Roberts' house to pick up my share of meat. As we transferred the vacuum-sealed parcels from her deep freeze to my car, I was flooded with an unexpected sense of pride and appreciation. It was not unlike the satisfaction of pulling the season's first carrot from a patch of tended earth. I drove away vowing to honor the animal whose frozen muscles rattled in the trunk of my car.

Back in my kitchen, I pluck fresh thyme leaves from their stems, zest a lemon, and crush garlic with the blade of a knife. I rub the mixture over the now-thawed short ribs before placing them in a heavy pot for searing. With the addition of onion, fennel, and celery, the house blooms with scents that are rich and full. I pull a wooden spoon from a crock near the stove, and stir. This moment—the smells and the spoon, which once belonged to my mother—pulls me to the center of a childhood memory: I'm standing at the knee of my mom as she prepares dinner with meat from the ranch. Onions and garlic sweat and perfume the air. I've got a spoon in my hand and an apron tied in a bow at my back.

I pull my attention back to the stove, give the mixture a final stir, and cover the pot. My two-and-a-half-year-old daughter wanders in, pulling a small red chair behind her. She scrambles up and asks for a peek. It's bison, I tell her. From a ranch I visited. She sniffs and grins.

In a couple of hours, I'll call my family to dinner and we'll sit down to a meal of slow-cooked short ribs. As we eat, I'll explain that, not long ago, this majestic animal—Josiah's bull—was grazing on Colorado prairie grass and wearing ear tag #142.

THE NEED FOR CUSTOM SLAUGHTER

By Barry Estabrook

From atlantic.com

Humane slaughter—an oxymoron? Not necessarily so, argues
Barry Estabrook—former *Gourmet* contributor and small-
scale Vermont farmer—whose focus on sustainability makes a
natural fit for *The Atlantic*'s thoughtful online food coverage.

I stood behind Monte Winship on a frigid morning last
December as he raised his .25-caliber Winchester rifle and
aimed at Léo, a two-and-a-half-year-old Holstein steer.

In an era when Food and Water Watch, an environmental group,
reports that four giant corporations—Tyson, Cargill, Swift, and
National Beef Packing—process 84 percent of this country's cattle,
the scene in that snow-covered field in Vermont is increasingly
rare: an animal was about to be humanely slaughtered on the very
farm where it had been raised.

Winship and his old, lever-action rifle represent the polar opposite of the huge, 5,000-animal-per-day meatpacking plants that
were so graphically brought to the country's attention in Eric
Schlosser's *Fast Food Nation*. "There aren't many of us left," said
Winship, who is in his fifties. "When I was a kid, every town had
someone doing this job."

In the jargon of the meat business, Winship's work is considered
"custom slaughter." He is a freelancer, traveling from farm to farm,
killing cattle and hogs and transporting their gutted carcasses to a
nearby facility to be cut into parts, wrapped, and frozen. As a means
for converting a living steer into meat, the practice has a lot going
for it. For one thing, it is as humane as killing an animal can be.

"It's the best way to slaughter them because you don't have to transport them," Temple Grandin, the renowned author, livestock handling expert, and associate professor at Colorado State University, told me. Being trucked long distances and then herded shoulder-to-shoulder into confined areas with strange sights and noises is a huge stress on animals, she said. A cow killed on its home turf doesn't know what hits it. "If on-farm slaughter is done properly, it's very, very humane," Grandin said.

It is also a way for a skeptical consumer to make sure the animal had access to pasture and did not spend its final months in a feedlot pumped full of hormones and eating an unnatural diet of corn fortified with antibiotics.

A humane death for Léo; healthy meat for the consumer. What's not to like? Plenty, according to the United States Department of Agriculture—the same folks whose rigorous standards all but guarantee that yet another *E. coli* outbreak hits the news every week. Because the USDA refuses to give on-farm slaughter its little purple stamp of blessing, it is illegal to sell meat butchered this way. Léo's meat would be consumed only by the family of the farmer who had raised him.

On-farm slaughter is one solution to the problem of how to have local, sustainable meat properly killed and butchered, but legal questions aside, it has a major drawback. "Once you get into more than a few animals," said Grandin, who is never one to mince words, "you'd have a dirty mess."

An alternative is to take animals to small slaughterhouses for killing and processing. But even as consumer demand has soared, the number of local processing facilities nationwide has plummeted. More than 1,500 have closed in the last two decades, according to the American Association of Meat Processors, which represents small- and medium-sized processors. As Patrick Martins of Heritage Foods USA, the sales and marketing arm of Slow Food USA, told Food and Water Watch, "The lack of slaughterhouses is the biggest bottleneck in the food business."

Such back-ups create huge problems. In one case, a dozen Vermont farmers pooled their resources to purchase a truck to serve the lucrative New York and Boston markets, where their products sell for three times the going rate in rural Vermont. But the scarcity of slaughterhouses means the animals must be trucked alive out of the state to be processed, which is both inconvenient and expensive. The situation is even more dire in New York State, where only 41 slaughterhouses remained in business in 2008, down from more than 120 in the 1980s. Pam McSweeny, a New York farmer who raises organic meat, has to truck her animals 10 hours to Pennsylvania and back to have them processed, a huge expense.

To get around such backlogs, some small, sustainable producers have opened or purchased their own facilities. These include Will Harris's White Oak Pastures, Georgia's largest grass-fed beef producer; Sallie Calhoun, owner of Paicines Ranch, a grass-fed cattle operation in San Benito County, California; and Joel Salatin of Polyface Farm in Virginia, made famous in Michael Pollan's *The Omnivore's Dilemma*.

Many of the problems forcing small operations out of business (and preventing would-be investors from building new plants) can be traced back to red tape imposed by the USDA. According to the Food and Water Watch report, the USDA's regulations favor huge facilities that can spread the costs over hundreds of thousands of animals. Complying with policies is too onerous for many small operators. Extensive record-keeping and ever-fluctuating safety criteria add additional burdens. And Food and Water Watch adds that there have even been accusations of USDA inspectors singling out small facilities for harsh treatment because they make easier targets than national corporations backed up by staff scientists, legal experts, and well-paid government lobbyists.

Having witnessed the process firsthand, I would have had no qualms about eating beef from Léo. The steer dropped and lay motionless in the snow, dead before Winship's shot had finished echoing. After the carcass was hoisted by the hind hooves with a front-end loader, Winship skinned and gutted it, retaining the heart, tongue, liver, and kidneys. He used a saw to cut the carcass in half lengthwise, and after that he sliced each half in two. The four quarters—over 800 pounds of beef—were loaded into Winship's pickup truck. In all, 90 minutes had passed.

I followed Winship for about 30 miles to a building off to the side of a winding gravel road. The unimposing structure, not much bigger than a two-car garage, was the headquarters for the company that had hired Winship, Rup's Custom Cutting, a mom-and-pop business run by Rupert LaRock and his wife, Jeanne. The spotlessly clean facility is regularly inspected by health officials, so apart from the manner in which he had died, Léo would comply with all state and federal policies regarding the sale of meat. LaRock, a butcher for 41 of his 55 years, hoisted Léo's quarters onto meat hooks connected to an overhead rail. He immediately started spraying them with a high-pressure hose, commenting on the size and high-quality of the carcass, but nonetheless grumbling, "Cows get so dirty this time of year." I could detect no traces of filth.

Because of the slaughterhouse shortage, LaRock is run off his feet. He processes only one cow per day. "And it gets busier all the time," he says. If you want Rup's to butcher, wrap, and freeze one of your steers, you have to book an appointment three to four months in advance.

For those of us who want to eat local, sustainably raised meat, LaRock has some words of encouragement. "Every time there's an *E. coli* scare, my phone starts ringing. There's so much demand out there that they are going to have to open on-farm slaughter to commercial sale soon."

EATING ANIMALS

By Jonathan Safran Foer

From *The New York Times Magazine*

Novelist Foer (*Everything Is Illuminated*) stirred up a hornet's nest with his impassioned 2009 book *Eating Animals*—part memoir, part dialectic, spiced up with his trademark stylistic flair. Here's a taste. . . .

Seconds after being born, my son was breast-feeding. I watched him with an awe that had no precedent in my life. Without explanation or experience, he knew what to do. Millions of years of evolution had wound the knowledge into him, as it had encoded beating into his tiny heart and expansion and contraction into his newly dry lungs.

Almost four years later, he is a big brother and a remarkably sophisticated little conversationalist. Increasingly the food he eats is digested together with stories we tell. Feeding my children is not like feeding myself: it matters more. It matters because food matters (their physical health matters, the pleasure they take in eating matters), and because the stories that are served with food matter.

Some of my happiest childhood memories are of sushi "lunch dates" with my mom, and eating my dad's turkey burgers with mustard and grilled onions at backyard celebrations, and of course my grandmother's chicken with carrots. Those occasions simply wouldn't have been the same without those foods—and that is important. To give up the taste of sushi, turkey or chicken is a loss that extends beyond giving up a pleasurable eating experience. Changing what we eat and letting tastes fade from memory create a kind of cultural loss, a forgetting. But perhaps this kind of forgetfulness is worth accepting—even worth cultivating (forgetting, too, can be cultivated). To remember my values, I need to lose certain tastes and find other handles for the memories that they once helped me carry.

My wife and I have chosen to bring up our children as vegetarians. In another time or place, we might have made a different decision. But the realities of our present moment compelled us to make that choice. According to an analysis of U.S.D.A. data by the advocacy group Farm Forward, factory farms now produce more than 99 percent of the animals eaten in this country. And despite labels that suggest otherwise, genuine alternatives—which do exist, and make many of the ethical questions about meat moot—are very difficult for even an educated eater to find. I don't have the ability to do so with regularity and confidence. ("Free range," "cage free," "natural" and "organic" are nearly meaningless when it comes to animal welfare.)

According to reports by the Food and Agriculture Organization of the U.N. and others, factory farming has made animal agriculture the No. 1 contributor to global warming (it is significantly more destructive than transportation alone), and one of the Top 2 or 3 causes of all of the most serious environmental problems, both global and local: air and water pollution, deforestation, loss of biodiversity. . . . Eating factory-farmed animals—which is to say virtually every piece of meat sold in supermarkets and prepared in restaurants—is almost certainly the single worst thing that humans do to the environment.

Every factory-farmed animal is, as a practice, treated in ways that would be illegal if it were a dog or a cat. Turkeys have been so genetically modified they are incapable of natural reproduction. To acknowledge that these things matter is not sentimental. It is a confrontation with the facts about animals and ourselves. We know these things matter.

Meat and seafood are in no way necessary for my family— unlike some in the world, we have easy access to a wide variety of other foods. And we are healthier without it. So our choices aren't constrained.

While the cultural uses of meat can be replaced—my mother and I now eat Italian, my father grills veggie burgers, my grandmother invented her own "vegetarian chopped liver"—there is still the question of pleasure. A vegetarian diet can be rich and fully enjoyable, but I couldn't honestly argue, as many vegetarians try to, that it is as rich as a diet that includes meat. (Those who eat chimpanzee look at the Western diet as sadly deficient of a great pleasure.) I love calamari, I love roasted chicken, I love a good steak. But I don't love them without limit.

This isn't animal experimentation, where you can imagine some proportionate good at the other end of the suffering. This is what we feel like eating. Yet taste, the crudest of our senses, has been exempted from the ethical rules that govern our other senses. Why? Why doesn't a horny person have as strong a claim to raping an animal as a hungry one does to confining, killing and eating it? It's easy to dismiss that question but hard to respond to it. Try to imagine any end other than taste for which it would be justifiable to do what we do to farmed animals.

Children confront us with our paradoxes and dishonesty, and we are exposed. You need to find an answer for every why—Why do we do this? Why don't we do that?—and often there isn't a good one. So you say, simply, because. Or you tell a story that you know isn't true. And whether or not your face reddens, you blush. The shame of parenthood—which is a good shame—is that we want our children to be more whole than we are, to have satisfactory answers. My children not only inspired me to reconsider what kind of eating animal I would be, but also shamed me into reconsideration.

And then, one day, they will choose for themselves. I don't know what my reaction will be if they decide to eat meat. (I don't know what my reaction will be if they decide to renounce their Judaism, root for the Red Sox or register Republican.) I'm not as worried about what they will choose as much as my ability to make them conscious of the choices before them. I won't measure my success as a parent by whether my children share my values, but by whether they act according to their own.

In the meantime, my choice on their behalf means they will never eat their great-grandmother's singular dish. They will never receive that unique and most direct expression of her love, will perhaps never think of her as the greatest chef who ever lived. Her primal story, our family's primal story, will have to change.

Or will it? It wasn't until I became a parent that I understood my grandmother's cooking. The greatest chef who ever lived wasn't preparing food, but humans. I'm thinking of those Saturday afternoons at her kitchen table, just the two of us—black bread in the glowing toaster, a humming refrigerator that couldn't be seen through its veil of family photographs. Over pumpernickel ends and Coke, she would tell me about her escape from Europe, the foods she had to eat and those she wouldn't. It was the story of her life—"Listen to me," she would plead—and I knew a vital lesson was being transmitted, even if I didn't know, as a child, what that lesson was. I know, now, what it was.

Listen to Me

"We weren't rich, but we always had enough. Thursday we baked bread, and challah and rolls, and they lasted the whole week. Friday we had pancakes. Shabbat we always had a chicken, and soup with noodles. You would go to the butcher and ask for a little more fat. The fattiest piece was the best piece. It wasn't like now. We didn't have refrigerators, but we had milk and cheese. We didn't have every kind of vegetable, but we had enough. The things that you have here and take for granted. . . . But we were happy. We didn't know any better. And we took what we had for granted, too.

"Then it all changed. During the war it was hell on earth, and I had nothing. I left my family, you know. I was always running, day and night, because the Germans were always right behind me. If you stopped, you died. There was never enough food. I became sicker and sicker from not eating, and I'm not just talking about being skin and bones. I had sores all over my body. It became difficult to move. I wasn't too good to eat from a garbage can. I ate the parts others wouldn't eat. If you helped yourself, you could survive. I took whatever I could find. I ate things I wouldn't tell you about.

"Even at the worst times, there were good people, too. Someone taught me to tie the ends of my pants so I could fill the legs with any potatoes I was able to steal. I walked miles and miles like that, because you never knew when you would be lucky again. Someone gave me a little rice, once, and I traveled two days to a market and traded it for some soap, and then traveled to another market and traded the soap for some beans. You had to have luck and intuition.

"The worst it got was near the end. A lot of people died right at the end, and I didn't know if I could make it another day. A farmer, a Russian, God bless him, he saw my condition, and he went into his house and came out with a piece of meat for me."

"He saved your life."

"I didn't eat it."

"You didn't eat it?"

"It was pork. I wouldn't eat pork."

"Why?"

"What do you mean why?"

"What, because it wasn't kosher?"

"Of course."

"But not even to save your life?"

"If nothing matters, there's nothing to save."

Attack of the Anti-Meat Crusaders!

By Lessley Anderson

From chow.com

Though chow.com has expanded beyond its original base of
die-hard street eaters, it's still an audience of wide appetites
and strong opinions. Instead of polarizing the meat-eating
issue, senior features editor Lessley Anderson brings
balanced reflection to this book review.

Meat eating is under attack! And yet you may not have
noticed all the noise—new, shocking reports from the
World Bank, United Nations, and more—because you were too
busy mawing on that delicious artisanal bacon.

The upshot is that, by some estimates, livestock farming produces more greenhouse gases than all the world's transportation
systems combined. Factory farms are responsible for 99 percent—
yes, 99 percent—of all the meat in the U.S.

Then there's the newish (November) nonfiction book by hot
young writer Jonathan Safran Foer, *Eating Animals*, which details
more horrors of factory farming. Like how just one pig farming
operation (Smithfield) produces more tons of shit than does the
entire human population of California and Texas combined, and
how that untreated waste has nowhere to go other than sprayed in
a fecal mist into the air and waterways.

The timing of this stuff is really weird. We are arguably in a
meat-obsessed cultural moment. Trendy Williamsburg restaurants
like the Brooklyn Star features few dishes in which the main course

is not wrapped in bacon. Hell, Fig in Santa Monica serves bacon wrapped in bacon. *The New York Times* even coined the phrase "hot butchers" to describe chefs like Ryan Farr of San Francisco, who teach sold-out classes in sausage making to slavering packs of meat nerds. Then there are Crif Dogs kimchee hot dogs, Shake Shack burgers, David Chang's pork belly, Donald Link's Boudin Balls. We can't get enough of it. It's just so damn cool.

Of course, for all of us ordering charcuterie plates, there's a caveat: we eat sustainably-raised meat. The pork skins Farr uses for his chicharonnes aren't from a factory farm, they're from pasture-raised pigs from Becker Lane Organic Farm, Dyersville, IA. The philosophy many of us have is that promoting the *right* kind of meat is helping fight the good fight against the *wrong* kind of meat produced by big agribusiness.

"I do feel like the environmentalists, vegetarians, and sustainable meat people do have a common enemy, and it is factory farmed meat," says Sasha Wizansky, editor of *Meatpaper*, a print magazine that chronicles meat culture.

But you, with your artisanal bacon, are you really above the fray? *Spoiler Alert*: Foer's book says we're full of shit.

Reason Number One:
All "Ethical Omnivores" Cheat.

Admit it: Not all the meat you eat is sustainably raised.

"How effective would the Montgomery bus boycott have been if the protesters had used the bus when it became inconvenient not to?" writes Foer. Zing!

"If I'm down in Mexico City or Barcelona, Japan, and there's really good street food, I'm going to eat it, and if I don't know where the meat's coming from, I'm still going to eat it," Ryan Farr told CHOW. And what about that pho place you love to go to for lunch? Is its beef grass fed? Or how about when you felt too stingy to buy the heritage turkey for Thanksgiving, because it was like, 80 times more expensive than the conventional one?

Reason Number Two:
Organic, Free-Range, and Cage-Free Mean Jack.

These words do not mean healthy, happy animals. Here's the deal, once again (we've all heard it before): To be considered free-range, a chicken must have "access to the outdoors." This, according to Foer and plenty of others who've covered this, is interpreted cynically by the poultry industry. Like, there's a little door or window that gets opened sometimes, that shows a little patch of earth onto which the chickens in their gloomy, overcrowded sheds of doom, will never tread.

"Cage-free" means they're not in cages, duh. But it doesn't mean they're on dirt. And how about the killing floor, where most birds are dragged through that lovely fecal soup? No cages there, either!

Organic, Foer points out, just means they were fed organic food, had "access to the outdoors" (see above), and weren't fed antibiotics or growth hormones. Not that they were treated humanely or safely during their lives and deaths.

Reason Number Three:
Any Meat Eating Promotes More Meat Eating,
and Most Meat Is Factory Farmed.

You get invited to somebody's house for dinner. They know you eat meat. Of course you're not going to be an asshole, and tell them that you only eat meat from such and such farms.

"This effort might be well-placed, but it is certainly more invasive than asking for vegetarian food (which these days requires no explanation)," writes Foer. "The entire food industry (restaurants, airline and college food services, catering at weddings) is set up to accommodate vegetarians. There is no such infrastructure for the selective omnivore."

So you eat what they put in front of you. And what they put in front of you is Tyson chicken or Smithfield ham.

And yet, all these very good arguments being what they are, I have not gone vegetarian. Why? For me the main reason is that becoming vegetarian means not supporting the small farmers who are trying to make a difference in our screwed up system of meat production. People like Mark Pasternak, of Devil's Gulch Ranch, who raises pigs in Sonoma County for many great local restaurants, while also offering nature education summer camp for kids. Or heritage poultry farmer Frank Reese, whom Foer profiles in his book as being one of the few farmers in the U.S. raising non-genetically modified chickens. (His birds don't have enormous breasts, and instead, have big legs from all the walking and running around that they do.)

Yes, there's the argument that there aren't enough of these farmers (or enough farmland) to supply all the meat in our country if overnight the entire U.S. population decided to boycott factory farms. But most nutritionists and doctors agree that we need to cut way back on the amount of meat we eat. And, furthermore, the best way to inspire real change is to find leaders and role models like those guys who create new paradigms consumers and lawmakers can aspire to. Or at least that's my opinion.

As Foer and the recent reports make clear, it might be mission critical to planet Earth that factory farms stop right now. But let's face it: Our culture is currently madly in love with meat. Not a day goes by that I don't get another email from a PR firm about a new product flavored with bacon, or see a menu featuring chicken liver mousse on the appetizer list. That's the reality. So now let's work with it. This is just a starting point, something I've been thinking about for a long time. So let's discuss: Where do you get your meat? Do you buy Safran Foer's arguments?

Dear Zagat

By Tim Carman

From *Washington City Paper*

As the Zagat restaurant guide dynasty continues to expand, a
nagging discontent with its influence has pervaded the food
world. *City Paper* food editor Tim Carman investigates just
how the guides are put together—and how reliable they are.

The Zagat guide turned 30 years old this year, and in honor
of the occasion, I'd like to give founders Tim and Nina
Zagat a hearty thanks for all their years of service to the restaurant
industry. And, if I may, I'd like to offer some friendly advice, too: You
can go away now.

Ten years ago, back before everyone had access to a world of
opinion via some device tucked into purse or pocket, diners relied
on your slim red eponymous guide, which compiled restaurant
ratings based on public opinion. It was your slap against the imperial voice of the critic. The Zagat book would be the voice of the
people, guiding diners by the collective wisdom of the people,
even if you would never tell us how many people actually voted
for any one restaurant.

But now, nearly a decade into the 21st century, the people no
longer need Zagat to compile data, crunch it, and cough it up in
cute little numbers of dubious quality. They can compile their own
dining information of dubious quality without all the opaque,
Wizard of Oz, man-behind-the-curtain nonsense that you have insisted on for three decades.

The truth is, the Zagat guide belongs to a time when tourists
and urban newcomers, looking for some guidance on restaurants,

had nowhere else to turn. For these folks, the Zagat guide was like asking 1,000 random strangers, "What's your favorite restaurant?" and then tabulating the results.

Except it wasn't. The Zagat survey has never been random. Its respondents are, in the language of pollsters, self-selected. Or perhaps mostly self-selected. That's the problem: Few people outside of Zagat's New York offices know who actually votes and how those voters are selected.

Nina and Tim Zagat, a pair of former lawyers, have indicated in the past that they'd send out hundreds of thousands of surveys to law firms, medical offices, and other white-collar institutions where people, presumably, have the disposable income to eat out often enough to provide the Zagats with the free data they need to sustain their empire. But Zagat also solicits online reviews. Are those included in the final ratings? That would seem to be the case, but one restaurateur complained to me that some never appear on the site.

THE ZAGATS ARE LIKE a couple living in a walled compound, sealed off from some of the major developments of the past decade. The generation that willingly accepted unverified pronouncements from established authorities has moved into retirement homes. The younger generation is far more interested in its own opinion, which it shares in virtual communities like Yelp, MySpace, and Facebook. It values transparency among peers (if not in the comments sections of blogs), and its members are strung out on the 24-hour news cycle, which has them addicted to the latest 140-character information bomb from Twitter.

We do not live in a Zagat World anymore.

This epiphany came to me via the 2010 edition of the Washington, DC/Baltimore Zagat guide. There, on page 10, are the 40 highest-rated restaurants in the D.C. area in terms of food. At the top, for the second year in a row, is Makoto, a 25-seat Japanese restaurant in Palisades that prepares a pristine, multicourse *omakase* menu based on the seasons and the chef's whims. The place earned 29 out of 30 points for food from Zagat raters, just barely beating out the Inn at Little Washington, which is rather impressive given the latter's bona fides. In 1994, the *International Herald Tribune* named the Inn one of the 10 best restaurants in the world, and it has remained a darling of critics. Celebrities and politicians hop in helicopters to dine at the Inn at Little Washington. Washingtonians consult their GPS to figure out how to find Makoto.

You might be wondering how a niche restaurant like Makoto, with such a minuscule seating capacity, could generate enough votes to win the top spot two years running in the D.C. Zagat guide. There's an easy answer: It didn't. Makoto won the 2009 Zagat survey for food. The ratings in the 2010 book merely repeat those from last year's survey, although the casual reader would be hard-pressed to know this important fact.

THE ONLY WAY I LEARNED about the duplicate ratings was through Michael Birchenall, editor and publisher of the local trade magazine *Foodservice Monthly*. After reading a blog item that I wrote about Makoto's strange stranglehold on Zagat, Birchenall combed through his old guides and discovered an interesting trend: Those restaurants that topped the Zagat ratings in the odd years were the same ones that topped them in the even years. A spokesperson for Zagat confirmed his findings.

"As Michael Birchenall pointed out to you, we compile new survey results and prepare a new guide for Washington, DC/Baltimore every other year," e-mailed Tiffany Barbalato, director of communications for Zagat. "This is why the winning restaurants and top lists you refer to in the 2010 guide are the same as last year's."

Barbalato, in the same e-mail, alerted me to this line in the latest guide: "This 2010 Washington, DC/Baltimore Restaurants Survey is an update reflecting significant developments since our last Survey was published." (Those significant developments, incidentally, are mostly the addition of new, unrated restaurants with an editor-written description.) Barbalato offered up this lone, coyly worded sentence as evidence that Zagat doesn't try to dupe its customers about the duplicate nature of the even-year guides.

I had my doubts that this anemic sentence was pulling its weight, so I called a few restaurateurs and asked them if they knew about Zagat's duplicate ratings. "I did not know that," says Jeff

Black, 46, the owner of four restaurants, including BlackSalt and Addie's, who's been working in the hospitality business since age 13. "That's kind of lame."

"Oh, really?" says Barton Seaver, chef at the new Blue Ridge in Glover Park. "OK, that's a dinosaur. . . . We're living in an era where Todd Kliman [of the *Washingtonian*] reviews a restaurant as it happens" via Twitter.

Their alarm at this news is understandable. Many restaurants have shorter life spans than the average prime-time program, which means that these places grow, mature, and gray quickly. A Zagat rating based on a year-old survey—or older—is the equivalent of judging this season's *Mad Men* by the episodes of the previous season. Take, for example, the rating in the 2010 Zagat guide for Black's Bar & Kitchen. Jeff Black's Bethesda operation scores a respectable 24 for food, but that rating is based on a survey likely tabulated when Mallory Buford was executive chef in mid-2009. Black's is now on its third different executive chef since Buford left. "Things do change [at restaurants]," Black says, "and they change quickly."

Makoto may be one of the few exceptions to that rule. Time doesn't stand still here—but it actually seems to expand, as if you get two minutes for every 60 ticks around the clock. Part of the sensation can be traced to a pair of unyielding policies at Makoto: You must take off your shoes in the anteroom and don slippers, and you must silence your cell phones. These house customs leave your toes swaddled in pillowy comfort and leave *you* to contemplate the finer things about the restaurant experience: your food, your dining companions, and your deepest, most neurotic thoughts.

Depending on the quality of the latter two, it's often best to focus on the food. Yoshi Itoh, chef and co-owner of Makoto, has developed a disciplined kitchen that can quickly produce a small banquet of plates, some so good you'll wonder why there's not a line snaking around this restaurant every night. Deep-fried soft-shell crabs breaded with pebble-sized crumbles of rice cracker. Strips of medium-rare tenderloin so rich and tender they practically slide down your throat with the soy-based sauce. Wasabi-smeared slivers of fresh fish perched atop the fluffiest sushi rice you've ever seen, each piece of nigiri expertly balancing its heat with its sweet.

And yet for all its devotion to the fine art and technique of Japanese cooking, Makoto is not one point away from perfection, at least not according to my own internal guide. The tuna served as part of my sashimi course during a recent visit was mealy and gummy, while the flounder was flavorless. The dessert of shaved ice, flavored with fruit and Grand Marnier, was refreshing enough but, frankly, has worn out its welcome after countless appearances on Makoto's *omakase* menu. Then there's the squadron of female servers, who balance the gentility of a geisha girl with the fastidiousness of an English nanny. I can't tell if they want to sit with me or tell me to clean up my room.

So HOW DOES A PLACE like Makoto reach the pinnacle of the Zagat food ratings? If you research the published literature on Zagat, you'll come across stories of restaurateurs trying to game the voting system. They'll blast e-mails to the diners in their database, reminding them to cast their votes before the Zagat survey period ends. Their message is implied but clear: Stuff the Zagat ballot box for their restaurant. Some restaurateurs might even offer discounts, or other gifts, to those diners who cast ballots, despite the fact that this kind of tit-for-tat vote solicitation can get you banned from the Zagat book.

Jeffrey Buben, owner of Bistro Bis and Vidalia, knows for certain that some restaurateurs try to outsmart the Zagat system. He's one of them (though without the promise of any kitchen bribe). In the past, he's placed little promotional tents on the tables or slipped cards into the checks, asking diners to vote in the next Zagat survey. His goal is to land a Top 5 ranking in Zagat's food category. He doesn't apologize for it, either. "That's what grass-roots PR is all about," Buben says. He leaves it up to the Zagat data-crunchers to weed out the questionable ballots, which they claim they can do.

Makoto has accomplished exactly what Buben was aiming for. The restaurant opened either in 1992 or 1993 (neither Makoto manager Michiko Lecuyer nor anyone at the restaurant could remember), and for its first few years, it never even appeared in the

Zagat guide. But then in 1997, it suddenly scored 28 out of 30 points for food, tying it for second place with L'Auberge Chez Francois in the entire D.C. market. Makoto has never slipped lower than third place since then, a run of more than 12 years.

Lecuyer credits the kitchen for Makoto's long ride atop the charts. The chefs select only the freshest seasonal ingredients, from fish to vegetables, no matter what the price, she says. The cooks also prepare the *omakase* plates with a nod to authenticity. "We serve the food we want to eat," Lecuyer says, "the way we want to eat it. . . . Our customers get it and understand it. That's why we've been highly listed."

Now, if there's one question you don't want to ask the owner or manager of an elegant Japanese restaurant like Makoto, it's this: Do you beg or cheat for Zagat votes?

"We don't do that," Lecuyer says, noting that servers aren't allowed to talk to customers. "We don't know who is doing the survey and is not doing the survey. We don't know."

Such ignorance may be a blessing to Makoto, but it's a bane for diners who want to know how legitimate Zagat's ratings are. Team Zagat in New York won't answer any questions about its survey methodology, and Tim and Nina Zagat turned down my interview request. It's more of the same stonewalling that has worked for 30 years for the Zagats and their guides, which now cover subjects ranging from dining to golf in more than 100 countries. The company's attitude forces you to make a snap decision: You either trust it or you lump it.

A lot of people are opting for the latter. According to a *New York Post* article from earlier this month, not only are Zagat sales "down dramatically," but the company moved too slowly online, "allowing Yelp and others to dominate the market." Zagat, the paper wrote, laid off about 16 people in May. The founders themselves seemed to see the writing on the wall a year earlier: The Zagats tried to sell their company for a reported $200 million last year but couldn't find any buyers in that price range and pulled Zagat off the auction block.

It's easy to see why people choose Yelp, Chowhound, Urban Spoon, and OpenTable over Zagat, both the guide and the online site. The obsolete-before-you-buy-it Zagat book is $14.95 a shot, and Zagat.com charges nearly $25 a year to access its complete site, including those ratings that can be seriously outdated. Plus, the mere act of creating an account with Zagat.com requires that you provide the kind of personal information—mailing address, telephone, birth year—that other sites have decided to forgo.

By contrast, Yelp, Chowhound, Urban Spoon, and other sites are free, and most already have established communities where members interact with each other on particular topics and restaurants. Even better for diners looking for recommendations on Yelp or OpenTable, they can see exactly how many people have commented on a particular restaurant—and how those reviews have been averaged into an overall rating. Even the minimal transparency on these sites makes Zagat seem like Stalinist Russia.

"Zagat is not a primary source [for information] anymore," says Dean Gold, the chef and owner of Dino in Cleveland Park, which scores a decent 21 rating for food from Zagat. Adds Gold, a college-trained statistician: "Zagat, of all the major sources, probably has the lowest levels of reliability" because of its self-selected survey base, which provides little to no information on the people who actually cast ballots.

At this point, OpenTable may be the most reliable of the sites that aggregate restaurant ratings. Site administrators send review surveys only to those diners who have honored their OpenTable reservation, and the diners have approximately 30 days to fill out the forms. This process guarantees two things, says Ann Shepherd, vice president of marketing for OpenTable: 1) that every review is actually based on a meal eaten at the restaurant; 2) that the meal was eaten recently, while the memory of it is still fresh.

Those are two promises that you will never hear from Zagat, a guide that looks destined to follow so many other print publications into oblivion.

ZAGAT'S 2010 MAKOTO blurb shows why the guides are "refrigerator-magnet poetry," "dubious," good only for a "lonely traveler . . . searching for a good place to sup before masturbating himself to sleep."

Grade Creepiness: As first pointed out in *SmartMoney* magazine in 2007, Zagat food grades have spiked dramatically over the years for restaurants in the New York guide. Same goes for the D.C. area: In the 1992 guide, only 13 restaurants earned grades of 25 points or higher (out of a possible 30). In 2010, more than 60 restaurants topped the 25-point mark. Even more startling, 72 percent of D.C. restaurants with actual ratings in the latest guide earned a grade of 20 or higher, which means that nearly three-quarters of our eateries are "very good" or better. No one sucks here anymore.

The Method, Man: Readers have no idea how many votes are required before the results are considered statistically relevant to merit a Zagat grade (Zagat's Barbalato told me that Makoto edged Inn at Little Washington, 28.9024 to 28.8495, but would not say how many votes were cast). What's more, they have no idea if the grade represents the votes of the restaurateur's spouse and 100 close friends or a statistically sound sample of D.C. area diners. All they know is this: The voters are self-selected, which is a pool almost guaranteed to skew results. Readers don't even know if voters actually *ate* at the restaurants in question. OpenTable, by contrast, posts reviews only from diners who have honored their online reservation.

Cut-and-Paste Prose: Zagat editors take a ransom-note approach to writing descriptions of the restaurants in their guides. Compare that to consumer-oriented sites, such as Yelp or Don-Rockwell, where amateur critics can relate their entire dining experiences without fear that an editor will place a dis about "uncomfortable seating" right next to some yahoo's Pollyanna piffle about a "wonderful experience." Zagat is refrigerator-magnet poetry at a time when people want the Library of Congress at their fingertips.

You've Been Duped: For those who purchased the 2010 edition of the Washington, D.C./Baltimore Zagat guide, the Makoto entry might seem familiar. For good reason. It's the exact same entry as last year's. The exact same awkwardly phrased copy. The exact same dubious grades. And yet you'd be hard-pressed to learn from the introduction that the 2010 guide is merely an update. Here's the truth: The even-year Zagat guides are based on the surveys from the previous year. Do you know how much a restaurant can change in two years, let alone two months? Would you trust a review from a year ago on Yelp?

Solitary Confinement: Zagat bases your estimated check on a single dinner and drink, plus tip, which is rather symbolic. Social network sites want to create a community around a common interest in food, which explains not only Myspace Local's recent move into online restaurant reviews but also local restaurateurs' embrace of Facebook and its ability to connect supporters. Zagat, by contrast, still conjures up images of the lonely traveler, that burgundy guide tucked into his back pocket, searching for a good place to sup before masturbating himself to sleep.

Caught in a Binder: Like newspapers and magazines, Zagat is dependent on print, where presumably the company still earns most of its revenues, despite the fact that its most timely and user-friendly information (menus, maps, and recent reviews) is found online. Zagat withholds survey ratings from its free Web pages in hopes that you'll plunk down $24.95 a year to find out what the voting public, in whatever numbers, thought of places like Makoto over a year ago. It's a hopeless online business plan, but it's probably a better deal than the $14.95 you pay for the actual paperback guide.

EL BULLI GETS BESTED

By Carla Capalbo

From zesterdaily.com

What does the title World's Best Restaurant really mean?
Capalbo, one of several seasoned journalists on the staff of
this intriguing new food news site, roots out the back story on
the changing of the guard.

W hen superstar chef Ferran Adria's restaurant, El Bulli, was dethroned after four years at the top of the San Pellegrino World's 50 Best Restaurants classification on April 26 in London, the invited audience of professional foodies gasped. The annual award is based on the votes of an 806-strong international jury of food critics, chefs, restaurateurs and food enthusiasts called the Academy. This year the prize-giving was held in the magnificent medieval Guildhall in the city's historic center.

The upset was caused by a spare 42-seat restaurant in a warehouse on the docks of Copenhagen run by Rene Redzepi, a 32-year-old chef whose idea of a spring salad includes beech leaves, axel berry shoots, pine shoots and unripe white strawberries in a dressing made from grill-charred cucumber skins.

The cuisine at Redzepi's Noma focuses on a continuously researched range of Scandinavian foods. "As soon as they named Ferran as No. 2 in the countdown, I knew the winner had to be Noma," said Alessandro Porcelli, a longtime collaborator with Redzepi on the concept of Nordic cuisine.

"That sends a really strong message that high gastronomy is going in a new direction, toward place-specific, seasonal ingredients, including wild and forgotten ones, cooked in more natural yet highly creative ways."

"This will be a great inspiration for cooks all over the world to look for interesting ingredients in their own backyards and use them in new ways. It's no longer all about technique and technology," Porcelli added.

THE NEWS OF NOMA'S VICTORY spread like wildfire via the Internet, Twitter and the traditional press. Within 24 hours, the restaurant received a staggering 140,000 requests for dining reservations, more than enough to fill the 45-seater at lunch and dinner for six years. As Redzepi took the stage to get his award, he and four of his sous chefs donned white T-shirts with a photograph of a smiling black man printed on them. "This is a team prize, the result of seven years of working together," Redzepi said. "It's a testament to what you can do working with people you love, with whom you can develop yourself," he added, before explaining the T-shirts pictured their dishwasher, Ali, who had been refused a 24-hour visa to be at the award show.

Adria, who is closing El Bulli at the end of next year, gave an emotional speech as he accepted Restaurant Magazine's prize for Chef of the Decade. "El Bulli will never be a restaurant again, so it won't be able to get a prize as one again," he said, as the audience rose to its feet to applaud him. "But this prize is in my heart, and my career is linked to this prize."

Now IN ITS NINTH EDITION, the World's 50 Best classification has been steadily gaining importance. "For the most ambitious chefs, this list has become the key to who's who in the food world," says chef-patron Davide Scabin, of Combal.Zero in Turin, listed at number 35, up seven places from 2009. "It now matters more for us to be in the 50 Best than to acquire other Michelin stars. There's also an element of national team competition: This year, five Italian restaurants are in the top 50, and that's exciting. It's a stimulus to keep improving." The Americans have eight in the 2010 top 50, the French six, the Spanish five, the British three. The remaining restaurants come from countries that include

Finland, Brazil, Mexico, Japan, Sweden, Singapore, Australia and South Africa. The highest scorer for the U.S., and receiver of the special Acqua Panna Best Restaurant in North America award, is Alinea, at number 7, up three places from last year. Its brilliant chef, Grant Achatz, was visibly moved at the success and warm reception he received. Other high-flying Americans present included Thomas Keller for Per Se (at number 10) and the French Laundry (32), David Chang, for Momofuku Ssam Bar (26), and Daniel Boulud, for Daniel (8). Boulud also hosted the chef's lunch the next day at his elegant, soon-to-be-opened, Bar Boulud in Knightsbridge.

The Michelin system, with its legions of faceless inspectors and penchant for the pompous and the prissy, is not always in tune with the direction today's most innovative restaurants are taking. Its rating structure is often too cumbersome and its criteria too rigid to follow the thrust of the ground breakers. Le Chateaubriand, an unstuffy 1930s bistro in an outer arrondissement in Paris, is a case in point.

Chef Inaki Aizpitarte is selftaught and hugely inventive. His food is imaginative, improvisational, and instinctive—adjectives more often used for a jazz musician than a cook. From his tiny, chaotic kitchen he prepares just one multi-course meal a day, take it or leave it. He has no Michelin stars, but came in 11th in the World's 50 Best this year—after jumping in at number 40 in 2009.

It's not just for the chefs' egos that the listing matters; the World's 50 Best is proving a winner in terms of business, too. "Many of our new customers come thanks to the list, and they're arriving from all over the world," said chef Yoshihiro Narisawa, whose Tokyo restaurant Les Créations de Narisawa was awarded Best Restaurant in Asia for the second consecutive year.

If most reactions to the new order have been positive, the World's 50 Best has its detractors. Comments on the Le Figaro website and in French blogs suggest some French diners just can't accept a non-Michelin, non-French-starring list, especially one that comes out of Britain. Despite being classified in the 50 Best, several of France's senior chefs, including Pierre Gagnaire, Joel

Robuchon and Alain Ducasse, were noticeably absent from the awards ceremony. Grunts and jeers were also heard from some in Italy and other Old World countries whose traditional food is often considered a sacred—and untouchable—part of their cultural heritage.

Chang expressed another point of view: "I think Noma's win shows that the days are over when a chef's image will be constructed around a single person's ego, when it was all about me, me, me, me! Redzepi's acceptance speech proves you need to keep your team together to create a top restaurant. And that's a great lesson."

Anonymous Online Reviews Affecting Twin Cities Eateries

By Rachel Hutton

From *City Pages*

Whom should you trust when picking a restaurant—
a professional dining critic, or a tip from a "real" diner on an
online review site? *City Pages* food editor Hutton examines the
impact of such amateur reviews on her local Minneapolis/St.
Paul restaurants.

They gripe about their server tacking the gratuity onto their bill, without realizing that the sum was actually the valet parking charge. They fault the pulled pork for being "too shredded," when, by definition, that's exactly what pulled pork is. They complain that the appetizer is too small—"a ¾-inch diameter of food on a big plate, about ¼ of what I would expect"—not recognizing the absurdity of such a large portion of foie gras. They air their criticisms to everyone on the internet, but rarely share them directly with the chef. These are the anonymous commenters on local restaurant review sites, message boards, and blogs: a source of both delight and ire to the local restaurant community.

Restaurants have long been subjected to professional critics— I dug up a *New York Times* review published in 1859. But increasingly restaurateurs find themselves being critiqued by anyone with an internet connection. Few other professions face such public scrutiny. You don't read many blogs that assess the efficiency of a particular computer programmer's code or the speed at which a certain farmer milks his cows. While service-industry workers certainly deal with their share of public feedback, the skills of hairdressers, tailors, and mechanics are perceived to be a bit more mysterious than those of chefs. How many people cut their own hair, sew their own clothes, or fix their own cars, compared to those who make their own dinner?

Thus an inordinate amount of online chatter—on blogs, message boards, and review sites—is devoted to restaurants. When I last checked the review site Yelp, it listed 130 reviews in Minneapolis's Beauty and Spas category, 225 in Nightlife, 476 in Shopping, and 898 in Restaurants. The commentary is by and large positive, and restaurants for the most part are grateful to have their praises sung further and faster than they would by word-of-mouth. Several restaurateurs I spoke with said they also appreciate critical but respectful online feedback as a tool to help them improve their business.

But negative anonymous reviews are murkier territory. Everyone is entitled to an opinion, certainly, and relaying one's experience with sub-par food and service can be a valuable warning to would-be diners. But many restaurateurs say they have received criticism they felt was false, unfair, or malicious—which they had little ability to correct or refute. They were deeply troubled to know that, with a cursory Google search, such messages could reach potential customers for the foreseeable future.

Lenny Russo, chef-owner of the upscale Midwest-focused eatery Heartland, says that often the inaccuracies he sees in online comments are minor. A person might, for example, describe a meal at Heartland that included rice and pineapple salsa—two foods the restaurant doesn't serve. "Maybe it was wheat berries or barley, and it was squash that they thought was pineapple," Russo says. "Hopefully the people reading understand that the writer is ignorant."

But he has also seen broad mischaracterizations of his restaurant spread rapidly around cyberspace. He was particularly exasperated by one commenter who complained about Heartland's small portions: "I think I could have gotten more food walking around the taste testers at Sam's Club," she penned. "She didn't really understand what we were doing," Russo says.

Chef Russell Klein, who owns Meritage with his wife, Desta, recalls one incident in which a family brought along a baby who cried loudly throughout their leisurely meal. The adults made no effort to quiet the baby as it continued to disturb other guests' enjoyment of the restaurant's quaint, romantic ambiance. Looking out for the interests of other diners—some of whom had certainly paid for babysitters—Klein says Desta politely asked the woman if she'd like to take the baby out in the hallway to soothe it. The woman responded by making a scene about being "kicked out" and writing a rant that she posted on several restaurant-related sites.

I looked up the screed: "She was the meanest and rudest restaurant owner I had ever seen!" it reads. "A person who can not comprehend that a 10-month-old baby is not able to behave at 7 p.m. can no way make the rest of the customers happy." Although Desta did post a response, the original comment remains. "If somebody puts something out that's biased, unfair, or untrue," Klein says, "it lives forever."

Russo says he's learned to ignore criticism—he gets his fair share from the comments section of his blog on StarTribune.com—though he and other restaurateurs are especially sensitive to unfair comments about their customers or staff. Erica Christ, owner of the Black Forest, recalls one online commenter who complained that a server was flirting with diners at another table and described the server's appearance so specifically that she was easily identifiable. Elijah Goodwell, manager of the Birchwood Cafe, says he was particularly upset by disparaging remarks about two groups of valued customers: cyclists, who were described as "older flabby spandex-wearing bikers jockeying for first place like it was the friggin Tour de France," and kids, of which the commenter wrote: "OMG! Do they really have to eat out? Can't you leave them at home and throw them some kibble when you return?"

THE ANONYMITY GRANTED to bloggers and commenters who write under pseudonyms does have advantages to face-to-face conversation. If someone isn't comfortable with confrontation, Duplex chef Andrew Smith points out, anonymous complaints may be more authentic and direct than those made in person. "'Fine' in Minnesotan means 'it sucks,'" he notes.

But anonymity also means not having to take responsibility for one's words. Opinions need not be justified with knowledge. "You can say whatever you want on a blog and you don't have to research or fact-check or have to be qualified to offer an opinion," Russo says. "Some of it borders on libel." Anonymous critiques also tend to be harsher than bylined comments. Anna Christoforides, owner of Gardens of Salonica, says that she's seen far too much of such internet bullying. Her husband/co-owner has been referred to as a "soup Nazi" and "freaky" on local restaurant comment forums. "The public seems to have lost all of its sense of decorum and diplomacy," she says. Klein concurs: "The viciousness that people display online that they wouldn't say in person is pretty disturbing, actually."

Anonymous comment forums can also foster smear campaigns. "If somebody had a bone to pick with you for whatever reason, they could go online and say some nasty things about your business," Klein says. He wonders if the animosity of former colleagues at W.A. Frost may have prompted some to write negative reviews of Meritage. Goodwell says it's harder for him to trust online comments, not knowing the commenter's agenda, and describes the situation's inherent imbalance. "They have less to lose than we do," he says. "Their reputation isn't involved."

Worst of all, online disputes may be moving off computer screens and manifesting themselves in physically destructive acts. Earlier this fall, Heidi's chef-owner Stewart Woodman published some unflattering remarks about another local chef on his blog, Shefzilla.com, and shortly thereafter his restaurant was egged. The timing and narrow target of the vandalism suggested it may have been retaliatory.

Smith notes that the rise of the "entry-level foodism thing" has shifted the way food is perceived in our culture. "Interest in food has increased astronomically, so you have people who are really into it but don't really know that much about it," he says. He compares the tirades of the notoriously temperamental television celebrichef Gordon Ramsey to those of online commenters. "Those folks who are the chefs on TV actually have a background in cooking and knowledge to compel their rants," he says. "Some of the people don't have the background of knowledge but do try to copy the attitude."

So how do restaurateurs respond to comments they feel are out of line? "If they attack me personally in a vicious way, I don't respond," Russo says. "For the most part people read that stuff and they don't give it a second thought." On some sites, responding to a comment will move it to the forefront of a discussion; if left alone, comments tend to migrate to less noticeable placement over time. "If you respond, you inject life into it, and the person is probably enjoying your response," Russo adds.

Parasole, the restaurant group that owns Manny's, Chino Latino, and Salut, among others, has jumped into social media with more enthusiasm than any other local restaurateur. (Even founder Phil Roberts, who is in his 70s, has taken to Twittering.) Each of the company's restaurants has one youthful staffer devoted to updating its Facebook page and monitoring online commentary. Kip Clayton, who handles the company's business development, says that he has occasionally responded to online complaints on behalf of the company. For example, when commenters griped about the long lines and ticket times at Burger Jones, he explained that the restaurant was receiving three times the traffic they anticipated and were struggling to keep up. (Even for experienced restaurant owners like Parasole, some aspects of the business can be hard to predict.)

Still, it's nearly impossible for restaurateurs to respond online and not have their remarks seem defensive. Lisa Edevold, co-owner of Tiger Sushi, discovered the challenges of counteracting negative online comments when a few loyal customers mentioned that they had seen some not-so-positive reviews of Tiger on Yelp and offered to submit their own reviews to balance them out.

Shortly after the loyal customers posted their reviews, several were removed. Looking into the situation, Edevold found a discussion on the site among hard-core Yelpers who accused Tiger of posting "fraudulent" reviews, because several had been written by first-time Yelpers. (Determining authentic reviews isn't Yelp's only business challenge. The company recently came under fire for allegations that its sales reps were offering to make negative reviews less prominent for businesses who advertised with Yelp, as well as accusations that employees were posting negative reviews about businesses that didn't advertise.)

"Now when people tell me they love my restaurant and ask what they can do to get the word out, I tell them to stay away from Yelp, because they don't seem to welcome newcomers to their site," Evevold says. "We just stopped all Yelp activity after I read that, thinking that any more interaction with them would just be dangerous."

LIKE IT OR NOT, social media and anonymous online chatter aren't going away. "We have to figure it out or we'll be left behind," Clayton says. "I'm not sure how we're going to communicate with twentysomethings otherwise. Young people depend more on each other than on a Target commercial to tell them where to shop."

Still, every restaurateur I spoke with wished that online commenters would first try to address their concerns in the moment. "That gives us the opportunity to make it better," says Goodwell. "We're human. We're going to make mistakes. But we really care that people have a good experience."

Mike Phillips, chef at the Craftsman, laments the tendency for dissatisfied customers to express their concerns online instead of in person. "No one wants to talk to anyone anymore," he says. "They want to hide behind a computer and say things." Phillips also encourages commenters to be aware of the power of their words—they can have an impact on a restaurant's bottom line. "A lot of people's jobs are at stake," he says.

Russo, too, says he can't understand why unsatisfied customers don't speak up. ("Maybe because I'm Italian and I'm from New Jersey," he says, "I'll tell anybody anything.") "I would have made an attempt to do a better job for you. I'm not going to charge you for something you didn't enjoy. Do they think the chef is going to come out and sock them in the eye?" Russo says he'll oblige a customer's wish, even if it goes against his recommendation. "Order steak well done?" he says. "That's wrong. But I'm doing it anyhow because that's the way you asked for it." Somewhat facetiously he adds, "You want me throw it on the ground and step on it?" (I dare somebody to hold him to that one.)

Like most new technologies, anonymous online comments can be both a blessing and a curse. Restaurant-goers may find them helpful in making dining decisions—as long as they know they're coming from a trustworthy source. And restaurateurs appreciate the increased feedback—with a few reservations. "It provides more publicity and more information for people," Klein acknowledges, "but it can be really frustrating to have people who don't know a whole lot about what we do evaluate us." He urges commenters to keep things in perspective. "There are also times that people can be downright mean and vicious, and you want to remind them, 'It's just dinner. Tomorrow it'll be shit—literally.'"

Dining Around

FRIED IN EAST L.A.

By Jonathan Gold

From *LA Weekly*

Longtime *LA Weekly* critic, and winner of a 2007 Pulitzer Prize
(the first dining critic to be so honored), Jonathan Gold is
like the Philip Marlowe of the LA dining scene, with a restless
curiosity about *all* its eateries, from the trendiest café to the
humblest food stand.

It is late, and my family is asleep in the car, and I am lean-
ing against a chain-link fence on a sleepy Eastside street.
At the shuttered bakery on the corner, some of the night crew has
just shuffled into work, but I am here for the makeshift line of
folding tables along the sidewalk, the line of folding chairs, the
bowls of salsa teetering on the oilcloth. A woman bent over blue
flames prepares to make my dinner.

She fries tortillas in hot oil for a second or two, just long enough
to soften them, dips them in a dish of ruddy sauce, and splashes a
few drops of oil onto a second griddle. Tortillas fly onto the hot
metal. A moment later, the air is thick with the dark, musky scent of
toasting chiles. She inverts the tortillas, flips them around a bit of
cheese, and maneuvers them onto a plate in what seems like a single motion. They are the best enchiladas I have ever tasted.

Until recently, the center of the Eastside street-food universe
was located in a small parking lot on Breed Street in Boyle
Heights, a nocturnal band of vendors drawing customers from as
far away as Riverside and San Diego, serving sticky, sizzling,
crunchy, meaty snacks from all over Mexico; salsas hot enough to
burn small, butterfly-shaped patches into the leather of your shoes;

and quart-size foam cups of homemade orange drink. Over here were *huaraches*; over there Mexico City–style quesadillas; crunchy flautas; sugary churros; gooey tacos al vapor. The vendors never stayed open quite late enough, but Breed Street had become something of an institution, a place to take out of town visitors, a great quick dinner before a show. Sometimes there were even clowns.

The Breed Street experience was not exactly dependable—you never knew if a visit was going to result in a delicious bowl of *barbacoa* or a desolate patch of asphalt—and after local officials rousted the gathering for good a couple of months ago, it looked as if the party was over. To some of us, luxury dining means being able to find your favorite tamale vendor two nights in a row. But this is 2009—the tools of social networking are no farther away than the cell phone in your back pocket. A few weeks ago, some of the scattered vendors from the old parking lot began broadcasting their locations on Twitter, one of them as @antojitoscarmen, another group of them as @BreedStScene, and as with the introduction of Kogi merely one year ago, the intersection of technology and street food enabled something new. With Twitter, it doesn't matter if that tamale vendor has set up at the corner of Olympic and Soto, at a Maravilla service station or in front of a nightclub down on Whittier.

So a weekend taco crawl might begin with a visit to the @BreedStScene guys, chiefly Nina's, whose *gorditas* and *huaraches* were the stars of the Breed Street gatherings, and whose scarlet *pambazos*, chorizo-and-potato sandwiches dunked in chile and fried until the sauce hardens into a crackly gloss, are among the best in town. (Nina's dry salsa of toasted seeds and chile is the perfect condiment.) Somebody will slip you a tiny pill cup filled with the hominy stew *pozole*, and you'll probably have a bowl of that too, as well as one of the Mexico City–style quesadillas, which are like demonically good Hostess Fruit Pies filled with squash blossoms and melted cheese. Kids run around glugging orange soda, teasing their little sisters with Mickey Mouse dolls.

Lupe's Crepes, the next stand over, specializes in sweets: bubbly pancakes or fried bananas dressed with caramel sauce and condensed milk. Rodolfo's Barbacoa sells soupy lamb stew. The rogue cart around the corner does street dogs and tacos *al vapor*, scooping soft, unctuous masses of cow's head from steam-table bins hidden under a clean, white towel. A block away are those enchiladas, part of a smaller, quieter scene, another entrepôt of *huaraches* and quesadillas. If you ask for tamales, somebody fetches them from a silent man in a car.

When you approach Antojitos Carmen, several blocks north and east, the first thing you may notice, once you get past the woman selling purses, are the big griddles dotted with chalupas, tiny tortillas smeared with puréed beans, drizzled with cream, and moistened with red or green salsa—the green chile is the spiciest thing you will eat tonight, unless you dipped into the sauce labeled "*muy picoso*" at Nina's, in which case you're already back home, recovering. And you can eat a dozen chalupas in a flash. Once you abandon yourself to the magnetic chalupa forces you will be lured across the river again and again—the CIA could learn something about mind control from antojitos masters.

And Antojitos Carmen itself? Homemade walnut *atole*, fluffy *pambazos* and the best Mexico City huaraches on the street: crisp-edged surfboards of toasted masa sluiced with an ink-black stew of *huitlacoche*, painted with red chile, *crema* and green chile to resemble the Mexican flag. The scion of the family that runs the stand, Abe Ortega, perpetually wearing an outsize Dodgers jacket, hands you a raisin-studded gelatin dessert and grins.

New Zion Barbecue

By Patricia Sharpe

From *Saveur*

Moonlighting from her three-decades-plus gig as food columnist of *Texas Monthly* magazine, Patricia Sharpe opens a window onto authentic Texas barbecue for *Saveur*'s nationwide readership.

The time is 5:30 on a cool Friday morning, and, as the old saying goes, it's as dark as the inside of a black cat. A little breeze riffles the tall pines lining a country road in Huntsville, a town of 35,000 in southeastern Texas, and an insomniac mockingbird sings somewhere deep in the shadows. Although every cell in my body is screaming for caffeine, I've somehow managed to show up on time at the small parish hall behind New Zion Missionary Baptist Church. Soon a pair of headlights appears in the distance: Robert Polk has come, as he does three days a week, to fire up the barbecue pit.

Looking with resignation at the soot-covered, nine-foot-long metal drum cooker in front of him, the taciturn 44-year-old outlines the task ahead. "First, I have to shovel the old ashes out and put them in the trash," he tells me. "Then I put some oak logs in the firebox," he says, referring to the metal receptacle that serves as the pit's fireplace. He gets a roaring blaze going and lets it cool down before he scrapes the grill racks clean. Then he disappears into the kitchen and returns with four enormous beef briskets that have been sitting in the refrigerator overnight while a seasoning rub from a closely guarded recipe seeps into every fiber and pore. After heaving the meat onto the racks, Polk settles into a rusty metal folding chair a few feet away. The sun has come up, and the day is getting warmer; the pit radiates a slumber-inducing heat. "I'll keep an eye on it, but I might nod off a little," he says. He's entitled. By 11, when the customers start showing up, things will be too busy for so much as a coffee break.

New Zion—more generally referred to as "that church that sells barbecue"—is one of the most renowned yet improbable members of the Texas barbecue hall of fame. I've been making regular pilgrimages here from my home in Austin, a good three hours away, for nearly 15 years, and each time I do I wonder why I've waited so long to come back. Everything about the trip is gratifying: driving out through the remote region known as the Piney Woods, spotting the smoke rising above the trees, comparing notes with other customers ("How'd y'all hear about this place?"), and finally sitting down in a rickety little church building to devour some of the most tender, flavorful barbecue in the state.

The transaction is about as straightforward as it can be: the church cooks mouthwatering meats, sides, and pies, and the public queues up for the privilege of consuming them. That's all there is to it. Basically, the church runs a barbecue joint like thousands of others in Texas, but something about the whole experience far surpasses the sum of its exceedingly modest parts. Walking across the remnants of purple carpet that have been placed on the ground around the pit to keep the dust down, I feel as if I'd been hired as an extra for a Texas-based episode of *The Andy Griffith Show* or perhaps been asked to pose for a Norman Rockwell painting. A feeling of déjà vu—of having stepped back into that elusive, simpler time, a time when community and fellowship fueled the state's great barbecue tradition—envelops me, but with one key difference: this is for real.

If you want to find out more about the place that wags inevitably refer to as the Church of the Holy Smoke, it's a good idea to get acquainted with the Reverend Clinton Edison, the fatherly, 56-year-old pastor who presides over New Zion's congregation of 40 or so mostly elderly members. I ask him how the barbecues got started, and he treats me to an hour-long yarn.

As best he can figure, it was 1976—although some say 1979—when a painting contractor named D. C. Ward volunteered to paint the church, to which he and his family belonged. At noon on the first day of work, his wife, Annie Mae, set up a smoker on the church lawn to barbecue some meat for Ward's lunch. Savory aromas wafted through the air. "Once she fired that pit up," Edison says, "people started stopping by and asking if they could buy some barbecue." Annie Mae sold a little meat, then a little more, and pretty soon it was all gone. "My poor husband never got anything to eat," she is quoted as saying in one of the yellowed news clippings tacked to the dining room's walls. The following Sunday, Annie Mae asked the pastor at the time whether she could sell barbecue and give the proceeds to the church. He handed her $50, and with that sum she started what could be described as the longest-running church fund-raiser in the state's history.

The Wards handled the whole shebang at first, but before long most of the congregation was pitching in. Lunches and dinners were served on paper plates on the church lawn for a couple of years, until the health department cracked down and said they had to move the operation indoors. Fortunately, the church had raised enough money by then to build a wood-frame parish hall with room for a handful of tables and a kitchen. Things took off in a serious way: on some days, the line of barbecue supplicants stretched out the door to the church parking lot. Annie Mae and half a dozen church ladies would bustle around the kitchen in their print dresses and aprons, preparing side dishes and desserts: tender, unfussy pinto beans that had soaked and simmered for hours; potato salad made with Idaho russets, mashed by hand and flavored with plenty of dill pickle relish; pecan pie with a famously high pecan-to-goo ratio; eye-rollingly good, cinnamon-y sweet potato pie; and more. The recipes were Annie Mae's, and she resisted innumerable entreaties from customers that she share them. As Edison recalls, "She would say, 'It's not a secret; we just don't tell anyone.'"

New Zion's pièce de résistance, though, was its barbecue, prepared in smoke-belching pits by D. C. Ward and the church men. In the early years, they used direct-heat smokers, in which the coals are placed right under the grill racks; it's a difficult, labor-intensive way to cook, as the meat can easily dry out if the cooks aren't careful, but done right, it delivers an intensely smoky taste. Later the church switched to indirect-heat barrel smokers, with the firebox off to the side. Beef brisket—loose textured and abundantly fatty even after it's been trimmed—was always the centerpiece, but there were also meaty pork ribs that you ate using two hands, as you would corn on the cob, along with chicken, its skin burnished and golden and its meat falling from the bone in pearlescent hunks. Links of slow-smoked pork-and-beef sausage—made in nearby Bryan, Texas—added a salty, peppery kick to the ensemble.

Annie Mae and D. C. Ward did things their own way, which is to say, not in the style you might expect to find at most East Texas barbecue joints. For one thing, they cooked their brisket and ribs for a comparatively short time, not until it fell apart in tender shreds. For another, they didn't serve their brisket precut and slathered with the smash-up of condiments, from ketchup and Worcestershire to barbecued meat drippings and black coffee, that's become the thick and hearty style of sauce now common across the state. Instead, the Wards cooked their meats for anywhere from four to six hours, until they were succulent and smoky, and served their sauce—the kind of thinnish, tomatoey, russet-colored brew shot through with vinegar that you used to find in Central Texas—on the side or, if the customer preferred, ladled onto the plate. The signature flavor came from Annie Mae's special mix of salt, pepper, and secret seasonings, which was not only rubbed on the meats but also added to the barbecue sauce and the beans, as it still is today. "About the only thing it's not in is the tea, and we're working on that," a cook named Clayton "Smitty" Smith tells me.

In 2004 the Wards, well into their 90s, retired to Houston, where they still live. Horace and Mae Archie, longtime church members, took over the management of the meals and oversaw them until last year, when Mae died of a heart attack. After that, Edison himself took on the job of running the business. "I told everybody we would keep it going as long as the Wards were alive or until the old building falls down," he said. Given a dwindling and aging congregation, he has had to hire help from outside the church in order to keep up with demand.

Over time and with practice, though, the group of six has coalesced into an efficient, tight-knit team. During the day I spent hanging around the kitchen, I watched with admiration as they sliced brisket, ladled sauce, toted steaming platters of sides, and weaved around one another with seeming extrasensory perception. Robert Polk, the pit master I met earlier this morning, comes in carrying a gorgeous brisket fresh from the smoker and hands it off to Smitty, who starts slicing it to make sandwiches and plates. The rest goes into a supersize crock pot, where it stays warm throughout service. Ann O'Bryant, a woman in her 40s who does most of the cooking, tells me that she prepares sides "just the way Mrs. Ward did," and Henry Ford, 16, the newest member of the team, moves quickly as he washes dishes and cleans up. Reverend Edison, under the watchful eye of his wife, Wyvonnia, who helps him manage the place, runs the cash register. He also comes in early to make a few desserts, having added his own, excellent buttermilk pie to the repertoire.

By around one o'clock, the rush has died down, and I come out from behind the counter where I've been shooed so that I'd be out of the way. I find Edison at a kitchen counter putting away leftovers. I have a couple of final questions for him, including one that you could almost call theological: What does the future hold?

"Well," he says, "our first goal is to give this place a good facelift." I confess that I find this alarming. While I can't deny that the church hall could use an upgrade—the flooring is cracked, the curtains are faded—too much spiffing up could destroy the joint's scruffy charisma.

Perhaps Reverend Edison senses that I'm quietly freaking out. "We're not going to do much; people come for the history," he says, as he stretches a sheet of plastic wrap around a bowl of potato salad and puts it into the refrigerator. Aside from a little sprucing up, the reverend says, he and his flock plan to keep things exactly the same. Thank heaven.

KYOTO'S TOFU OBSESSION

By Adam Sachs

From *Bon Appetit*

If the term "globetrotter" hadn't already existed, it would
have to be invented to describe Adam Sachs. Few travel
writers delve so eagerly into the local tastes of a destination.
He doesn't just dine in Kyoto, he seeks out the artisans who
create its signature foodstuff.

Mitsuyoshi Kotzumi squeezes a soybean between his fingers and looks pleased.

"*Unyuu*," he says—a Japanese onomatopoeia that means (more
or less) the sound of something firm but pliant being squished.
This, according to Koizumi, is what a perfect soybean sounds like
when it's ready to become tofu.

"Like gummy candy," he says, handing me the wet soybean.

It is 5:30 a.m. on my first full day in Kyoto. I am wearing a hairnet, standing in a narrow, steamy kitchen overlooking the Kamo-
gawa River, pinching a soaked bean. Why am I here? The reason is
bean curd.

Koizumi-san is a tofu maker at Kinki, an artisanal shop where I
have come to witness the daily predawn alchemy by which raw
soybeans are transformed into squares of the firm-but-creamy
building blocks of *kyo-ryori*, the cuisine of Kyoto. Ancient land of
culture, temples, and gardens, once the imperial capital of Japan for
1,000 years, Kyoto is a city with a healthy obsession for tofu.

But stay, carnivorous reader. Don't turn the page. It's not what
you're thinking. Believe me—I'm not a morning person, and before coming here, I was never an avid tofu-seeker. The fresh Japan-

ese version is a far more noble creature than the often bland loaves sold in American supermarkets. The difference in taste? Chalk and cheese, I'd say, though that would be unfair to chalk.

Here, tofu is a delicate handmade food, produced every morning in small shops and large industrial kitchens throughout the country. Each region makes its own styles of tofu, but Kyoto is to tofu what Naples is to pizza, New York to bagels. The Kyoto variety—perfected over centuries by Buddhist monks, in imperial kitchens, and in neighborhood shops like this one—is the accepted standard; it is regarded as the best in Japan and thus the world.

While tofu has become a mass-produced staple stateside, only now are we waking up to the allure of nonindustrial tofu. Japanese restaurants like EN Japanese Brasserie in New York feature fresh tofu on their menus. Reika Yo, the proprietor of EN, told me it took her a while to educate people about how tofu was eaten in Japan. I'd had great tofu dishes in the formal *kaiseki* restaurants and raucous *izakayas* of Tokyo. But Tokyo is so overwhelming; the discreet pleasures of humble tofu are easily lost in the culinary cacophony. I knew that in quieter Kyoto I'd find (and be able to focus on) the real thing.

Back at Kinki, Koizumi and a few colleagues dart around the kitchen while loungy Blue Note jazz plays on the radio. Through a window, gawky herons are visible gliding across the river. On the far bank, the first stirrings of the morning bicycle traffic. Kyoto is a modern city, with modern sprawl, apartment towers, and a subway system. But it is also a place of serene gardens, of temple life, and of little streets like this one, where you can walk alone in the early morning and observe craftsmen keeping alive old traditions inside *kyomachiya*, the city's traditional wooden townhouses.

My translator this morning is Derek Wilcox, a Poughkeepsie-born chef who works at Kyoto's Kikunoi restaurant. "It has more *presence*," Wilcox says, trying to explain the special properties of Kyoto tofu. "It's not just this empty block of protein that you flavor with something else."

The thing that turns *tonyu*, or soy milk, into tofu is called *nigari*. Crystals of magnesium chloride act as a coagulant, much as rennin makes cheese curds out of cow's milk. The familiar, firm, square-cut variety is called *momen-dofu*, meaning "cotton tofu," as it was traditionally pressed over a porous cloth. *Kinugoshi-dofu* means "silken tofu," and while silk isn't actually used to prepare it, the name makes sense: It is a wet, jiggly tofu with the silken creaminess of a custard—the best a soybean can be.

Wilcox and I leave the staff at Kinki to their morning work. Walking north, we take a meandering course from the river toward Nishiki Market, Kyoto's famous covered street of food stalls, pickle sellers, tea vendors, fishmongers, a 400-year-old knife shop, and, of course, tofu—lots of tofu.

As we walk, Wilcox talks me through what he calls "Kyoto Tofu 101." In addition to *momen-dofu*, the most flexible, and *kinugoshi-dofu*, the most refined, we find *age-dofu* (tofu sliced into sheets and deep-fried), *atsu-age dofu* (thick deep-fried tofu), *oboro-dofu* (with a scooped, crumbly texture like cottage cheese), and *yaki-dofu* (grilled tofu). This being Japan, there are dozens of variations and riffs within this framework, and hundreds of ways to cook it: cold tofu, boiled tofu, *dengaku* (skewered and grilled), fried tofu balls, and on and on.

Our lesson is cut short by the sight of Hara Donuts, a happy little take-away place with three giggly girls frying donuts. The house specialty is a tofu donut made with sweet soy milk and okara, the fiber-rich by-product of tofu production. In the interest of research, Wilcox and I eat several. "Almost healthy," he says. The girls giggle more.

"Hippie, crunchy, pinko-leaning, in America, we have all these associations for tofu," says Chris Rowthorn, an expat writer who lives in Kyoto and runs personalized tours around Japan. "But in Japan, you'll see the hardest construction workers or truck drivers walk into a restaurant and order a block of cold tofu."

Rowthorn and I meet for lunch at Tousuiro, a tofu restaurant in a narrow alley off Kiyamachi Street. The *kaiseki*-style tofu menu begins with a pretty plate of *zensai*, Japanese amuse-bouches: *tamago* (omelet) folded with sea bream eggs and tofu; a small pile of grainy *okara*; and a green-pea-flavored tofu cut into the shape of a Japanese maple leaf. Next comes cold *yuba*, or tofu "skin," piled up like soft-serve, topped with purple-flowering miniature *shiso* leaves and resting on a bed of crushed ice. In every course, tofu pops up like Peter Sellers playing multiple roles in the same movie, a versatile actor showing off its range with various accents and guises. Sea bass is pressed into a block with tofu. *Oboro-dofu* has a consistency somewhere between *burrata* and panna cotta.

After a dessert of soy-milk ice cream, Rowthorn and I chat with the restaurant's manager, Nagashi Yoshida.

"Originally, tofu came from China," Yoshida-san explains. "It was first brought to Nara, which was then the capital of Japan. There were a lot of priests there, so it became associated with Buddhism. When the capital moved to Kyoto, the priests came, too, and brought tofu culture with them."

Whenever you talk to people about tofu in Kyoto, this is what they mention: the city's history, the vegetarian diet of monks, the mountains that surround the city, and the clean water that runs down from those mountains. One night, I sleep at a 191-year-old *ryokan*, or traditional inn, called Hiiragiya. Each room is a sanctuary: tatami mats, wooden baths, and sliding doors that open onto a little private garden. Samurai slept here. Charlie Chaplin had stayed in my room.

In the morning, I sit wrapped in my yukata robe and eat the traditional dish called yudofu—squares of tofu boiling in a nabe pot over a small flame. Later, I follow the Path of Philosophy to the grounds of the Nanzenji Temple, where there is another kind of shrine: Okutan, a 360-year-old tofu restaurant. Here, charcoal is brought in, as well as a bowl of broth to simmer tofu.

The mood is meditative, yet even in my contemplative state I think maybe that's enough simmered tofu for a while. But this is before I go to dinner at Kichisen, where chef Yoshimi Tanigawa proceeds to blow my mind.

Michael Baxter, an American who lives here and writes a blog called kyotofoodie.com, introduces me to Kichisen. Baxter is sort of obsessed with the place—and the chef—and it's easy to see why. Tanigawa is an intense, funny genius who once defeated an Iron Chef on the Japanese program, and whose *kaiseki* restaurant is run with martial precision. Baxter and I eat Tanigawa's version of *yudofu*: a clay pot with tofu that's whiter and shinier than any I've seen. The tofu is dipped into dashi with *kujo-negi* (local scallions) and covered in bonito flakes. The broth is rich, but the smoothness and taste of the tofu itself is remarkable—bright, creamy, sweet.

The tofu, Tanigawa tells us, comes from Morika, a famous shop on the outskirts of town. Instead of *nigari*, Morika uses calcium sulfate as the coagulant, which for some reason produces a smooth tofu that holds its shape in the hot bath of *yudofu*.

"We opened Morika about the time Commodore Perry came to open Japan," Genichi Morii tells me when I visit him the next day at his shop. Perry's arrival in the 1850s ended two centuries of self-imposed isolation. When he sailed home, Perry's ships are said to have delivered to America its first soybean plants. A century and a half later, soybeans are America's biggest crop, supplying much of Japan's demand, and Morika is still here making tofu. "Whatever you do, you must love it," says Morii. "You've got to love tofu to make it."

I think about that love and dedication—centuries of bean curd!—when I find myself at Yubahan, a small *yuba* maker in an old *kyo-machiya* on a placid backstreet in the center of town. Here, early in the morning, a young man tends to two dozen large vats of simmering soy milk. Slowly, a skin forms on the milk's surface. And slowly, slowly, the kid deftly runs a wooden dowel over the milk and pulls up a thin, delicate sheet of tofu skin, as his family has been doing here since 1716. I eat a bowl of *yuba* and watch the boy watching the vats. I think about the ritual slowness of this work. The *yuba* is warm and soft on the tongue. This is what Kyoto does so well: coaxing the boring-looking soybean to greatness, bringing out its essence, and finding there something simple, pure, and *oishii*—delicious.

Time to Respect the Ramen

By Kevin Pang

From the *Chicago Tribune*

Tribune dining reporter Kevin Pang's eclectic background—
born in Hong Kong, raised in Seattle, college and first job in
Southern California—makes him a natural for navigating
Chicago's multi-faceted food culture. A dose of hipster
humor comes in handy too.

Not too long ago, I stared longingly out the window of a Tokyo hotel, my eyes laser-focused on a ramen noodle cart by the train station.

A half-dozen people stood in line, mostly men in dark business suits. They waited and waited, then plopped themselves onto stools outside when summoned by the ramen chef. Sufficiently intrigued, I found myself in line among the suits. Ten minutes later, the cook presented a perfectly composed bowl, primary colors popping, a half-dozen ingredients resting in their respective nooks atop a steam-billowing tangle of noodles.

The bowl satisfied every taste sense man is blessed to experience. The soy-sauced broth was savory and pure. The noodles: smooth on the intake with an appealing chew. Alternating bites of bean sprouts, braised pork, seaweed and hard-boiled egg ensured every bite highlighted a different flavor.

My brows beaded with sweat, my heart rate rose, my virginal experience of real Japanese ramen shook me to the core. Ramen was the first food I learned to cook at age 10—drop noodle brick in boiling water, empty sodium packet—and here it was, in the middle of Tokyo's Shinagawa neighborhood, a dish redefined.

This following statement I shall defend to the death: When ramen is good, it's in the top three of the most extraordinary, soul-satisfying foods in the world. Admittedly, ramen gets a bad rap stateside. It conjures images of college dorms and food-drive donation bins. When you can get Sapporo Ichiban noodles—10 for a dollar—at Walgreens, there's a whiff of cheapness ramen can't escape.

But the last decade has seen ramen's street cred rise in cities such as New York, Los Angeles and Seattle. It's a mystery why Chicago isn't a ramen hotbed.

Two theories as to Chicago's underwhelming ramen representation: Among Asians in Illinois, there are more Indians, Chinese, Koreans and Filipinos than Japanese. A bigger reason is that ramen is a laborious, time-consuming dish that, to prepare well, a restaurant has to pretty much make the dish its singular focus.

There's this terrible movie called "The Ramen Girl," in which Brittany Murphy's character apprentices at a Tokyo ramen shop. There was one memorable line from the ramen chef, though: "A bowl of ramen is a self-contained universe with life from the sea, the mountain and the earth, all existing in perfect harmony. What holds it all together is the broth. The broth gives life to the ramen."

As great broths go, three in our area are worth noting.

Takashi Yagihashi's cooking can be described as white-tablecloth Japanese through a French prism, but the Sunday brunch menu at his Bucktown restaurant, Takashi, is closest to his native roots. It's the one day of the week he serves ramen.

For Takashi, growing up in Mito, a town outside Tokyo known for its abundant pink plum blossoms, ramen was omnipresent.

"My house was on the same block as a ramen shop. We'd get so hungry after baseball practice we'd go there for a snack, then I'd eat dinner again," Takashi said. "I wanted to introduce what you can eat in Japan if you traveled there."

The number of regional ramen styles in Japan number in the dozens, but the most prevalent is Tokyo-style shoyu, the Japanese word for soy sauce. Like a Chicago hot dog, you'll always find the same six ingredients atop a shoyu ramen: bamboo shoots, scallions, seaweed, hard-boiled egg sliced lengthwise, braised pork and Naruto-style fish cake (characterized by its pink swirl design).

The day I visited, it so happened that Rick Bayless and his wife, Deann, were also dining at Takashi, sharing a bowl of the shoyu ramen ($13). I could hear him from a few tables away raving about the noodles. We compared notes after the meal.

"There's something so elementally true about getting and understanding what role broth plays and how incredibly satisfying that is," Bayless said. "I like the very gentle spicing in it, that hint of star anise. It's gentle, doesn't hit you over the head. That to me is the perfect Sunday morning: that Tokyo ramen."

Takashi's name is attached to the noodle bar on the seventh-floor food court inside Macy's Loop store. The ramen at his Bucktown restaurant, though, is miles better, because he's overseeing the broth's 24-hour cooking process.

Chicken and pork bones are boiled for hours. Bonito flakes (classic Japanese flavoring agent of dried shaved tuna), kombu (kelp) and dried sardines are added, giving the stock that savory taste sensation of umami. From there, the stock base goes in any number of directions—the popular shoyu, or the version I ordered, miso ramen. (True miso is a thick paste made from fermented soybeans, not the gunky powder turned soup.)

The miso ramen ($13) arrived studded with sweet corn, bean sprouts and wakame, sweet strips of seaweed.

I slurped louder than culturally appropriate. This is, in fact, acceptable behavior. Slurping accomplishes two duties: It cools the noodle, and the extra intake of oxygen supposedly amplifies flavor, the same way it would with wine.

A sure sign of unadulterated slurping was the dots of broth that soon splattered on the table and my shirt. The broth had a nutty, earthy flavor that soothed on that chilly day (miso ramen is indigenous to Hokkaido, Japan's northernmost island, known for its long, frigid winters). Therein lies the difference between 10-cent instant ramen and Takashi's broth: One is just salty, the other a deep, resonant flavor made possible by a secret ingredient called Father Time.

Bill Kim's most excellent *Urban Belly* offers a lighter take on ramen ($13). Authenticity is not a concern for Kim, a Korean-American who can deftly meld far-off Asian flavors. His dashi-based pork broth (bonito flakes and kombu) features Vietnamese pho spices, lime juice and fish sauce. Kim's ramen tilts more refreshing, though the richness from the pork belly tips it back the other way.

Kim tipped his hand: "We all go to Santouka. A good Asian will know to go to **Santouka** in Mitsuwa."

Santouka is the chain ramen franchise from Japan, inside the food court at Arlington Heights' Mitsuwa Marketplace. Its special toroniku shio ramen was so spectacular I asked the Santouka manager its secrets. I was hit with a big, fat "no, thanks."

The manager is a young Japanese fellow who allegedly speaks no English. Even with the lure of positive press, the manager's English-speaking subordinates claimed that he was under no authority to divulge proprietary company secrets and, therefore, *get off my lawn!*

This much I could derive: Their special toroniku shio ramen ($8.99) has buttery, luscious slices of pork cheeks that fell apart with no teeth resistance. The broth is wintry white, as if the noodles were soaked in buttermilk, then flecked with sesame seeds. It's reminiscent of tonkotsu ramen, the Southern Japan-style broth made by boiling pork bones for a *long time* (not to be confused with tonkatsu, the panko-breaded fried pork cutlets).

Don't let anyone tell you otherwise: In the ramen world, tonkotsu is king among kings.

The top of the broth glistened; an emulsified pork fat spillage that would put Greenpeace volunteers on high alert. The toppings came separately on a side plate—wood-ear mushrooms, scallions, bamboo shoots, fish cake and the fatty pork—to be dumped into the ramen by the diner.

It was profoundly delicious. The broth's porkiness was so rich and intense I inhaled every last sip. The toothsome noodles were made using alkaline salt, which gives them an eggy-yellow hue. Beneath the savoriness, there's a gentle sweetness to it all. In all my visits to Santouka, it accessed the same lobe and cortex that flooded back memories of ramen carts outside Tokyo train stations.

After I slurped the last of the noodles, a residue of slick, porky balm had formed around my lips. That was my favorite part.

WORLD'S BEST SOMMELIER VS. WORLD'S WORST CUSTOMER

By Frank Bruni

From *Food & Wine*

Former *New York Times* dining critic Frank Bruni—author of
the memoir *Born Round: Secret History of a Full-Time Eater*—
knows a thing or two about restaurant impersonations. Here
he deliberately sets out to test the mettle of a top Manhattan
wine steward.

I vetoed the Champagne that Le Bernardin's Aldo Sohm
suggested at the meal's start, telling him my mood wasn't
so bubbly. Rejecting his advice again, I insisted on having a red instead of a white for the charred octopus, then I staged a tabletop
tantrum over the price of the Montrachet that he initially paired
with the monkfish.

As dinner progressed and Sohm's face turned an increasingly
flustered shade of red, I accepted only one of his recommendations, a sake for a smoked-salmon carpaccio bejeweled with glittering salmon caviar. Otherwise, I grimaced and protested while
he stammered and perspired. I wanted to see how well the "world's
best sommelier" could roll with the punches—and just how many
of them he could take.

That's what had brought me and a companion to Le Bernardin,
one of Manhattan's most esteemed restaurants for more than two
decades. We were staging a sort of contest, which pitted a pesky,
deliberately obnoxious naysayer (i.e., me) against a wine savant of
world renown. The restaurant's venerated chef, Eric Ripert, and a
few of his lieutenants knew about our ploy. But they hadn't

informed Sohm, whose reactions to me would ideally reveal something about the flexibility of wine pairings and the deliberations of a master sommelier.

Sohm, 38, is certainly a master. Born, raised and educated in Austria, he moved to New York in 2004 to work with Kurt Gutenbrunner at Wallsé and the chef's other restaurants, then left to take charge of the wine program at Le Bernardin in 2007. While working full-time there, he boned up for sommelier competitions and bested rivals from around the globe in Rome in 2008, winning top honors from the Worldwide Sommelier Association. He was judged on his ability to recognize wines in blind tastings, to edit a wine list and to suggest pairings for food.

It was the last of these talents that I focused on, assessing the agility and inspiration with which he navigated Le Bernardin's list of about 750 wines from 14 countries. The wine list emphasizes France, but I wasn't going to let Sohm do that. Nor was I going to let him return too frequently to his homeland, which he's been known to do.

"We're yanking you out of the Alps, Aldo," I made clear at the start, when he tried to substitute an Austrian Muskateller for the spurned glasses of Champagne. So he toggled to the island of Santorini and a 2008 Thalassitis from Gai'a Wines. He likened the body, bite and citrus notes of the Greek white to a French Chablis. But why was it the right wine for our canapé of raw tuna pressed in briny kombu seaweed?

"Acidity and minerality," he said, explaining that the wine should brighten and sharpen the taste of the fish the way a splash of lemon and a scattering of coarse salt would.

Bit by bit, Sohm detailed his philosophy on wine-food pairings, saying that not only should the wine burnish the food, but also the food should burnish the wine.

"Food and wine are in a marriage where both should get better," he said. "It's a two-way relationship."

"But shouldn't it be a three-way?" I asked. He blushed. I explained: "Shouldn't you consider the drinker, too, and what his or her taste in wine is?"

"That's true," Sohm conceded, then added that he was only now learning what kind of wine drinker I was.

I accelerated his education, telling him I'd long been prejudiced in favor of drier wines. That inclination, not just orneriness, was why the Greek white had worked better for me than the Austrian.

It was also one reason I waved away the floral Tramin Gewürztraminer from the Alto Adige region of Italy—the Alps, mind you—that he paired with the exquisite octopus, a Mediterranean-meets-Asian dish combining Bartlett pear with fermented black beans and a squid ink-and-miso vinaigrette. I told him to give me something drier and demanded a red to boot. So he presented two California Zinfandels, which he said would be fruity enough to match the dish. But the first one—a 2006 late-harvest wine from Dashe Cellars—had definite sweetness. The second, a 2005 from Martinelli's Jackass Vineyard, didn't, though there was a price for that.

"Seventeen percent alcohol," Sohm noted, thus commencing a tutorial on another crucial aspect of wine pairings during a meal that includes a half dozen courses or more: pacing. The wines, in sequence and aggregate, shouldn't exhaust a diner's palate or leave him too tipsy.

Without being asked to, Sohm chose as many wines for under $100 a bottle as wines that hit or exceeded that mark, even though roughly 80 percent of Le Bernardin's list falls in the higher-priced category.

But for another stunner of a dish, supple pan-roasted monkfish in a gingery sake broth studded with honshimeji mushrooms, Sohm got a little bit ritzy: He wanted to pour glasses of a premier cru 2006 Chassagne-Montrachet from Domaine Bernard Moreau Les Chevenottes. It was white Burgundy at its most regal, and it cost $150 a bottle.

"Too much!" I declared, trying for the vocal equivalent of a pout.

So he trotted out another white Burgundy, because he said the sake in the dish called for a wine with soft tannins. This one, a 2005 Philippe Colin Maranges, was $75, and, though it paired beautifully with the fish—making the broth's flavor seem deeper and earthier—it had less elegance than its regional kin. Sohm studied me as I registered the difference.

"When you've driven a Ferrari and you go back to a Mercedes, you can feel a little lost," he consoled me. "That doesn't mean the Mercedes isn't any good." The Maranges was in fact excellent, and its crispness made it in some ways a better match for the monkfish than the Montrachet. We also preferred it to a California Pinot Noir that he threw into the mix at the last minute.

I noticed that the redness in Sohm's face had faded somewhat, and that he now seemed much too calm. So I became even more strident and implacable for Ripert's final savory course, an upscale surf and turf of grilled escolar and Kobe beef with pungent anchovy-butter sauce.

"No Bordeaux!" I said, dismissing his pick. "No red wine, period.

"And no white, either," I pronounced, my voice turning sinister. "In fact, no wine. I want a pairing of hard liquor. It can be in a cocktail. It can be served neat. Your choice."

Sohm looked baffled. Nervous. Then he vanished.

When he reappeared—too soon, and with a stride too brisk and steady—he had in his clutch a bottle of Zacapa rum from Guatemala, aged up to 23 years. He said it just might work with the Kobe and escolar, and sure enough it did, providing precisely the sweet-with-unctuous charge that distinguishes a classic union of Sauternes and foie gras. And because the rum had been aged so long, it was gorgeously smooth.

By that point, Sohm had taken us to eight countries, presented us with about a dozen grape varietals and, most impressive, maintained extraordinary grace under pestering. What could be left?

As it turned out, beer. In part because of its carbonation, which can cut richness and settle a full stomach, Sohm sometimes likes to throw it in toward the end of a long meal, and on this night he offered a Westmalle Dubbel Trappist beer from Belgium for a milk-chocolate pot de crème topped with maple-syrup caramel. The dessert neatly underscored the vaguely chocolaty aspect of many dark brews. Sampling the food and the beer together, I was put in mind of a chocolate egg cream.

Visions of a Jewish deli staple at a haute French restaurant? The evening's last laugh belonged to Sohm, who bid us good night with beads of perspiration on his forehead but a triumphant gleam in his eyes.

Nights on the Town

By Patric Kuh

From *Saveur*

Author of *The Last Days of Haute Cuisine*, chef / writer Kuh—
otherwise known as the dining critic for *Los Angeles*
magazine—here opens a nostalgic window on the glamour
days of L.A.'s restaurant scene.

I love dusk in LA, that moment just before restaurants open for dinner. A waiter runs to work, toting his white shirt on a hanger. A kitchen crew wolfs down a quick meal at the empty bar. A parking valet rolls out the pavement stand. The scent of night—blooming jasmine is in the air, and all over the city, against an evening sky whose colors are unique to this part of Southern California, the lights are coming up. They click on in the recessed nooks of a sleek sushi joint. They sparkle on a chandelier in an old-school French restaurant somewhere in the San Fernando Valley. They shine from sconces in a west side bistro. And, everywhere, there's the neon: "Cocktails," "Steaks and Chops," "Seafood." Night falls, and, feeling the first pangs of hunger, you are faced with that most pleasant of quandaries in LA: Where should we eat?

As a restaurant critic, I spend hours each day driving around this city, asking myself that very question, the same one Angelenos have asked themselves since the earliest days of fine dining in LA. And I spend just as much time sitting in crowded restaurants, considering the service, the food, the setting, and wondering what makes restaurant culture here so different from that of any other city in the world. It's no secret that LA's upscale restaurants tend to be more casual and more outwardly trendy than those you find in other great food cities, or that the cuisine here is often lighter and more far ranging. But, why? What made it so?

It's okay not to have too much of a history in Los Angeles. In fact, being without one is something of a tradition. The past here need reach no further back than the moment the lead character (in drop-dead heels, please) steps off the 20th Century Limited at Union Station and onto the palm-lined street. Over the course of the past hundred years or so, when it came to restaurants in LA, things could quickly get funny. Nothing was native here, so borrowed themes took on their own, distinctive character.

Consider L'Orangerie, the venerable and now defunct French restaurant on La Cienega Boulevard. Until it closed, a few years ago, you could treat yourself to a fine meal there, shielded from traffic by boxed hedgerows, and find that the evocation of the court of Versailles was in no way hampered by the working oil wells down the street. And still today, in the Atwater Village neighborhood, one can have a good prime rib at the Tam O'Shanter, an institution that dates from 1922 and has an interior modeled after a Scottish peasant hut: sagging roof, bulging walls, soot-darkened mantel. The original designer, Harry Oliver, didn't have any actual link to the Scottish Highlands; he'd perfected the look on Culver City movie lots.

Some call that superficiality; I call it lightness, the defining characteristic of LA dining. The knock against us as a city is that we're not real epicures, that we are health-obsessed weenies who care only if there's a star in the vicinity and will hardly eat because we must be doing squat thrusts at dawn up a canyon. The truth is that we are engaged by food but pair that passion with a sense of fun. It's not fakeness that bothers us but fakeness without heart.

True, like every other place in America, we once had our potted-palm dining rooms where classical French food might be enjoyed, but one can only wonder whether the Angelenos who ate at those places took all that saucy food at face value or whether they thought it was just a bit of show business. With the rise of the motion picture industry in the 1920s, fantasy became part of the landscape of everyday life in LA, and the theme restaurant took root. At the Jail, a restaurant that opened in 1925 in Silver Lake, the waiters dressed as inmates. At Ye Bull Pen Inn, which opened in 1920 downtown, customers dined in rows of livestock stalls. No matter what the theme, most places served comfort-food classics, like fried chicken and steak. But at Don the Beachcomber, which opened in 1934 and kicked off a nationwide tiki trend, the Polynesian menu matched the setting.

And while not every eatery in town banked on fantasy—downtown LA in the 1920s was crowded with sterile-looking cafeterias that catered to the sober tastes of the hundreds of thousands of Midwesterners who were flooding into the city at the time—the movie business was the engine that drove our fine-dining culture for much of the 20th century. In the early years, the stars gathered at night in places like the swank Cocoanut Grove, in Midtown's Ambassador Hotel, where their comings and goings, documented in newsreel images in thousands of movie palaces, kept the rest of the country fixated on what was happening out here. In those flickering images was the inkling that Los Angeles, once a remote, dusty pueblo, was now a place with a vibrant culture all its own. It would take a few years, however, for that culture to find expression in food.

WELL INTO THE 20TH CENTURY, the fanciest restaurants in LA, like those in the rest of the country, were still looking to Europe for their models. Places like Perino's—an Italian-owned restaurant on Wilshire Boulevard with a lengthy, haute-Continental menu—were still considered the epitome of stylishness in the 1940s and 1950s. When it came to food, imported cuisine was fine, but Angelenos of certain means eventually came to expect something more—a little sleight of hand, a memorable character. Romanoff's, which opened in 1941 on Rodeo Drive in Beverly Hills, delivered both, in the person of owner "Prince" Mike Romanoff. The self-styled Russian royal was actually Herschel Geguzin, an orphaned son of a Cincinnati tailor. Everyone knew he was a fraud, but no one cared. On the contrary, guests seemed to admire him for his chutzpah.

Mike Romanoff's success also owed to this: he knew that for all of Hollywood's glamour, the inner workings of the city amounted essentially to a bunch of hard-nosed men eating lunch. Romanoff's, accordingly, was a boys' club, complete with stiff drinks, deep booths, rich French food, and waiters who were models of discretion. Cigarette girls roamed the big back room; the coveted five tables opposite the Art Déco bar were reserved for the real movers and shakers, and for Romanoff himself. In 1949, M.F.K. Fisher, not yet a doyenne of the food world but a recently divorced sometime screenwriter, expressed admiration for the restaurant's breeziness and pragmatism. "The attitude seems to be," she wrote in her book An *Alphabet for Gourmets*, "that all humans must eat, and all humans must make money in order to eat, and therefore the two things might as well be combined."

Romanoff had recognized an essential facet of LA culture, but an older restaurant had already begun to break through and represent something even more intrinsic about Los Angeles. The Brown Derby had opened across the street from the Cocoanut Grove back in 1926; with its exterior shaped like a giant bowler hat, it seemed to hint at the extravagances of the theme restaurant, and, filled with movie stars, it certainly had élan, but over the years it had gained a reputation for its tasty food. It wasn't fancy: pan-fried corned beef hash was a popular dish, as was the grapefruit cake with cream cheese frosting. The most famous dish, the Cobb salad, didn't skew European at all. It is hard to think today of iceberg lettuce, watercress, chicory, romaine, bacon, and avocado as being original, but it was a brilliant combination, as perfect as blinis and caviar, hollandaise and *filets de sole*, and certainly more interesting than any ersatz European grandeur hashed up under dusty chandeliers.

While the Brown Derby had begun to unmoor LA's fine dining from Europe's, it took a restaurant called Chasen's to cut the ropes. In the 1950s, by which time LA had become an important enough city that the Dodgers decamped there from Brooklyn, this low-slung Beverly Hills restaurant was becoming the place to be seen. Its most famous dish wasn't *coquilles St-Jacques* or chicken quenelles; it was a bowl of chili sprinkled with diced raw onion. Running a close second was the hobo steak, a New York strip steak cooked tableside in copious amounts of butter. Like Romanoff's, Chasen's had a manly brusqueness, but unlike Romanoff's, it rejected dynastic pretensions. Actually, Chasen's wasn't really very good. (My aunt, a one-time Vegas showgirl and not one for moist-eyed nostalgia, once summed matters up saying, "Patric, the only things worth having at Chasen's were the garlic bread and the decaf.")

The only time I ever visited Chasen's was in 1999, four years after it closed. The restaurant where Ronald Reagan had proposed to Nancy, where Orson Welles had hurled a flaming chafing dish at the producer-actor John Houseman, was auctioning off all its furnishings. I walked into the massive structure on Beverly Boulevard, with its weird white columned exterior and its green-and-white-striped awning that stretched to the curb, and there it all was: the silver crab forks, the butter holders, the golden cocktail stirrers, laid out and tagged with lot numbers. In the dark, wood-paneled interior, I got a sense of why that bowl of chili with diced onions had been so important. It announced that fine dining, with all its trappings, could be made in America. What remained to be figured out was whether fine dining in Los Angeles could be made to reflect not just America but this particular corner of California.

IT COULD BE ARGUED THAT LA's unique brand of California cuisine was born on a patch of farmland outside Los Angeles, where a Cordon Bleu graduate named Michael McCarty and a chef named Jean Bertranou, who'd brought nouvelle cuisine to LA with his West Hollywood restaurant L'Ermitage, began farming ducks for foie gras. McCarty had fallen in love with French cuisine as a teenager but was intent on expressing that love in a local dialect. He opened Michael's in Santa Monica, three blocks from the ocean, in 1979. In a complete departure from the upscale chop house vibe of places like the Brown Derby, Michael's had a back garden that was suffused with sunlight in the afternoon. Yes, there was foie gras, but it was served by waiters in pink button-down shirts alongside California-made *chèvre* and wines. Whereas Chasen's could have been mistaken for Manhattan's '21' Club, Michael's couldn't have existed anywhere but Southern California.

The confluence of graceful outdoor living and expensive modern art, of baby vegetables and understated affluence, was the sexiest encapsulation of modern American cooking yet. But McCarty was more than a showman. He was a mentor who believed in his mission of channeling the rigors of French cooking into something new. The LA pastry chef and restaurateur Nancy Silverton— one of a number of now famous alums of Michael's, including the chefs Jonathan Waxman and Ken Frank—recalls McCarty's taking her aside and saying of the mousse she was making, "It's too French." The dessert was over-aerated, he explained; he wanted more concentration of flavor. The moment was an epiphany, Silverton says, a turning point that would lead her toward her signature, rustic style of baking. "Suddenly, I understood that there was a difference between a good French pastry and a good pastry based on French technique."

Michael's had started a transformation, but to start a revolution, it would take a chef who really had something to rebel against. In fact, it took a European truly to see Southern California's singular lifestyle and incomparable natural bounty for what they were. A few years before McCarty got his restaurant off the ground, a 30-year-old Austrian cook named Wolfgang Puck was living in a rented room with sheets on the windows and an *Emmanuelle* poster on the wall. Puck was a culinary hired gun. Before coming to LA, he'd worked at dowagers of haute cuisine like Maxim's in Paris and the Hôtel de Paris in Monte Carlo; once here, he got a job at Ma Maison, a Melrose Avenue restaurant that was the height of style in the mid-1970s. Certainly, the place was a change of pace for Puck: the dining room had an Astroturf floor, and the owner, a Frenchman named Patrick Terrail, was known to sport an elegant suit with sandals and white socks. But by Puck's own admission, the kitchen was still doing a butter-with-more-butter style of cooking.

Puck became famous at Ma Maison anyhow, publishing a popular book on French cookery in 1981 called *Modern French Cooking for the American Kitchen*. But with Spago, which he opened the following year, he became a legend. The first iteration of the eatery was located on Sunset Boulevard in what had been a Russian-Armenian restaurant. Puck saw it as something casual—the dining room had checkered tablecloths—and while there were certain connections to Alice Waters's Chez Panisse (the same German bricklayer had made both restaurants' pizza ovens, and they had the same enthusiasm for the produce of California), at first glance there wasn't anything momentous about it. But Spago was unlike anything LA had seen before. Here was a chef who had been raised on the French "mother sauces" and had chosen not to use them. Instead, he installed a grill and had a truckload of almond tree wood delivered weekly. In the kitchen, he fostered an atmosphere of pure improvisation. The chef Mark Peel, who had come over from Michael's to work as head chef, recalls the manic opening night. "We cooked with the menus propped in front of us to remember what the ingredients in the dishes were," he says. This was not cooking from a playbook that had been slavishly passed down from one chef to another.

By the time I moved here, in 1988, Los Angeles's role as a brilliantly inventive restaurant city had been cemented. I came as a cook, not a critic, carrying with me well-worn knives from Dehillerin in Paris, where I'd worked for Guy Savoy, and from Bridge Kitchenware in New York, where I was a line cook at the '21' Club. Now the energy was pointing west. Everything seemed to be in flux when I got here. Even at the city's older, well-loved places like Valentino, in Santa Monica, chefs were changing their stripes. When Valentino's owner, Piero Selvaggio, opened the place back in 1972, it was a typical high-end *ristorante* with plenty of tableside pyrotechnics. "We didn't use anything like buffalo mozzarella," he recalls. "Mozzarella was something breaded and fried." But by the time I visited, Selvaggio was wheeling an olive oil cart around his dining room, pouring samples over bruschetta so that customers could appreciate the differences between regional oils.

I got a job on the line at Citrus, a new restaurant that the French-born chef Michel Richard had just opened among the production houses and sound stages in the raggedy southern end of Hollywood. At Citrus, Richard wasn't just mining the local terrain for the freshest beets or handmade charcuterie; he was going to the Thai grocery down the block and coming back to the kitchen with lemongrass and coconut milk. He was shopping at Armenian markets and bringing back things like *katafi* (shredded phyllo dough), which most of us had never seen before, and wrapping local Dungeness crab cakes with the stuff. One day, he became fascinated by watching one of the Salvadoran prep cooks eating a chayote salad. A few days later, we were plating up chayote slaw.

That you could play with culinary genres like that had become a given. Everyone was blurring boundaries: there was Roy Yamaguchi mingling Hawaiian foods like ahi and macadamia nuts with

European techniques at his restaurant 385 North in West Hollywood (and later at the LA branch of Roy's); Nobu Matsuhisa melded Latin American ingredients with traditional sushi at his namesake restaurant in Beverly Hills; and at the Melrose Avenue eatery Border Grill, which opened in 1985, Susan Feniger and Mary Sue Milliken freely interwove strains of regional Mexican cuisines in homage to LA's countless great taquerías. In a way, this sort of eclecticism was right at home in a city where fantasy and invention, rather than history and tradition, had formed the foundation of high-end dining.

By the end of the 1980s, LA was home to innovative restaurants that boasted an equally novel asset: homegrown talent. When Campanile opened, a few blocks north of Wilshire Boulevard, in 1989, its planked salmon and its grilled prime rib with black olive tapenade—served in a rustic but elegant dining room in a faux-Tuscan complex with a verdigris cupola—caused a sensation. Its owners were Nancy Silverton and Mark Peel, chefs who had come up through the ranks of LA dining and not from New York, France, or Austria.

I've eaten at Campanile too many times to count, and every time I do, I feel grounded in this city. Los Angeles is a hard place to know—its fantasyland roots, its ethnic patchwork, and its almost too perfect sense of glamour all defy easy explanation. But sitting in a crowded dining room like Campanile's, I feel the disparate streams of LA's history coming together, and I can gaze around me, and at the plates of beautiful food, and say to myself, This is it. This is LA.

Au Revoir to All That

By Michael Steinberger

From *Au Revoir to All That: Food, Wine, and the End of France*

Has France—the country that gave the world *haute cuisine*—
truly ceded its place as the epicenter of all things culinary?
Known for his controversial wine columns in Slate.com,
journalist Michael Steinberger argues the case in fascinating
detail.

On an uncomfortably warm September evening in 1999,
I swapped my wife for a duck liver. The unplanned exchange took place at Au Crocodile, a Michelin three-star restaurant in the city of Strasbourg, in the Alsace-Lorraine region of
France. We had gone to Crocodile for dinner and, at the urging of
our waiter, had chosen for our main course one of Chef Émile
Jung's signature dishes, *Foie de Canard et Écailles de Truffe en Croûte
de Sel, Baeckeofe de Légumes*. Baeckeofe is a traditional Alsatian stew
made of potatoes, onions, carrots, leeks, and several different meats.
Jung, possessed of that particular Gallic genius for transforming
quotidian fare into high cuisine, served a version of baeckeofe in
which the meats were replaced by an entire lobe of duck liver,
which was bathed in a truffled bouillon with root vegetables and
cooked in a sealed terrine. The seal was broken at the table, and as
soon as the gorgeous pink-gray liver was lifted out of its crypt and
the first, pungent whiff of black truffles came our way, I knew our
palates were about to experience rapture. Sure enough, for the ten
minutes or so that it took us to consume the dish, the only sounds
we emitted were some barely suppressed grunts and moans. The
baeckeofe was outrageously good—the liver a velvety, earthy,

voluptuous mass, the bouillon an intensely flavored broth that flattered everything it touched.

We had just finished dessert when Jung, a beefy, jovial man who looked to be in his mid-fifties, appeared at our table. We thanked him profusely for the meal, and my wife, an editor for a food magazine, asked about some of the preparations. From the look on his face, he was smitten with her, and after enthusiastically fielding her questions, he invited her to tour the kitchen with him. "We'll leave him here," he said, pointing at me. As my wife got up from the table, Jung eyed her lasciviously and said, "You are a mango woman!" which I took to be a reference to her somewhat exotic looks (she is half-American, half-Japanese). She laughed nervously; I laughed heartily. As Jung squired her off to the kitchen, I leaned back in my chair and took a sip of Gewürztraminer.

By now, it was midnight, the dining room was almost empty, and the staff had begun discreetly tidying up. After some minutes had passed, Madame Jung, a lean woman with frosted blonde hair who oversaw the front of the restaurant, approached my table, wearing a put-upon smile which suggested this wasn't the first time her husband had taken a young female guest to see his pots and pans. Perhaps hoping to commiserate, she asked me if everything was okay. "*Bien sûr*," I immediately replied, with an enthusiasm that appeared to take her by surprise. I was in too much of a stupor to engage in a lengthy conversation, but had I been able to summon the words, I would have told her that her husband had just served me one of the finest dishes I'd ever eaten; that surrendering my wife (in a manner of speaking) was a small price to pay for such satisfaction; and that I'd have gladly waited at the table till daybreak if that's what it took to fully convey my gratitude to Monsieur Jung.

In the end, I didn't have to wait quite that long. After perhaps forty-five minutes, Jung returned my wife to the table. She came back bearing gifts: two bottles of the chef's own late-harvest Tokay Pinot Gris and, curiously, a cold quail stuffed with foie gras, which had been wrapped in aluminum foil so that we could take it with us. We thanked him again for the memorable dinner and his generosity, and then he showed us to the door. There, I received a perfunctory handshake, while my wife got two drawn-out pecks, one to each cheek. She got two more out in front of the restaurant, and as we walked down the street toward our hotel, Jung joyfully shouted after her, "You are a mango woman!" his booming voice piercing the humid night air.

Early the next morning, driving from Strasbourg to Reims in a two-door Peugeot that felt as if it was about to come apart from metal fatigue, my wife and I made breakfast of the quail. We didn't have utensils, so we passed it back and forth, ripping it apart with our hands and teeth. As we wound our way through the low, rolling hills of northeast France, silently putting the cold creature to an ignominious end, I couldn't help but marvel at what had transpired. Where but in France could a plate of food set in motion a chain of events that would find you whimpering with ecstasy in the middle of a restaurant; giving the chef carte blanche to hit on your wife, to the evident dismay of his wife; and joyfully gorging yourself just after sunrise the next day on a bird bearing the liver of another bird, a gift bestowed on your wife by said chef as a token of his lust? The question answered itself: This sort of thing could surely only happen in France, and at that moment, not for the first time, I experienced the most overwhelming surge of affection for her.

I FIRST WENT TO FRANCE as a thirteen-year-old, in the company of my parents and my brother, and it was during this trip that I, like many other visitors there, experienced the Great Awakening—the moment at the table that changes entirely one's relationship to food. It was a vegetable that administered the shock for me: Specifically, it was the baby peas (drowned in butter, of course) served at a nondescript hotel in the city of Blois, in the Loire Valley, that caused me to realize that food could be a source of gratification and not just a means of sustenance—that mealtime could be the highlight of the day, not simply a break from the day's activities.

A few days later, while driving south to the Rhône Valley, my parents decided to splurge on lunch at a two-star restaurant called Au Chapon Fin, in the town of Thoissey, a few miles off the A6 in the Mâcon region. I didn't know at the time that it was a restaurant with a long and illustrious history (among its claims to fame: It was where Albert Camus ate his last meal before the car crash that killed him in 1960), nor can I recollect many details of the meal. I remember having a pâté to start, followed by a big piece of chicken, and that both were excellent, but that's about it. However, I vividly recall being struck by the sumptuousness of the dining room. The tuxedoed staff, the thick white tablecloths, the monogrammed plates, the heavy silverware, the ornate ice buckets—it was the most elegant restaurant I'd ever seen. Every table was filled with impeccably attired, perfectly mannered French families. I hadn't yet heard of Baudelaire, but this was my first experience of that particular state of bliss he described as *luxe, calme, et volupté* (richness, calm, and pleasure), and I found it enthralling.

Other trips to France followed, and in time, France became not just the place that fed me better than any other, but an emotional touchstone. In low moments, nothing lifted my mood like the thought of Paris—the thought of eating in Paris, that is. When I moved to Hong Kong in 1994, I found a café called DeliFrance (part of a local chain by the same name) that quickly became the site of my morning ritual; reading the *International Herald Tribune* over a watery cappuccino and a limp, greasy croissant, I imagined I was having breakfast in Paris, and the thought filled me with contentment. Most of the time, though, I was acutely aware that I was not in Paris. On several occasions, my comings and goings from Hong Kong's airport coincided with the departure of Air France's nightly flight to Paris. The sight of that 747 taxiing out to the runway always prompted the same thought: Lucky bastards.

In 1997, a few months after I moved back to the United States, the *New Yorker* published an article by Adam Gopnik asking, "Is There a Crisis in French Cooking?" The essay was vintage Gopnik—witty, well observed, and bristling with insight. Gopnik, then serving as the magazine's Paris correspondent, suggested that French cuisine had lost its sizzle: It had become rigid, sentimental, impossibly expensive, and dull. The "muse of cooking," as he put it, had moved on—to New York, San Francisco, Sydney, London. In these cities, the restaurants exuded a dynamism that was now increasingly hard to find in Paris. "All this," wrote Gopnik, "makes a Francophile eating in Paris feel a little like a turn-of-the-century clergyman who has just read Robert Ingersoll: you try to keep the faith, but Doubts keep creeping in."

I didn't share those Doubts: To me, France remained the *orbis terrarum* of food, and nothing left me feeling more in love with life than a sensational meal in Paris. I refused to entertain the possibility that French cuisine had run aground; I didn't see it then, and I still didn't see it when Émile Jung took off with my wife two years later during that Lucullan evening at Au Crocodile. Sure, I knew that it was now pretty easy to find bad food in France if you went looking for it. I was aware, too, that France's economic difficulties had made it brutally difficult for restaurants like Au Crocodile to keep the stoves running. In 1996, Pierre Gagnaire, a three-star chef in the industrial city of Saint-Étienne, near Lyon, had gone bankrupt, and the same fate had almost befallen another top chef, Marc Veyrat. I also recognized that I was perhaps prone to a certain psychophysical phenomenon, common among France lovers, whereby the mere act of dining on French soil seemed to enhance the flavor of things. Even so, as far as I was concerned, France remained the first nation of food, and anyone suggesting otherwise either was being willfully contrarian or was eating in the wrong places.

It was the swift and unexpected demise of Ladurée just after the turn of the millennium that caused the first Doubts to creep in. Ladurée was a Paris institution, a charmingly sedate tea room on the rue Royale, in the eighth arrondissement. It was famous for its macaroons and pastries, and it also served one of the best lunches in Paris. I usually went with the artfully composed, perfectly dressed salade niçoise, which I chased down with a glass or two of Marcel Lapierre's violet-scented Morgon (a Beaujolais) and a deliciously crusty roll. At some point, I discovered Ladurée's praline mille feuille, which was also habit-forming: I would finish every lunch with this ethereal napoleon consisting of almond pralines, praline cream, caramelized pastry dough, and crispy hazelnuts. Of all the things that I routinely ate in France, it was the praline mille feuille that made me the happiest.

But returning to Ladurée, after a year's absence, I walked into a restaurant whose pilot light had been extinguished. The first sign of trouble was the lack of familiar faces: The endearingly gruff waitresses who had given the restaurant so much of its character had been replaced by bumbling androids. Worse, the menu had changed, and many of the old standbys, including the salade niçoise, were gone (so, too, the Morgon), replaced by a clutch of unappetizing dishes. The perpetrators of this calamity had the good sense to leave the praline mille feuille untouched, but I had to assume that it would soon be headed for history's flour bin. While Ladurée was an adored institution, it had no standing in the gastronomic world—no famous chef, no Michelin stars, no widely mimicked dishes. Even so, I now began to wonder if the French really were starting to screw things up—if French cuisine was genuinely in trouble. You might say it was the moment the snails fell from my eyes.

A few days after my dismaying visit to Ladurée, I was in the Mâcon area, this time with my wife and a friend of ours. As the three of us kicked around ideas for dinner late one afternoon, I felt pangs of curiosity. Did it still exist? If so, was it still any good? I quickly began leafing through the Michelin Guide, found Thoissey, and there it was: Au Chapon Fin. It was now reduced to one star, but the fact that it still had any was mildly encouraging. Several hours later, we were en route to Thoissey. By then, however, my initial enthusiasm had given way to trepidation. For the dedicated feeder, the urge to relive the tasting pleasures of the past is constant and frequently overwhelming. But restaurants change and so do palates; trying to recreate memorable moments at the table is often a recipe for heartache (and possibly also heartburn). And here I was, exactly two decades later, hoping to find Chapon Fin just as I had left it.

Well, the parking lot hadn't changed a bit—it was as expansive as I remembered it, and most of the spaces were still shaded by trees. Sadly, that was the high point of the visit. One glance at the dining room told the tale. The grandeur that had left such a mark on me had given way to decrepitude. Those thick, regal tablecloths were now thin, scuffed sheets. The carpet was threadbare. The plates appeared ready to crack from exhaustion. The staff brightened things a bit. The service was cheerful and solicitous—perhaps overly so—but they were doing their best to compensate for the food, which was every bit as haggard as the room. The evening passed in a crestfallen blur. What the hell was going on here?

En route back to Paris, my wife and I stopped in the somniferous village of Saulieu, at the northern edge of Burgundy, to eat at

La Côte d'Or, a three-star restaurant owned by Bernard Loiseau. He was the peripatetic clown prince of French cuisine, whose empire included the three-star mother ship, three bistros in Paris, a line of frozen dinners, and a listing on the Paris stock exchange. Loiseau's brand-building reflected his desire to emulate the venerated chef Paul Bocuse, but it was later learned that it was also a matter of survival: Business in Saulieu had become a struggle, and Loiseau was desperate for other sources of revenue. The night we had dinner in Saulieu, the food was tired and so was he. It was another discouraging meal in what had become a thoroughly dispiriting trip. Maybe the muse really had moved on.

IN 2003, the *New York Times Magazine* published a cover story declaring that Spain had supplanted France as the culinary world's lodestar. The article, written by Arthur Lubow, heralded the emergence of *la nueva cocina*, an experimental, provocative style of cooking that was reinventing Spanish cuisine and causing the entire food world to take note. El Bulli's Ferran Adrià, the most acclaimed and controversial of Spain's new-wave chefs, was the focus of the article and graced the magazine's cover. Lubow contrasted Spain's gastronomic vitality with the French food scene, which he described as ossified and rudderless. "French innovation," he wrote, "has congealed into complacency . . . as chefs scan the globe for new ideas, France is no longer the place they look." For a Francophile, the quote with which he concluded the article was deflating. The Spanish food critic Rafael García Santos told Lubow, "It's a great shame what has happened in France, because we love the French people and we learned there. Twenty years ago, everybody went to France. Today they go there to learn what not to do."

But by then France had become a bad example in all sorts of ways. Since the late 1970s, its economy had been stagnant, afflicted with anemic growth and chronically high unemployment. True, France had a generous welfare state, but that was no substitute for creating jobs and opportunity. By the mid-2000s, hundreds of thousands of French (among them many talented chefs) had moved abroad in search of better lives, unwilling to remain in a sclerotic, disillusioned country. France's economic torpor was matched by its diminished political clout; although prescient in hindsight, its effort to prevent the Iraq war in 2003 struck even many French as a vain-glorious blunder that served only to underscore the country's weakness.

A sense of decay was now pervasive. For centuries, France had produced as much great writing, music, and art as any nation, but that was no longer true. French literature seemed moribund, ditto the once-mighty French film industry. Paris had been eclipsed as a center of the fine-art trade by London and New York. It was still a fashion capital, but British and American designers now seemed to generate the most buzz. In opera and theater, too, Paris had become a relative backwater. French intellectual life was suffering: The country's vaunted university system had sunk into mediocrity. Even the Sorbonne was now second-rate—no match, certainly, for Harvard and Yale.

Nothing in the cultural sphere was spared—not even food. The cultural extended into the kitchens of France, and it wasn't just haute cuisine that was in trouble. France had two hundred thousand cafés in 1960; by 2008, it was down to forty thousand, and hundreds, maybe thousands were being lost every year. Bistros and brasseries were also dying at an alarming clip. Prized cheeses were going extinct because there was no one with the knowledge or desire to continue making them; even Camembert, France's most celebrated cheese, was now threatened. The country's wine industry was in a cataclysmic state: Declining sales had left thousands of producers facing financial ruin. Destitute vintners were turning to violence to draw attention to their plight; others had committed suicide. Many blamed foreign competition for their woes, but there was a bigger problem closer to home: Per capita wine consumption in France had dropped by an astonishing 50 percent since the late 1960s and was continuing to tumble.

This wasn't the only way in which the French seemed to be turning their backs on the country's rich culinary heritage. Aspiring chefs were no longer required to know how to truss chickens, open oysters, or whip up a béarnaise sauce in order to earn the *Certificat d'Aptitude Professionnelle*; instead, they were being tested on their ability to use processed, powdered, frozen, and prepared foods. France still had its outdoor markets, but *hypermarchés*—sprawling supermarkets—accounted for 75 percent of all retail food sales. Most ominously, the bedrock of French cuisine—home cooking, or *la cuisine familiale*—was in trouble. The French were doing less cooking than ever at home and spending less time at the dinner table: The average meal in France now sped by in thirty-eight minutes, down from eighty-eight minutes a quarter-century earlier. One organization, at least, stood ready to help the French avoid the kitchen and scarf their food: McDonald's. By 2007, the chain had more than a thousand restaurants in France and was the country's largest private-sector employer. France, in turn, had become its second-most-profitable market in the world.

Food had always been a tool of French statecraft; now, though, it was a source of French humiliation. In July 2005, it was reported that French president Jacques Chirac, criticizing the British during a meeting with Russian president Vladimir Putin and German chancellor Gerhard Schroeder, had harrumphed, "One cannot trust people whose cuisine is so bad." In the not-so-distant past, Chirac, simply by virtue of being France's president, would have been seen as eminently qualified to pass judgment on another country's cuisine—and, of course, in disparaging British cooking, he merely would have been stating the obvious. Coming in the summer of 2005, Chirac's comment revealed him to be a man divorced from reality. Was he not aware that London was now a great food city? Just four months earlier, *Gourmet* magazine had declared London to be "the best place to eat in the world right now" and devoted an entire issue to its gustatory pleasures. As the ridicule rained down on Chirac, his faux pas assumed metaphoric significance: Where once the mere mention of food by a French leader would have elicited thoughts of Gallic refinement and achievement, its invocation now served to underscore the depths of France's decline. *They've even lost their edge in the kitchen.*

French cooking had certainly lost its power to seduce. Several days after Chirac's gibe made headlines, members of the International Olympic Committee, despite having been wined and dined for months by French officials, selected London over Paris as host city for the 2012 Summer Games—fish and chips over foie gras.

There were other indignities, less noted but no less telling. In October 2006, New York's French Culinary Institute marked the opening of its new International Culinary Center with a two-day extravaganza featuring panel discussions, cooking demonstrations, and gala meals. The FCI was one of America's foremost cooking schools, but it was also a wellspring of French cultural influence— a culinary consulate of sorts. Its faculty included Jacques Pépin, André Soltner, and Alain Sailhac, three expatriated French chefs who had helped unleash America's food revolution. To assure a suitably splashy debut for its new facilities, the FCI brought ten eminent foreign chefs to New York. Amazingly, though, the list was headed not by a Frenchman but by three Spaniards: Adrià, Juan Mari Arzak, and Martín Berasategui. Not only that: the other seven chefs were Spanish, too. The French Culinary Institute threw itself a party and didn't invite a single chef from France.

All this was a reflection of what was happening in France. Twenty-five years earlier, it had been virtually impossible to eat poorly there; now, in some towns and villages, it was a struggle to find even a decent loaf of bread. The France memorialized by writers like M. F. K. Fisher, Joseph Wechsberg, Waverley Root, and A. J. Liebling; that inspired the careers of Julia Child, Alice Waters, and Elizabeth David; that promised gustatory delight along every boulevard and byway—that France, it seemed, was dying. Even those epiphanic vegetables were harder to come by. When Waters started regularly visiting France, she would smuggle tomato vine cuttings home to California; now, she smuggled vine cuttings to her friends in France.

It saddened me to see this way of eating, and being, disappearing. In France, I didn't just learn how to dine; I learned how to live. It was where my wife and I had fallen in love, a bond formed over plates of choucroute, platters of oysters, and bowls of *fraises des bois* (Ladurée pastries, too). When we began traveling to France as a married couple, great meals there weren't just occasions for pleasure; they were a way of reaffirming our vows. The calendar indicates that our children couldn't have been conceived in France, but from the moment they were able to eat solid foods they were immersed in our Francophilia. They became acquainted with crème caramel before they ever knew what a Pop-Tart was. But it now appeared that the France I grew up knowing would no longer be there for them.

A Remembrance of Things Present

By Alexander Lobrano

From *Gourmet*

Forget the Michelin-starred gastronomic temples with their
cutting-edge cuisine, countends Lobrano, an American food
and travel writer based in France. Paris is still studded with
wonderful vintage restaurants—if you know where to look.

On a stifling August night in 1974, I was led down a steep
flight of stairs into a vaulted basement in the Latin
Quarter. In my madras jacket, I immediately felt like a dork.
Everyone else in the dining room was wearing jeans, and my mor-
tification was magnified by the fact that both of my brothers were
also wearing madras, while my sister was sporting a daffodil-yellow
frock. Plunged into the heart of bohemian Paris, a place I'd always
dreamed of, I was suddenly desperate to be elsewhere and furious
with the aunt who'd told us we couldn't miss this restaurant, a real
old-fashioned bistro that had been a memorable find on her most
recent trip to Paris.

Still, I liked the slightly musty smell of the room, which reminded me of a country well, and the sour stink of the Gauloises
that were sending up small curls of blue smoke from every table
but ours. The bread was delicious, and it was a relief when the
waiter understood Mom's French, especially since a wonderful
salad of sliced tomatoes in a silky mustard vinaigrette—so simple,
but so good—arrived a few minutes later, along with a pocked
white porcelain plate of sizzling snails for Dad, who insisted I try
one (I gulped it down with a big sip of water). Then, after a stately

pause, the graying waiter returned with a heavy copper casserole, which he set at my end of the table. Lifting the lid, he released a fleeting cloud of steam. The mingled aroma of wine, beef, and onions was so intoxicating it seemed an eternity before everyone had been served and I could dig in. I burned my tongue, never quite realizing that I was experiencing my first round of primal pleasure at table. Nothing had ever tasted as good to me as the shiny mahogany sauce, an amazing mixture of wine and butter, that glazed the tender chunks of beef on my plate. That *boeuf bourguignon*, served at a long-vanished restaurant on a street I barely remember how to find, left me with an irresistible craving for more—more Paris and, most of all, more French food. So much so that 21 years ago I moved to Paris.

Last fall, I decided that spending all my time chasing talented young chefs around the city as they moved from kitchen to kitchen (usually before opening places of their own) was only part of the culinary equation. I set out to rekindle an old flame, tracking down those restaurants that, while not especially chic anymore, deliver the kind of soul-satisfying *boeuf bourguignon* on which French cuisine was built. I started with **L'Ambassade d'Auvergne**, which continues to serve some of the best regional food in Paris. Anyone who loves real French cooking cannot afford to live in fear of fat. At this outpost near the Marais, creamy lentil salad comes with a healthy dollop of goose fat, while blanched cabbage leaves are layered with a fine filling of pork, salt pork, pork liver, Swiss chard, and fresh bread crumbs before being popped into a hot oven where all the flavors fuse into a superb terrine—a brilliant work of edible masonry. The "embassy" also understands basic tableside theater: After serving a generous length of grilled *auvergnat* sausage, the waiter returns with a copper saucepan and a wooden spoon to whip the *aligot*—that heavenly concoction of potatoes, cheese curds, and garlic—into a cascade of melting sheets, a coup de théâtre that dazzles the occasional tourist while reassuring the serious Parisians that French cuisine is still alive and well.

Running late for my next stop, I rush into *La Grille*, a peculiar dining room (it reminds me of Miss Havisham's) festooned with lace, straw hats, and dusty dolls, as my friend waves away my apologies. "What a wonderful idea to eat here," she says. "I'd forgotten about this place—so much character." Geneviève and Yves Cullerre have run La Grille for nearly half a century, turning out almost anthropological classics like duck terrine with hazelnuts, mackerel poached in white wine, and his plat de résistance, a superb grilled turbot in black fishnet stockings (thanks to the scoring of the grill) with a sublime beurre blanc. I live in dread of the inevitable day when the Cullerres retire to some sunny place by the sea. Then again, I might just tag along.

I also hope that Michel Bosshard ("Boboss") at **Auberge Le Quincy** won't hang up his indigo cotton apron anytime soon. With his blue-framed glasses and teasing style, Boboss is as much a part of the ambience as the bric-a-brac that fills this cubbyhole of a restaurant. After greeting me with a big slice of *saucisson* to nibble on while reading the menu, he insists I have the *caillette*, an Ardèche specialty of small patties of grilled pork, pork liver, Swiss chard, and herbs that have been rubbed with fat from the caul (the lacy membrane enclosing an animal's abdomen). I'd been dreaming all day about the foie gras, but he is firm. "If you hate the *caillette*," he says, "I'll bring you some foie gras." But I don't, not this *caillette*—whose bed of mesclun dressed with vinaigrette is the perfect "grassy" foil for the rich meat. I move on to rabbit cooked in shallots and white wine, ending the meal with one of the best chocolate mousses in Paris—all fine with Boboss.

For a meal that's equally animated but more anonymous, I love **La Tour de Montlhéry**, one of the last of the night restaurants that fed the workers at Les Halles before the market decamped to the suburbs. Like the décor, the menu here is as authentic as a Doisneau photo—grilled marrowbones, *oeufs en gelée*, calf's liver with bacon, and massive *côte de boeuf*, all accompanied by a cheap but harmless Beaujolais from the barrels inside the front door.

Atmosphere is also the lure at the magnificent **Le Train Bleu**, inside the Gare de Lyon rail station. The nice surprise here, though, is that aside from being the best place in town to savor the visual opulence of fin de siècle Paris, the ornate dining room also serves some surprisingly good French food. Ignore the contemporary dishes (like scallops sautéed in tamarind-spiked *jus de poulet*) and go straight for the escargots or oysters to start, followed by grilled sole, steak tartare, or the succulent leg of lamb, which is carved tableside on a silver-domed trolley and served with a delicious potato gratin made with Fourme d'Ambert, a wonderful blue cheese from Auvergne.

As an American, I remain neutral in the ancient quarrel between the French and the English but still find it curious that the French derisively call the Brits "rosbifs" (roast beefs) when they're such avid *boeuf* lovers themselves. Just watch the way hungry Gauls go for the hearth-grilled *côte de boeuf* at **Robert et Louise**, a rustic hole-in-the-wall in the Marais with exposed half-timbers and a grumpy house poodle. Almost everything here—from the crusty sautéed potatoes that come with the storied rib steak to the great dishes like boudin noir and confit de canard—is cooked over an open fire.

Beef is also very much the focus at **Au Moulin à Vent**, in the Latin Quarter, where the walls are decorated with shiny copper saucepans and the menu is vast. Make it easy on yourself and go for either the Salers beef chateaubriand with homemade béarnaise sauce or the veal kidney flambéed in Armagnac. But be sure to start your meal with the frogs' legs *à la provençale*, little bites of juicy meat on tiny bones in a wonderfully garlicky sauce—the best to be found anywhere. No place in Paris quite channels the jubilation that ended the privation of the World War II years like this standard-bearer from 1946.

I have a soft spot for *Chez Georges*, a bistro that succeeds brilliantly by flatly ignoring the passage of time. The last time I ate there, I had exactly the same meal I'd had 15 years earlier, when I met Julia Child, who also loved this place. "It's not often I get real bistro cooking anymore," she told me before ordering a frisée salad with lardons ("It never tastes as good at home as it does in France," she insisted) and calf's liver with bacon. I had the *blanquette de veau*. Just before dessert, a French designer stopped by to pay his respects, congratulating Madame Child for "civilizing" the American palate. After he'd gone, she asked, "Who was that? Oh dear, I hope this place doesn't become fashionable." Well, it has, as a quick look at the antiques dealers and fashion-house bigwigs filling the banquettes makes clear, but the kitchen turns out the same guilelessly retro cooking it always has.

For anyone who lives in Paris, few things are more treacherous than the nostalgia trap, that fretful and despairing mind-set that insists that everything tasted better in the past. Sometimes, though, restaurants change for the better, as I find with **Josephine Chez Dumonet**, a beautiful 1898-vintage place near the famous Poilâne bakery. Now under the management of Jean-Christian Dumonet, a second-generation owner, I find the food fresher and more vivid than it has been in a long time. The clientele has changed, too. Just as I finish a homemade *terrine de campagne*, a ripple rises up in the dining room. Joey Starr, France's most notorious rapper, dressed in immaculate dove-gray sweats and a Yankees baseball cap, is shown to the table next to mine. After my meal—panfried foie gras; monkfish with white beans; and, finally, a plate of cheese from the nearby Quatrehomme *fromagerie*—Starr and I exchange sheepish grins as our Grand Marnier soufflés arrive at exactly the same time.

Later, walking home, I am elated that France's bad-boy rapper also chose this place. I have no doubt that Paris's old-fashioned restaurants will survive, and I also know that the *boeuf bourguignon* I ate in the Latin Quarter 35 years ago had been every bit as delicious as I'd remembered. Maybe even better.

Address Book

L'ambassade d'Auvergne 22 R. du Grenier-St.-Lazare, 3rd (01-42-72-31-22). Auberge le Quincy 28 Ave. Ledru-Rollin, 12th (01-43-28-46-76). Chez Georges 1 R. du mail, 2nd (01-42-60-07-11). La Grille 80 R. du Faubourg-Possionniere, 10th (01-47-70-89-73). Josephine Chez Dumonet 117 R. du Cherche Midi, 6th (01-45-48-52-40). Au Moulin a Vent 20 R. des Fosses-St.-Bernard, 5th (01-43-54-99-37). Robert et Louise 64 R. Vielle-du-Temple, 3rd (01-42-78-55-89). La Tour de Montlhery Chez Denise 5 R. des Prouvaires, 1st (01-42-36-21-82). Le Train Bleu Gare de Lyon, 12th (01-43-43-09-06).

Someone's In the Kitchen

The Perfect Chef

By Todd Kliman

From *The Oxford American*

Todd Kliman's day job—as dining editor for the *Washingtonian* magazine—was almost beside the point. His casual fascination with the food at a local Chinese restaurant eventually deepened into an obsessive quest, tracking down an elusive genius who didn't want to be found.

Before I got in my car and drove to three different states to find him, before I began tracking his whereabouts on the Internet and running down leads that had been passed to me by people I had never met, before I had to admit that I had become a little crazed in my pursuit and that this was about more than just him, but about me, too—before all that, Peter Chang was simply somebody whose cooking I enjoyed.

I was just starting out as a food critic, and had learned through a tipster that a talented chef had taken over the kitchen of a restaurant in Fairfax called China Star, in the suburbs of Northern Virginia, forty minutes from Washington, D.C. In the world of serious food lovers, in an age of rapid information sharing, the real excitement over a new place happens far in advance of the published review in the paper or magazine and at a subterranean level, below the awareness of ordinary folks, those people possessed only of a mere casual interest in food and restaurants. Someone gets a tip and passes on the news, and a following quickly builds—a kind of culinary equivalent of insider trading.

Despite my newness to the job, or perhaps because of it, I had made myself an inviolable rule about tipsters, and that was to take every one of their recommendations seriously. Often, this resulted in driving an hour and a half for dispiriting Thai or dessicated barbecue, and I would feel toyed with and mocked; driving home, I would curse my rule and vow never again, only to get back in the car and hunt down the next lead that came my way, because the truth was that I could be disappointed nine out of ten times but the tenth time, the success, would fill me with such a sense of triumph that it was as if those earlier disappointments had never occurred. As a critic, I was inevitably thought to be gorging myself on the good life, on endless quantities of champagne and caviar and foie gras, each meal richer and more luxurious than the last, but after a while, and to my great dismay—because I had made another vow, which was to not become jaded by an excess of pleasure—these meals blended into indistinction. No matter how exquisite something might be, a diet made up exclusively of exquisite dishes inevitably becomes normal, and normal is boring. The unrequited love is always more interesting than the requited love, and, as it had been with me and dating, so it was with me and restaurant meals. I lived for the chase.

In this case, my tipster was possessed of more than just the usual slate of dish recommendations. He had a backstory to pass on. This chef had won two major cooking competitions in China, a significant achievement by any reckoning, but especially in a culture that is disinclined to valorize the individual. He had cooked for the Chinese premier, Hu Jintao, had written culinary manuals, and had come to the U.S. to cook at the Embassy in Washington, which is where he had been working just prior to joining the restaurant in Fairfax. It all sounded promising.

NOT LONG AFTER, I showed up with a friend one afternoon at China Star, expecting some outward announcement of the great man's arrival, some manifestation of his specialness, only to find the usual list of beef and broccoli and orange chicken. But there was another menu, the Chinese menu, and on it was a parade of dishes I had never seen. Diced rabbit in hot oil. Sliced tendon of beef with cilantro. I didn't know where to start, so I started everywhere.

I sat with a friend at a corner table, our mouths afire from the incendiary heat of the Szechuan chilis, alterations that compelled me to keep eating long after I was no longer hungry—a desperate longing for that runner's high, that intoxication. At the same time, I was filled with a paradoxical sense that I had ordered too much and yet, somehow, not enough. I could have gone to China Star every day for a week and still not have eaten enough to know what Chef Chang's cuisine was or wasn't.

I returned not long after that initial encounter, ordered still more dishes, and felt, again, defeated. This time I was convinced there was a right way to order and a wrong way to order, and that I had ordered the wrong way. What was the right way? I wasn't exactly sure. But whatever it was, I felt certain that it was conveyed in clues offered up by the menu. The key was to decipher them, and I had not done that. Lacking any real guidance from the waiter (except to warn me that a dish was spicy, which in my eagerness to prove my bona fides—which was, really, to demonstrate that I was not the timid, fearful, judging Westerner that I might have presented, and had an active interest in duck blood and internal organs and other such delicacies—I conveniently ignored), it was easy to wind up with a table full of nothing but hot dishes, which was like reading only the dirty parts torn from a novel and concluding that the author has a one-track mind. I hastily devised a plan for my next visit: I would order both hot and cold (temperature) dishes, I would order both spicy and nonspicy dishes, I would seek, above all, balance—the balance that was, surely, there in the menu but that I had, foolishly, missed. I would enlist a group of friends to come along, reinforcements for a campaign that had become more complicated than I had counted on, their presence at the table less about communality and sharing than about subterfuge—masking my intent and allowing me to cover as much culinary ground as possible. I would do it right.

I WOULD DO IT RIGHT, and in fact, I did do it right, though I did not do it at China Star. I returned to the restaurant with my five-member crew, only to learn that Chang had moved on and was cooking at a place in Alexandria, fifteen minutes closer to Washington. The restaurant was called TemptAsian Café—in intention and appearance no different from tens of thousands of Americanized Chinese restaurants across the land. When I stopped in with my wife one night, two people were waiting for carryout orders, and hearing the manager call out the contents of the stapled bags for a man in running shorts—chicken and green beans, orange beef, General Tso's chicken—I thought I might have been mistaken in thinking this was Chef Chang's place. I whispered my doubts to my wife. A cheerless and brusque waitress materialized, directed us to a table, and handed us a couple of Americanized Chinese menus. Now I was certain this could not have been where the estimable Chef Chang had landed.

"Do you have a Chinese menu?" I asked.

She gave me a scrutinizing once-over, her brow knitting. It was as if I had mispronounced the password, proving myself an interloper, undeserving of being handed the Chinese menu. For a long moment, she regarded my face, not simply for evidence of my seriousness but rather, it seemed, for evidence of my worth.

Stupidly, I smiled. Or rather, *reflexively* I smiled, because I had not wanted to smile. Even as I was smiling, I had not thought I was smiling, but I am an American, and that is what we Americans do in any situation where we are being denied what we think we indisputably deserve access to. We smile. Even when we do not know the native language. Even when we commit egregious acts of cultural ignorance. The smile, we think, is our badge, our passport— the smile will erase everything else we have done or, as the case may be, not done; the smile will put us over; the smile will deliver us to the vital center.

I smiled, and the waitress turned and left. My wife and I raised an eyebrow at each other across the table, wondering what exactly had just happened. "Well, I guess it's just gonna be beef and broccoli then, huh?" she said.

And then, just as abruptly as she had left, the waitress returned and grudgingly handed over the Chinese menus, which, in contrast to the bound and printed regular menu, had been cobbled together hastily via the aid of a computer. This was more like it. Here were many of the dishes I had eaten at China Star, plus a good number more that I hadn't seen before, like a dish of fish with sour mustard greens that was preceded by a red asterisk, the universal warning that the preparation listed is going to be hot.

I pointed to the number on the menu, trying to order.

The waitress frowned. She directed me to something tamer, without an asterisk. I persisted, and she touted more aggressively the merits of the dish she had suggested. I knew from experience that we had begun that verbal joust that sometimes takes place in ethnic restaurants that don't know and don't court Westerners, and that each eager parry was going to be met by a forceful thrust. In some restaurants, the trick was to make multiple visits within a short span of time, demonstrating your sincerity by virtue of familiarity; then, and only then, was the staff likely to relent and allow you access to the real stuff, the good stuff, the stuff you'd truly come for. But I didn't want to wait. In my mind, I had already bypassed this tedious and time-consuming process by having eaten twice at China Star.

When I asked for the grilled fish with cold rice gluten, her eyes bulged for a split second before she shook her head no.

No, you don't have it in? I wanted to scream. *Or no, you're not going to serve it to me, regardless?*

What the hell did I have to do to earn the restaurant's trust to be able to taste Chef Chang's food again?

Whether my inner torment was visible on my face, and she had taken pity on me, or whether I had demonstrated a willingness to try any number of dishes that would have put a scare into most Westerners, or both, or neither, I don't know, but she relented and decided to bring out the fish with sour mustard greens.

It was wonderful, sour and spicy in a way that dishes featuring fish almost never are, but even if it had been merely ordinary, I would have made sure that we devoured all of it, in this way making the very unsubtle, I hoped, point that we were deserving of being shown the full extent of the chef's repertoire of dishes.

WHAT FOLLOWED WAS extraordinary: Chinese cooking like I had never tasted, better than anything Chef Chang had prepared at China Star—or maybe it was that I had learned how to order from him, in much the way that you need to read two or three books by Faulkner just to begin to grasp even a little of what he is up to.

There was a plate of cold beef that the chef had intended for us to fold into a fried wrapper of dough, a little sandwich. A seemingly simple thing, except that the thin-sliced beef, tender and almost gelatinous, had been scented with the famous *ma la* peppercorn. The *ma la* peppercorn is not strictly about heat; for that, for pure heat, Chef Chang had also used the red Szechuan chili peppers. *Ma la* numbs the lips as you eat, a sensation that can only be likened to the novocaine you get in the dentist's chair, though without the dawning sense of dread that invariably follows an injection. Why would this be desirable? Why would a chef want to numb a diner's lips? Because the numbing is also a cooling, and that cooling works in opposition to the scorching heat of the other pepper, producing an odd yin and yang, just as the sweet, doughy, chewy wrapper was set off in contrast to the slippery, savory beef.

Out came a rattan basket of fried fish the color of a blazing summer sunset. Wait, was this the roasted fish with green onion we'd ordered? The name was a misnomer, it turned out. And the description on the menu had not fully prepared us for the taste of this fish. Wait, was that cumin? Cumin, in a Chinese restaurant? On fish? It was odd. It was haunting. I couldn't stop eating it.

After a while, I knew that I was eating it not because I was hungry, but because I was eager to learn it, to burn the precise, sensory details of the taste into my memory, the way you do with anything that's good that you've never before tried, any experience, any phenomenon. With a book, you read and re-read sentences; with a dish, you eat and eat and eat, long after you're full. Being overstuffed, for the food lover, is not a moral problem. It's a practical problem.

We had not yet finished the fish when the pancakes arrived. I had had pancakes at Chinese restaurants before, delicate crepes into which you stuffed slices of crisp-skinned duck, or greasy discs of dough that had been flecked with bits of diced scallion. But never anything this dramatic. Never these big, poofy balloons that drew the eye of everybody in the dining room, and which gave up a little plume of steam when they were pricked with a chopstick.

It was a law of reviewing that if you made three visits, almost without fail, one of those meals would turn out to be a disappointment, even if the restaurant was a good restaurant. Each meal here, though, was wonderful, and I began to feel not just that I was learning his dishes, but that I was advancing deeper into Chef Chang's canon and learning *him*.

I wrote my review, which in every other instance meant that I was done with the place and had moved on to the next restaurant to be written about, to Thai, to Lebanese, to sushi, to Salvadoran. But with TemptAsian, I did not move on.

I wanted more, so shortly afterward, I organized a group to descend on the restaurant when I learned that Chang had, again, and rather more mysteriously this time, left. Three departures in two years. Even by the diminished standards of the industry, whereby a chef at one location for two or three years is regarded as a crusty vet, this seemed like a lot.

It was at this point that the gossip and speculation began to float my way, in beseeching e-mails from diners who, like me, had also fallen under the spell of the bewitching cooking of the curiously peripatetic Chef Chang. *His green card has expired, and he's on the lam. He can't stay for long in one place—as soon as he's reviewed, he has to leave. No, no: He's running from a vindictive former employer, out to exact revenge upon his star chef for leaving. Wrong, all wrong—he's had his taste of Western-style freedom and celebrity, and can no longer abide working for owners who do not treat him as the glittering talent he is.*

Strangest of all was the theory that was trotted out by one of these obsessives: *He fears success.*

In the absence of a place to eat his cooking and commune with him, the obsessives needed an outlet to express their sense of neurosis. They turned to e-mail. They took to the web. Where would Chef Chang turn up next? *Would* he turn up next? Could this have been—no, don't speak it—the last chance to taste his pepper-fired genius?

I passed along some of these e-mails to my wife, with wry notes attached to the top, wry, distancing notes about these cult-like pronouncements. I was laughing at the lengths that ordinary folks could go in their love for a few dishes. The truth, though, was that I was just as caught up in this as they were.

He turned up, many months later, at a dismal-looking place, again in Fairfax, called China Gourmet, with garish green pile carpet that had lost most of its nap and a drink menu featuring Mai Tais.

The owner had been following Chef Chang for some time now, he confessed to me over the phone, having attended an "extraordinary" fourteen-course banquet at the Chinese Embassy and then, later, having become a regular at both China Star and TemptAsian Café. So the owner was one of us, I thought, except that he had been studying more than just the intimate magic of *ma la* and finger peppers. He'd purchased this particular restaurant because it was less than a mile from where Chang's daughter attended high school. He gave Chang the go-ahead to hire his own staff, which meant the chef could hire his wife, Hongyong, a specialist in cold dishes. Having intuited that control was important to the chef, he even allowed him to choose the restaurant's new name: Szechuan Boy.

There was a sweetly childlike quality to this name, but also something grandiose, an atypical rejection of the Chinese need to recede into the background. This was a passionate embrace of foreground, a bold assertion of his individuality and independence. The place belonged to him, the chef, the Szechuan boy.

I MADE MY FIRST VISIT three days after Chang started, a marked contrast to the three weeks I ordinarily waited before dropping by a restaurant for my initial assessment. At his other stops, I had gone with one other person, but now I took groups, the better to sample a raft of dishes in a single sitting. I had learned from experience to be firm and insistent about what I wanted, to bark out instructions. I sounded like a stranger to myself, like a petty tyrant, or a football coach, but it worked. "Yes, sir," the waiter at Szechuan Boy said, over and over again, as I placed my exhaustive order. I was in.

My parents were my guests for that first meal. They had eaten a lot of Chinese food, from New York to San Francisco. My mother had taken classes in Chinese cooking. They regularly hosted dinners of Chinese corn soup, homemade egg rolls, steamed fish in ginger. And still nothing prepared them for their encounter with Chef Chang, for the cumin-scented ground-beef hash that we tucked into tiny steamed buns, for the chicken consommé seasoned with microscopic dried shrimp and topped off with delicately fashioned dumplings, for the *ma po* tofu with its squares of jiggly, custardy bean curd poking up from a broth so glossy and red it resembled a new fire truck. "It's like I've never eaten Chinese food before," my mother said, awestruck.

"This guy's a genius," said my father, who blasted anyone who deigned to attach that label to others he deemed unworthy: Bill Cosby, Bill Gates, Martin Scorsese.

Ordinarily, I would spread my visits out over the course of a month, but I was much too impatient to abide by my self-made rule this time. I went back a couple of nights later, and then a couple of nights after that, and then a couple of nights after that. Three times in one week, and then, because I couldn't help myself, I went back two more times the next.

"This is a druglike experience," said a friend one night, speaking slowly and absent-mindedly in the midst of eating the chef's version of pickled peppers, as if he were finding his bearings amid a hallucination.

Another night, I watched tears streak down a friend's face as he popped expertly cleavered bites of chicken into his mouth with his chopsticks. He was red-eyed and breathing fast. "It hurts, it hurts, but it's so good, but it hurts, and I can't stop eating!" He slammed a fist down on the table. The beer in his glass sloshed over the sides. "Jesus Christ, I've got to stop!"

Even when I wasn't eating Chef Chang's food, I was thinking about it, and talking about it, recreating those singular tastes in words and images. I talked about it constantly; I couldn't not talk about it. I wanted everyone I knew to try it, particularly since, as experience had taught me, he would not be here long and the moment was not likely to last. "I'll definitely have to make it out there," friends would say, and I knew from the complacency of their tone that they didn't get what I was telling them, that a great restaurant, of all places, is not static, it is constantly changing and evolving, and often for the worse, and that greatness, when you can find it—if you can find it—is an evanescent thing, kept alive by luck and circumstance and numberless mysteries we can't hope to understand, not unlike life itself, and we must heed the imperative to go, now, and give ourselves over to it.

Two weeks after my review came out, he was gone. Wherever he went, he left—that was nothing new, I'd intimated as much in the three-and-a-half-star piece I'd written. (Four stars is an exalted designation, rarely granted; restaurants with nine-buck entrées and garish green carpet are generally lucky to be considered for two.) What was new was the suddenness of it. I knew not to expect a long run, but even I was unprepared for this latest exit. The owner, in particular, must have been ambushed by it. After all he had extended to Chef Chang, all he had given away. . . .

Readers hounded me for weeks with e-mails, many of them suspecting that I'd perpetrated a hoax. This Szechuan Boy I'd written so gushingly about—what evidence was there to suggest it had ever existed? There was no sign out front and no printed menus inside. The owner had assured me for weeks that both would be arriving "any day now," and I had accepted his promises at the time as typical of a harried owner with a new restaurant, but now I suspected that he had been deliberately withholding his full embrace of his elusive chef, like a partner in a marriage who keeps a separate account. As for the vaunted Chef Chang—gone. If he had ever arrived in the first place. The majority of my readers were moneyed and comfortable, accustomed to going where they were told, and they took it on faith that a glowing review of a restaurant amounted to a guarantee, no different, that is, from a rave about a book or a CD or any other product that was regarded as a fixed and immutable experience. Life was messy, uncertain, chaotic, and full of mystery, yes, but a great restaurant meal was an oasis of calm and order, a bourgeois stay against randomness and darkness, and this is what I had promised them in touting this great talent. My explanations that Chef Chang had bolted for destinations unknown, upending the entire operation, seemed insufficient in the face of their bewilderment and rage. My readers did not want me to explain Chang. They wanted me to explain me. My judgment. My foresight. Heck: my stability. They had trusted me, and I had betrayed that trust. I had ruined their Saturday night. I had led them astray.

Among the network of Chang obsessives, there was no less tortured a search for explanations, albeit without the hostility. Could it be explained? I wondered. For years now, I had been trying to understand him and had gotten no closer to any kind of meaning as to who and what he was. There was the cooking, electric and inimitable, and available only in discrete installments that emphasized the fleeting nature of everything that matters. And that was all. And maybe that was enough, in the same way that a painter is the sum of his paintings and the life that matters, the person, is what you find and intuit in the canvases.

WORD CAME a couple of weeks later that Chang had left the area for good, and was now living in—and cooking in?—the suburbs of Atlanta, in Marietta, about twenty miles northwest of downtown.

So ends a crazy and intense chapter of my life, I thought—one whose passing I will mourn, even as I hold on fast to the memory of all those great meals. Things come and go, and nothing is forever, and we savor the good times when we can. Szechuan food was never the same again, every subsequent, subpar dish only reminding me what I'd once had, and how I would never have it again—the ache, the longing, that much more intense, because the gap between greatness and mediocrity was so profound.

I kept tabs on him from afar, growing jealous of Atlantans, jealous of their privilege, as I read the reports about his new restaurant. My memory overwhelmed me with a procession of bright and vivid pictures, and I was sitting down again to a meal of corned beef with cilantro and scallion bubble pancake and roast fish with green onion. I read the reviews over and over again, devouring the words, as if reading were akin to eating, as if the more I read, the more the descriptions would satisfy my desire for the real thing. There was something about these reviews that bothered me, though, and it only occurred to me after a fourth reading. What bothered me was that they were not as approving as my reviews had been, not nearly as comprehensive, not nearly as obsessive in nature, and the thought came to me that he was in the wrong place, that Atlantans did not love him enough, or understand him enough. It was not a professional thought, not something a restaurant critic, obliged to consider things with a certain objectivity and impartiality, is supposed to feel. A critic is not supposed to feel proprietary—and certainly is not supposed to feel protective—of a restaurant or a chef. That's when I knew that I had crossed a line, if only in my own mind. And that's when it occurred to me to get in the car and drive down to Atlanta.

TASTY CHINA WAS THE NAME. Grim-faced servers cleared tables with militaristic efficiency. From my corner table, in the back, I watched a huge white tureen being carried aloft through the sickly lit dining room like the crown prince, trailing a cloud of steam that I thought I could smell from several tables away: ginger, garlic.

The new place was a lot like the old place, a lot like all the old places. If I had been plunked down, blindfolded, at a table in front of a buffet's worth of his cooking, I would not have been able to tell where I was. Atlanta was Alexandria was Fairfax. The same strip-mall setting, the same bad lighting, the same attentive but impersonal service. And the same food, the same brilliant, mouth-numbing, heart-racing dishes.

It was strangely comforting, this sameness—because there was nothing about cilantro fish rolls and cumin-spiced fried fish and pepper-laced chicken that resembled chicken and mashed potatoes or meatloaf and gravy or any of the other dishes that I ordinarily thought of as constituting comfort food. But they were comforting to me, somehow, all the same. They had become comforting. Familiarity, in food, doesn't breed contempt; it breeds the opposite—it breeds contentment. I had eaten these dishes so many times that they had ceased to feel exotic—a function largely of novelty and newness—or ceased to feel *merely* exotic. Eating them again, here in Atlanta, was like running into old friends far from home. They eased my sense of dislocation, of being far from home, in a strange city, without connection. At the same time, they would always be a little different, because this was not the palate I had grown up with, and there were new things I learned each time I dug into them, subtleties of spicing, nuances of texture, the same way a classic story or poem is different upon each fresh reading.

The plates massed around me, threatening to crowd me out, a circumstance my waiter sought to ameliorate by pushing over an adjoining table, a solution I flatly rejected on the grounds that I would look like an even bigger glutton, and it dawned on me, finally. Driving south, I had been buoyed by a sense of adventure, of lighting out for a new world, and the thought of reconnecting, retasting, had seemed to ease some of the drudgery of a long road trip. But now, having travelled more than six hundred miles to his new restaurant, I realized: *I had traveled six hundred miles to a restaurant to eat dinner.*

And not only that, but I had just crossed a line from critic to fan in coming down here. I had formally acknowledged that an interest had become an obsession.

And that unnerving thought gave way to this unnerving thought: If the past was any guide, then Chef Chang would not last very long at Tasty China—the fact that reviews had already come out seemed to suggest that his days were numbered. And then what? Would I follow him to his next place? And the next place after that? Trail after him the way groupies did The Grateful Dead? The itinerant critic and the exile chef? The answer, I supposed, would determine just how much of an obsessive I had become.

HE LEFT, OF COURSE. He always left. It was not a matter of if, but when. When, in this case, turned out to be almost a year after he moved to Atlanta.

But this time, he did not stay in the area. He'd headed west: Knoxville, Tennessee, according to one of my tipsters.

"You're not going, are you?" my wife asked when I told her one night. We were out at dinner, on one of my appointed rounds: a generically stylish American restaurant with the same menu of rarefied, rustic dishes, it seemed, I had eaten for the last year or more. It was as if the chefs had all attended the same seminar.

"Probably not," I said.

My wife set down her martini thingie. "Here we go again."

"What?"

"Probably not means probably yes. You watch. You'll end up talking yourself into going."

"I mean, it's pretty far."

"Uh-huh."

"And it's not like I haven't ever had his cooking. . . ."

"Enjoy yourself."

WASHINGTON, ATLANTA, KNOXVILLE . . . and then where? Where would it end? *Would* it end?

Was Chef Chang destined never to find peace, never to find a permanent home, to tramp from town to town, state to state, a culinary mercenary, a tormented loner genius? I wondered if growing up in Hunan Province, he could have imagined a life like this: a cooking vagabond, hopscotching across America and the Deep South—a restless and hungry seeker, Kerouac with a wok. Was this the life he dreamed for himself? Trading one suburban strip mall for another, the places as indistinct as the landscape, homogenized and featureless? Lacing complex dishes with the famed *ma la* peppercorn for Americans who knew nothing of him or his country, who could not tolerate heat and would much rather he concentrated his attention on their General Tso's chicken?

This was the Chef Chang I had created in my imagination, in lieu of actual knowledge of the actual Chef Chang. A chef with poetry in his soul, a romantic figure who yearned to break free of all that constrained him, including the limits of his own imagination.

It troubled me to think that there might be another Chef Chang, or many other Chef Changs, that I had driven to Atlanta and now hopped a flight to Knoxville to eat the cooking of a man who was on the run from authorities, or who had gotten in deep with the wrong people and who did not pick up and leave because he sought a greater freedom, but who picked up and left because he was interested merely in survival.

Who else, I wondered, was following him?

Maybe he was the one and also the other, a romantic figure on the run. Maybe he was neither, and all the speculation was horribly off base.

I had driven to Atlanta with the idea that eating more of his food would bring me closer to understanding him and whatever compelled him to keep leaving places, but it hadn't even brought me closer to understanding why I picked up and followed him. I liked to think that I was recreating his own journey westward, tracing his steps in the hope of entering his mind and heart. I liked to think that, because otherwise I would have to come to grips with the idea that I was losing my mind, just a little. Washington, Atlanta, Knoxville. . . . Where would I stop? *Would* it stop?

I HAD ALWAYS THOUGHT the food was addictive—the way you ate more than you intended for no other reason than that the scorching heat set your heart to racing and caused you to sweat and gave you the feeling of release and exhilaration. Now I had to wonder if there was something addictive, too, in the quest itself. I reflected on that very question as I sat at my table at Hong Kong House, surrounded by half a dozen dishes, my heart racing, feeling happier than I had in weeks and maybe months, the simple contentedness that comes of knowing that you are in the right place at the right time.

I had suspected that this meal would be my last, that I was not long for the road, that I couldn't continue to follow him from city to city. He was the one in exile, not me. Enough. I'd had my adventure.

I said all this to my wife when I returned. She looked at me the way she often looked at me when I made a promise to stain a bookcase or embark on some other project of house beautification: *I'll believe it when I see it.*

And in truth, I knew when I said it that I had said it simply to have said it, to give the idea a spin, to look good; I was test-driving, I wasn't buying.

A year later, I learned that Chef Chang had bolted again. He had come east and was cooking in Charlottesville, Virginia, at a place called Taste of China. I was in Richmond, doing research for a book, when I got the news. *An hour away. He hasn't been this close since he was in D.C.* What came over me, then, was almost chemical, an emotional sensation akin to that triggered by the peppers, an involuntary systemic reaction. I was salivating.

I WAS STANDING OUTSIDE the bathroom at Taste of China with my cellphone pressed to my ear, assuring my wife that I was fine, that the trip had been a smooth one, when I spotted Chef Chang through the narrow window of the double doors and subsequently lost the thread of our conversation. It was the closest I had ever come to seeing him.

"Where are you?"

"Charlottesville."

"Charlottesville? I thought you were in Richmond."

"I was."

"And now you're in Charlottesville. . . ."

"I finished what I had to do in Richmond and decided to come home by way of Charlottesville and get some dinner," I said, adding that I was going to be back later than I expected. I was feeling like a cliché.

"Where are you having dinner?" she asked, just as a manager pushed through the double doors of the kitchen, exposing us to the echoing sound of clanging pots and pans and cooks barking instructions at one another. I craned my neck for a better glimpse. Out came two waiters bearing large trays on their shoulders and gesticulating wildly as they bickered in very loud Chinese, presumably about who was responsible for what.

"Don't tell me," she said, and I couldn't tell whether I was hearing admiration or dismay in her tone. Admiration and dismay? "Are you with him there in the kitchen?"

"No, I'm outside, peeking in."

"Are you going to talk to him?"

Talk to him. Such a simple idea. An inevitable idea, an entirely practical idea. Chef Chang and I had never met, but it seemed odd that I would not seek him out now, that I would just sit there at my table like any other customer in the restaurant instead of one who had intimate knowledge of his canon and who had studied his techniques and methods. Besides which, I was a restaurant critic in Washington, not Charlottesville, so what harm could be done in divulging my identity if I so chose? And why, at this point, after all these many trips, after Atlanta and Knoxville, would I not choose?

These were smart, sensible arguments my wife was making, but they were aimed at normalizing what was not normal. To talk to Chef Chang was to make purposeful a trip that had been conceived on a whim and a notion, since an interview could be useful, and might one day form the basis for a piece (I didn't have an assignment to come down here)—to talk to him, in other words, was to turn what was, in truth, a crazy pursuit of a man and a taste into something that could be spoken about in ordinary conversation without making me look like a loon.

Our bond, such as it was, was through food, through the silent communication of dish and diner, I said to myself. Not through talk; through taste. But this was an attempt at self-justification, an attempt to preserve some semblance of my critical distance, the wall I erected between the moments I described and my ability to be affected by them and, possibly, succumb to them.

What would happen if I went up and introduced myself? Would he bolt in the middle of dinner and never come back? Would he fling the contents of a hot wok in my face for making his life in Washington so difficult? Would he call the cops and accuse me of stalking him? And how would I plead, if he did? What would I say? What could I say? Taste of China was his sixth restaurant in four years. I had been to all of them. Where he went, I went. He cooked, and I wrote about him. I wrote about him, and he left.

Seeking him out was beside the point, I decided, which made what I did next so stupefying, as though I had contrived a passive-aggressive defiance against my own ruling. I ordered nine dishes. Nine dishes, for a table of one. The waiter had turned to walk away after dish four, and I had had to flag him down to return. He attempted to put the brakes on me after dish five, but I persisted. By dish number six he was shaking his head, his tired eyes widened in alarm. By the ninth, and final, dish he looked worried for me, worried for my soul, and I imagined as he turned to head back to the kitchen that he cursed my Western indifference to waste. What was I doing?

The plates gathered around me—scallion bubble pancake, corned beef with cilantro, cleavered whole chicken with finger peppers, cilantro fish rolls, roast fish with green onion—and this time I did not put up a fight when the adjoining table was shoved up against mine. I wanted Chef Chang to come out and see the spectacle in his dining room. I wanted him to come out and see my devotion, the depth of it, wanted him to know that I was no mere customer but a fervent loyalist. A critic, yes, but only by occupation. Our connection now, clearly, transcended those bounds.

He did not come out. It was okay. I understood. Maybe it was better this way. *Not through talk; through taste.* I did not come to Charlottesville for a meeting of the minds. I had come to Charlottesville because his food was a part of my life. His tastes had become my tastes. Where he went, I followed. I dug into a mound of cleavered chicken with peppers. My mouth went numb. Tears rolled down my cheeks.

Killer Food

By Dana Goodyear

From *The New Yorker*

New Yorker staff writer (and poet) Dana Goodyear has a knack
for profiles that capture the subject's personality. The real
story behind this hip new L.A. restaurant lies in the
personalities of its iconoclastic chef-owners.

One Wednesday in mid-February, Jon Shook and Vinny
Dotolo, the Bill and Ted of the Los Angeles culinary
scene, finished eating a couple of burritos at a stand in the Farmers
Market and headed for the parking lot. Dotolo—five feet six and
broody, with glasses, a multicolored sleeve tattoo, and a three-day
beard—yawned and stretched, exposing a pale, rusty-haired ex-
panse, before climbing dozily into Shook's truck. Shook, who is
also small, but chatty, with a homemade lexicon, had on shorts and
a T-shirt, with purple-and-black argyle socks yanked up above a
pair of pull-on leather boots. He was talking about a problem with
a line cook at Animal, the restaurant that he and Dotolo opened
nearly two years ago.

"Whoa!" Dotolo said suddenly, pointing at a mark on the forehead of a middle-aged woman in a station wagon nearby. "What is
that metal plate in her head? Man, is that a tattoo? Jesus Christ!
That's the craziest fuckin' thing I've ever seen." Shook stared.
"Yeah, it looks like it," he said vaguely, before someone realized it
was Ash Wednesday.

"*Oh*, it *is* Ash Wednesday," Shook said. That meant the next
week would be slow: the Lenten slump. "We're a meat-eccentric
restaurant," he said.

Meat is the main event at Animal. According to Michael Voltaggio, a young chef trained in the cerebral techniques of molecular gastronomy, Animal is distinguished by its "gnarly big plates of food where each dish has three thousand calories." (Voltaggio, whose menu at the Langham, a hotel in Pasadena, includes "A Study of the Vegetables of the Season," eats there once a month.) Animal's staples are outrageous concoctions that might be called whimsical if they weren't so rich: expertly prepared junk food made from exquisite ingredients. The petit basque, a bubbling crock of sheep's-milk cheese and thin-sliced chorizo, accompanied by grilled bread, is like a personal pizza; the poutine, with cheddar in place of the customary Montreal curds, has an oxtail topping the texture of chaw, and tastes unmistakably of chili cheese fries. For the restaurant's version of loco moco—a Hawaiian surfer meal composed of white rice, a hamburger, gravy, a fried egg, and sometimes Spam—Shook and Dotolo serve a heap of artisanal Anson Mills rice, a Niman Ranch beef patty, a quail egg, and a slab of Spam, all drenched with house-made teriyaki sauce. The tamest offerings are a flat-iron steak under a slick of truffle-Parmesan fondue, and a forty-six-ounce rib eye, which requires nearly an hour on the grill.

Animal is in an old Jewish district of Los Angeles, several doors down from Canter's deli, and next to Schwartz Bakery, whose owner is the restaurant's landlord. The lease stipulates that Shook and Dotolo cannot advertise as kosher, for competitive reasons, but there is not much chance of that. The restaurant uses three different kinds of bacon, and manages to incorporate pork into just about everything, including the bar of dense dark-chocolate mousse that is its signature dessert, and which customers often order with a glass of milk.

Faithful to its roots as a tubercular colony, Los Angeles is a city of juice fasts, tonics, and brown-rice cleanses; its image of itself depends on rigorous abstinence from comfort food. But there is a countercurrent of roadside stands, drive-ins, and food trucks, which, along with grilled pizza and Cobb salad, arguably constitute the true regional cooking of Southern California. Shook and Dotolo draw on this tradition freely. "You think about L.A. and it's, like, the junk-food capital—doughnuts, hamburgers," Shook says.

Animal serves both, though it is perhaps the only doughnut place in town that insists on making them "in season," which is winter. The chefs talk wistfully of opening an old-fashioned sandwich shop, and a second restaurant seems imminent, though they are cagey about their plans.

Animal is small and spare: a single room, with a framed lamb's skull and an old Muppets lunchbox with a picture of the namesake character providing much of the décor, and a slim panel of sound-proofing overhead, to absorb the music and the conversation, which are pitched loud. The tables are unadorned: no tablecloths, breadbaskets, or bouquets, just knives and forks and paper menus, printed daily, which warn about the chefs' resistance to requests for any alterations to the food. There are forty-seven seats, which, from the beginning, have been occupied by the city's hard-core eaters: pretty girls and mangy guys, who seem to be mostly in their thir-ties, or trying to recapture them. One recent Friday night, at nine o'clock, there was a three-hour wait for a spot at the bar; the host-ess took down cell-phone numbers and sent customers across the street to a dive where they could drink in the meantime. Shook and Dotolo cook the kind of food they like to eat, and the willing-ness with which their tastes have been embraced can still surprise them. "You see a table of, like, four hot chicks, they come in and suck down, like, two poutines, two foies," Shook says.

Not long ago, Thomas Griese, the sous-chef at Le Cirque in Las Vegas, who is twenty-four, was sitting at the bar, enjoying a meal of barbecued pork-belly sliders and crispy sweetbreads. "To any cook, that's a Sunday-evening meal," he said. "It's what I want to come home and eat after a nice service." Unlike most restaurants in town, which stop serving at ten o'clock, Animal is open late—till 2 A.M. on Friday and Saturday—and local cooks come by when they get off work. Voltaggio tends to order the biscuits with maple-sausage gravy and foie gras: the ultimate wee-hours, Denny's-style binge. "It doesn't sound like it's O.K., but that's why everyone wants to eat it," he said. "And they cook it perfectly." Akasha Rich-mond, who used to be the personal chef for Michael Jackson and Barbra Streisand, and now has a restaurant catering to health-con-scious Angelenos, takes her staff on field trips there. "It's bad-ass food," she said. "My line cooks love it." The charm is not universal, though. Reviewing Animal in 2008, S. Irene Virbila, the restaurant critic for the *L.A. Times*, praised Shook and Dotolo's technique but accused them of overkill: too much bacon, too much sauce, too much sugar, too much salt, not enough vegetables. "What's needed are some perspective and discipline," she wrote. One dish, the biscuits with gravy and foie gras, she deemed "too cloying to live."

Dotolo is the primary architect of the menu, and he is uncompromising about his food fantasies. When the restaurant first opened, he served a bowl of mulberries with a whole nectarine for dessert, and no knife. He wanted customers to pick up the fruit, bite into it whole, and feel the juice running down their chin. His inspiration often comes from eating; he and Shook claim that one year, early in their career, they spent a hundred and fifty thousand dollars dining out—at a time when they were living in a flophouse in Hollywood.

"I had this weird thing last night," Dotolo said recently. "I was, like, eating tofu and I was, like, thinking about how much it reminded me of, like, bone marrow and, like, brains and, like, that weird texture—like, soft, a little bit gelatinous. But the flavor of tofu is, like, so *yelchth*. I'll think about that now for, like, maybe a year before I think about something to do with it. I think it'd be fuckin' hilarious to do tofu at Animal, just because it throws people off so much." He thought for a second, and said, "Maybe you do tofu with meat."

SHOOK, TWENTY-NINE, and Dotolo, thirty, are known at times as the kids or the boys or occasionally the bookends, but always as the dudes. A short-lived reality show they starred in on the Food Network, in 2007, was called "Two Dudes Catering"; their cookbook, which came out the following year, is "Two Dudes, One Pan." In large part, they are treated indivisibly. When *Food & Wine* came up with a list of the ten best new chefs of 2009, Shook and Dotolo counted as one. A chef friend distinguishes between them by saying that Dotolo spends all his time thinking about his most recent meal, while all Shook thinks about is his next.

The pair exude an air of slovenly innocence, refusing to wear chefs' jackets and shaving irregularly; greasy baseball hats hold back their hair, which they at one time grew to shoulder length. Unkempt self-presentation is part of their appeal. The art dealer Earl McGrath, who met Shook and Dotolo ten years ago and often hires them to cook for parties, describes them with an epigram: "Look so dirty, smell so clean."

Shook was brought up Jewish in Ormond Beach, Florida (his parents have since become Lubavitchers); Dotolo is from an Italian family in Clearwater. They spent their adolescent years surfing and fishing and working on the margins of the food world. Dotolo was a dishwasher at a barbecue joint; Shook was the stockboy at a grocery store, which he hated, and then got a job washing dishes at a restaurant, which he loved. "They used to feed me," he says. "My favorite dish was a mashed-potato sandwich, 'cause they had French bread. That might have been the first time in my life I had French bread and real mashed potatoes." After that, he worked at an Outback and a mom-and-pop pizzeria, before deciding, when he finished high school, to go to culinary school in Fort Lauderdale. He met Dotolo there, at orientation, in 1999. Shook says, "He was, like, 'Dude, I just found this dope pizza place right up the road. Want to go check it out?'"

While still in school, Shook and Dotolo worked for Michelle Bernstein, a prominent chef in South Beach, at her restaurant, the Strand, and then went to Vail to cook. In 2001, they made their way to Los Angeles and started as line cooks at Chadwick, an elegant Beverly Hills restaurant owned by the chef Benjamin Ford. Chadwick eventually failed, but Ford kept the two on as caterers and odd-jobs men. Ford's father and stepmother, the actor Harrison Ford and the screenwriter Melissa Mathison, started hiring them, too. They became part of the family—gardening, babysitting, house-painting, and sometimes, when it was too cold to sleep in their pickup truck, spending the night on Mathison's couch. "I have this image of Vinny in his shorts, Vans, apron, tattoos, holding a spoon, saying, 'But should I call her first or should I wait for her to call me?'" she recalled.

In 2002, Shook and Dotolo launched Carmelized Productions, a catering company, and started hustling to get a television show, a demonstration of ambition that other chefs found off-putting and which they now regret. The pair spent a month in New York, painting Mathison's apartment there—and living in it, without furniture—while pitching executives from MTV and the Food Network. At a meeting with Pam Krauss, an editor at Clarkson Potter, they said they hoped to do a pop-up cookbook. Shook says, "She was, like, 'Scratch and sniff?' And we were, like, 'Oh my god, you get it!' She was, like, 'Get out of here, we'll never work together.'" (Several years later, Krauss edited "Two Dudes, One Pan.")

Catering a party at the director Brett Ratner's house, Shook and Dotolo met Benedikt Taschen, the publisher, and his wife, Lauren, who became their new patrons. They started to do parties for the Taschens at the Chemosphere, the futuristic John Lautner house they own off Mulholland Drive. "All our guests always want to hug them," Benedikt says. "They don't have an agenda. They have kind of a Forrest Gump approach."

For a while, Shook and Dotolo ran Carmelized Productions out of the space that now houses Animal. They filmed their show and shot photographs for the cookbook there; the plan was that, if necessary, they would move in and shower at a friend's house around the corner. But their hope was always to open a place of their own, an aspiration they realized with seed money invested by the Taschens. (Benedikt likes to come in at lunchtime, when Animal is closed, to eat and give them business advice.) Before the restaurant opened, Shook and Dotolo were sitting around with a couple of friends spit-balling names, and struck upon Animal. Dotolo's girl-friend, Sarah—not his wife—protested vigorously when she found out what they had in mind. "She was, like, 'No way,'" Shook said, smiling mischievously. That, of course, sealed it.

WHOLE-ANIMAL COOKERY began to find a place in high-end American restaurants about ten years ago. Shook and Dotolo's cohort of chefs—they call themselves the D.I.Y. generation, because they had restaurants before they had money—embraced it with gusto. Grappling with the product in its least-processed form appealed to them on an aesthetic level; the economics of using every part spoke to their thrift. Nate Appleman, a proponent of offcuts and charcuterie, who by his mid-twenties was part owner of a restaurant in San Francisco, says that the only way he could afford to serve the same meat as the French Laundry was to buy the entire beast and cook it all. Shook and Dotolo have served lamb-tongue ravioli, lamb-heart paprikas, devilled lamb kidneys, veal brains grenobloise. Not long ago, Dotolo told a food blogger for *L.A. Weekly* that he'd been experimenting with veal testicles, and would add them to the menu soon. "What they do at Animal is use the cuts nobody wants," Appleman says. "They're really pushing the limits. They had a dish on the menu that was thirty duck hearts in curry. It was hard even for me to get through." The ethos of this kind of cooking is undeniably macho (though some female chefs are known for it, too). Ford, who serves a variety of domestic hams and a whole-pig dinner at his new place, Ford's Filling Station, in Culver City, says he always tries to get a woman to read over his menu and make sure it's not too alienating.

In mid-February, Dotolo got his hands on a whole lamb from a local purveyor. "I can't say who, 'cause it's not approved, but it's fuckin' good," he said. "It's all fed on apples and pears and lettuces." Shook butchered it in the kitchen. They prepared the liver with roasted butternut squash and sage brown butter, and the leg with green-garlic tsatziki, farro, and rutabaga greens. "Now I just have two tenderloins and a neck to use," Shook said. They served the brain to Rory Herrmann, the chef de cuisine at Bouchon in Beverly Hills, when he came in to eat one night. "I cut the skull open—whack!—with an axe," Dotolo recalled. "Most guys use a band saw."

The next day, seven frozen pigs' heads arrived from Niman Ranch, and the following morning they went into a brine. They were for head cheese, which Shook and Dotolo were taking to a food festival in South Beach. In the afternoon, Shook opened the walk-in cooler and checked on the heads. One, in a pot, was already cooked; it was for the restaurant. "I was talking to my friend Tandy Wilson, at City House, in Nashville. I was, like, 'Man, your head cheese stays so fuckin' moist,'" Shook said. "We got real wasted and he said, 'Boy, the trick is to cook the head and leave it in the pot overnight.' So we tried it and it worked amazing."

In the kitchen, Dotolo stood over the cooked head—cartilaginous, magenta, baring its teeth—and rooted persistently around the cheek and neck for the prime bits. "We're partially professionally trained chefs, partially self-trained," he said, removing a delicate layer of skin, like a pink satin blanket, and tossing it into a garbage can. Then he tore a hunk of flesh from the jaw and shredded it with his fingers. "It's a pretty meticulous job," he said. "Some people don't see the worth in it. I think of it as the transformation of something you would never eat into something really tasty."

The food lovers of South Beach were, if not delighted, at least challenged. Shook said that everyone kept saying, "Head cheese? What's head cheese? Is that like blue cheese?" One woman, when Shook finally had a chance to explain, spat it out on the table and said, "Oh my fucking God, I've been kosher for thirty-two years." Shook giggled, recollecting. "Not any more you ain't!"

THE SATURDAY of Oscar weekend, the Animal boys had a gig catering a five-hundred-person party hosted by Moët & Chandon to honor the work of a celebrity photographer named Tom Munro. The guest list included Dustin Hoffman, Justin Timberlake, Seth McFarlane, and Garth Fisher, a plastic surgeon to the stars. Shook arrived at the venue, a gallery on Melrose Place, at four, wearing shorts. Out front were a red carpet, a disco ball, and moveable hedges; a decorator was tacking faux greenery to the lintel. The kitchen, in the back alley, consisted of a fryer and a grill underneath a tent, next to a Dumpster.

"Want to go on a long walk off a short pier?" Shook asked two of his line cooks, when they had finished setting up. He grabbed a lighter and the three of them set out jauntily down the alley.

An hour before the party, it was pouring rain, and Shook was in high gear, prepping food; interviewing the line cooks about their outfits, with an imaginary microphone; and dealing with the Fire Department. "You guys hungry?" he asked the inspectors, when they came to check out his set-up. They looked dubious—open fire, tent, gas tanks—until he fed them each an heirloom carrot coated with clarified butter and dipped in rye-bread crumbs, causing them to smile and go away.

Planning the party, the coordinator from Moët had specified an all-male serving crew: "Tall, handsome, good-looking *dudes*." Alex Meyer, a promising young line cook, showed up, dressed in black on black, to work as a waiter. He hit the floor carrying a tray of meatballs. Two made-up blond women cut through the crowd to reach him. "You're killing us," one said. "I'm not going to fit into this dress anymore." Victoria Keon-Cohen, an Australian model in town for a few months, popped a beer-battered squash ring, which she mistook for calamari, in her mouth. She said she was working to promote the cause of models eating, and speared a meatball from a passing tray.

At nine-twenty, a black Escalade appeared in the alley, and Madonna got out, wearing dark glasses. Twenty minutes and no hors d'oeuvres later, she was back in the Escalade. The cooks congregated at the mouth of the tent to have a look. One of them, Carlos, asked who she was. A line chef filled him in, and Carlos looked baffled. "The singer, not the mom of Jesus," the line chef said.

Back at the restaurant, Dotolo, in a camouflage hunting cap, was expediting orders from the kitchen. Just before midnight, Mario Batali came in with the chef Nancy Silverton, with whom he owns Osteria Mozza, a popular local restaurant. They were accompanied by Mozza's wine director, pastry chef, and sous-chef, and by a mixologist, a magician, and two musicians, one of whom was Mike Mills, the bassist of R.E.M. It was Batali's first time at Animal, and he was famished, having just come from cooking at a party for *Vanity Fair* advertisers. "Is there anything we shouldn't miss?" he asked the waiter. "The pork belly," the waiter replied.

"Five of those," Batali said.

"The poutine."

"Like the fries with the fat gravy? We'll take five."

"Five?" someone at the table said, alarmed.

"Shut the fuck up. O.K., three," Batali said, and glanced at the menu. "And two pig ears, two gnocchi, two sweetbreads, two quail, two fluke, and then, after *that*, two crispy rabbit legs, two pork ribs, two flat irons medium rare/rare, two veal breasts—what's loco moco? Two-a them. And I don't want any fuckin' vegetables." He took a swig from an open wine bottle.

In the kitchen, Dotolo slumped intently over the salad station, strewing balsamic onions over chicken-liver toast. To Batali's order, he added everything else on the menu. Shook took over expediting, and told the cooks to fire the ears, fire the quail, fire the sweet-breads and poutine. Dotolo looked up testily from his ministrations; he didn't want there to be too much food on the table at once. "Just 'cause you're hungry, doesn't mean we have to fuckin' kill 'em," he said. But Shook ignored him, and killed them anyway.

Sweet Life

By Francis Lam

From *Gourmet*

A former *Gourmet* contributing writer, now the food editor for
salon.com, Lam combines curiosity, enthusiasm, and stealthy
wit. As a CIA-trained chef himself, he gives us a unique chef's
perspective on the process of developing the menu for a hot
new L.A. restaurant.

Their Los Angeles restaurant, Street, is just weeks from
opening, and Susan Feniger and Kajsa Alger are living
the dream: wrangling with contractors, getting permits, and reporting break-ins. So this weekend, they're unwinding by trashing
Feniger's house—breaking cupboards, warping wallboards, burning
holes in the upholstery. The crash and bang of professional cooking
does not enter the home quietly, and these two are cranking out
recipes, testing and tasting and retesting them for their menu.

"Tomorrow we're testing food and beer; Sunday it's Cham-
pagnes, liquor, and food," Alger told me with military precision
when I met her. Then she smiled. "It always sounds so organized
when I talk about it. But when we're three cocktails in, not a lot of
food happens."

I'm up in the hills of L.A., in Feniger's home, learning how the
two partners decide what goes on the plate and which plates go on
the menu. Because a menu is a funny thing. When you're at the
table, with a drink in your hand and hunger in your belly, its purpose is obvious. For a chef, however, it might be a statement of vision or a document of her past. For the kitchen, it's a plan for how
to use precious space and manpower. For the accountant, it's all

numbers: What's going to sell well enough to keep the lights on? As chefs and owners, Feniger and Alger have to look at every dish from all of these angles, and so, as with all your favorite movies and all your favorite records, lots of ideas get left on the cutting room floor.

Like the hot dogs. A street-food-inspired restaurant should have some hot dogs on offer, right? So Alger did some research, which is to say she ate 42 hot dogs in one brutal day in Chicago, and followed that up with a 30-dog day in L.A. She and Feniger then developed enough hot dogs to occupy a whole section of the menu, only to realize (eventually) that, you know, people might not want to come to your restaurant and spend more than $2.50 on a hot dog. So they ditched them. The lesson: When writing your menu, be sure that you know your price point and your clientele's perception of value. And, apparently: Be ready to sacrifice your life for your restaurant.

The hot dogs were a dalliance they thought better of. But sometimes they'll fall a little in love with something even if they know they shouldn't. Alger takes leaves of collard greens and carefully cuts circles out of them while Feniger chops piles of limes, chiles, dried shrimp, coconut, and ginger and pulls out bowls of roasted peanuts and tamarind caramel made earlier. The Thai Bites are becoming unwieldy, each component crowding the cooler in its own container. And I imagine the poor pantry cooks, every time an order comes down, having to whip out all this stuff and arrange it neatly in ramekins as Alger was doing. Feniger smears a collard round with caramel, wraps it around the fillings, tries one, and offers it to me. Her eyes widen with excitement behind her Bunsen Honeydew glasses, and her words purr and gear up before being blurted out. "Fffffabulous!" she says. It's sweet, sticky, salty, sour, hot, and wild; crunchy and cool and sharp and round. It's crazy, and it shows on my face. Alger nods. "It takes up too much time and space, but it's worth it. We'll just have to drop two or three things from the menu so we can keep this one on," she says.

But it's not always the needs of the restaurant that dictate a dish. Sometimes, a dish can dictate the restaurant.

Twenty-five years ago, before she had four restaurants, before she had cookbooks and TV shows as one of the Too Hot Tamales, before she had managers and accountants and assistants, Feniger was just a young chef visiting a friend in India. He took her to a small village, where women offered them a dish of tapioca, chewy and sticky, festooned with pungent spices and *neem* leaves. It wasn't delicate, it wasn't pretty, it wasn't anything like the French cooking that she had trained for and maybe even understood. But in that moment, with those people, it was everything she wanted to eat, the most serendipitous and yet fundamental of shared experiences.

So when she decided that she wanted to see if she could go back to scratch and start a new restaurant on her own, without the whole apparatus that she and business partner Mary Sue Milliken had built up over the years, Feniger went back to India. She ate from 8 a.m. through midnight for 14 days, until she came back to that village. Those women were still there, making that dish, and Feniger decided Street would be where she would share those memories, those flavors you find when in a community that is not your own but that, with a bite or two, might become a little more so. "The thing with street food," Feniger says, "is that it's not food created for carts or trucks. It's food that came out of someone's home." No wonder, then, that people take their street food so personally. It's iconic; it's their culture.

"But how do you make sure your dishes are true to those cultures?" I ask. The easy answer is that Feniger and Alger called in ringers, experts who could train them in the flavors and techniques of cuisines they didn't know firsthand. But it's bigger than that. Alger is thoughtful, excited and challenged by this question, and finally says that the lines she won't cross are felt rather than delineated. They made Korean-style dumplings, for instance, flavored with cilantro. They loved them but couldn't find any cilantro in Korean cooking, so they dropped them, too. "The more we learn about these cuisines, the harder it gets," Alger says. "At first I might think, 'Let's do a stir-fried noodle dish.' And then we'd cook with a master who shows us twenty different variations, and all of a sudden something called 'stir-fried noodles' just sounds so amateurish. So we pick one and learn to nail it and it looks and tastes and sounds great, but now the kind-of-lame dishes we had penciled in next to it on the menu sound totally ridiculous."

But there's one dish they feel they've nailed for sure. Alger draws me to the stove and shows me a bowl of tapioca balls soaking in water. She fires up a pan, gets some ghee good and hot, pops some spices and chiles, and stirs in the starchy pearls. "When I first tried to make this, I was trying to chef my way through it too much," she says. It was looking too gluey, so she tried to sear it with high heat, but it became weirdly chunky. For this dish, she had to learn to cook against her instinct, to let it ride the way Feniger suggested, to let it get mushy, sticky, tacky. Alger hands me and Feniger spoons. It's like chewy butter, heat and cumin and grassy herbs. "Prrrrretty nice," Feniger says. She takes another bite. "Mmm! That's rrrrreally good."

The women pause to notice the sun going down, the light so low, so directed, so yellow and beautiful. We go outside to take a break and marvel, and Feniger's cat Squirt takes advantage of our distraction to nuzzle her nose right into a big bowl of bacon. They start to freak out. Then they stop and look at each other. "Do you . . . care?" Alger asks.

"Well . . . as long as we're not serving it to patrons," Feniger laughs. There are no health inspectors in the living room. This isn't Street food quite yet.

GINO CAMMARATA, GELATO KING

By Sarah DiGregorio

From the *Village Voice*

As restaurant critics for the *Voice*, DiGregorio and her
counterpart Robert Sietsema tend to cover the low-profile
restaurants that their uptown colleagues ignore—thereby
catching the real pulse of New York life. Case in point: this
profile of one Bay Ridge restaurateur.

Gino Cammarata talks to himself while he shops. Sniffing
an orange, peering at bottles of olive oil, he mutters un-
happily in Italian, remembering the smell of tangerine peel in October and the fragrance of ripening olive trees. "When I go
shopping, I go crazy," he says. If there's anything that would make
you an obsessive about food, it's growing up in Sicily, like he did,
on a farm where your father cultivates citrus, olives, and peaches.
Where your grandmother always has a surplus of fresh goat's milk.
Where you work in your uncle's restaurant, as a 10-year-old
gelato-making prodigy.

Cammarata, who moved to New York in 1970 when he was 15,
has just opened Piattini, a Sicilian-inflected restaurant in Bay
Ridge where he serves his now-famous gelato, along with dishes
like bucatina with sardines, linguini with bottarga, charcuterie, and
various fish and meat secondi. Cammarata's story is an immigrant's
tale of making it (and not making it) in New York, but it's also a
parable of the city's restaurant industry over the last 25 years—sky-
rocketing rents, condos replacing restaurants, and the little guys
ending up in Brooklyn.

The Cammarata family left their farm, and the "modern, American-style" gas-station-cum-restaurant owned by Gino's uncle, to settle on Sullivan Street in Greenwich Village. There, Giuseppe, Gino's father, got a job at Zampieri Brothers Bakery on Cornelia Street. "All his life, he was cold," says Gino, describing the chilly early mornings his father spent in the orchard. "And he always wanted to become a baker so that he could be warm."

Imagine leaving a small Sicilian farm town and arriving in Greenwich Village in the '70s. Hippies filled Washington Square Park—Gino thought they were exotic and fabulous: "The long hair! The guitars! I never wanted to go back to Sicily. I thought, here, I wouldn't have to go to school." The food was a different matter. In those days, the pasta was mushy and the tomato sauce sour. He started eating nothing but ham and eggs. On the weekends, he delivered bread from Zampieri to legendary venues like the Rainbow Room and the Waldorf-Astoria, chatting up the chefs along the way. After starting at 1 a.m., he always reached a certain midtown Italian steakhouse around 6 a.m., where the chef would give him a glass of wine.

On a recent Tuesday, the day Piattini is closed, I stopped by the restaurant to talk to Gino and check out his gelato machine. Gino is a garrulous, sturdy, middle-aged man, in a loose, white linen shirt tucked into chinos, with a gold chain around his neck. He's prone to proclamations like, "Good food, good wine, and good women, that's all I want!"

Gino pats his gelato maker as you would a good dog. He bought the squat, Italian-made machine in 1987, and has been lugging it around with him ever since—wherever Gino and that machine go, his followers scamper behind, seeking out what is considered the best gelato in the city. "It's my Ferrari," he says of the contraption. The machine churns out nine-liter batches, turning Gino's mixtures of milk, cream, and flavorings like ricotta, licorice with mint, hazelnuts, and Sicilian pistachios into miraculous confections. The cassada—a frozen version of the Sicilian cake of ricotta and candied fruit—is a dense, creamy concoction that tastes more like ricotta than ricotta.

Back in 1982, Giuseppe—along with Gino, his brother, Enzo, and their mother, Maria—went out on their own and opened an Italian gourmet shop and restaurant called Siracusa, after the region where the family came from. This was just as well, because a year or two later, Zampieri Brothers closed to make way for condos. Siracusa was situated on Fourth Avenue near Astor Place, a kind of culinary no-man's land at the time, populated with bookstores.

At Siracusa, Gino was in the kitchen with his parents, while Enzo worked the front of the house and the wine program. The restaurant sold Italian groceries and served Sicilian standards. In 1984, in the *Times's Diner's Journal,* Bryan Miller praised the gelato, the pastas—like fettuccine with porcini—and the Italian wines (a bottle of Barbera d'Alba for $9!).

But as the restaurant became more popular, the family dressed it up until it resembled, in Gino's words, a grand hotel lobby. The look didn't work for the neighborhood, so when the lease was up in 1992, the family closed Siracusa, made repairs, and revamped the dining room. They reopened as Bussola Bar & Grill, which had a more casual, affordable approach.

Still, the house specialty was Gino's gelato, and when Ruth Reichl visited in 1997 for a Diner's Journal, she gave the pasta with bottarga special mention, before noting, "The Cammaratas have always made great gelato. That has not changed." Alas, when 9/11 rolled around, business suffered. Then, in the old familiar story, the landlord cranked up the rent from $5,000 a month to $35,000. The neighborhood was gussying up, and the Cammaratas could no longer afford to be Manhattan restaurateurs. They closed Bussola Bar & Grill in 2002. Later, the space became Ippudo.

"It was so sad. [The restaurant] was my life, me and my brother," Gino says. He disappeared from the city for five years, working on the line as the pasta guy at a resort in the Hamptons. Then the resort was sold to make way for, yes, condos.

So Gino did what many New Yorkers priced out of Manhattan did before him—he moved to Brooklyn. (Actually, he already lived in Bensonhurst.) He and his trusty gelato machine set up in an unlikely location: a tanning salon in Bensonhurst, selling gelato from a small window. But then he found a proper spot on Fourth Avenue and Marine Avenue in Bay Ridge, and he and Enzo decided to give it another go.

At Piattini, the gelato machine is ensconced in the back, behind a small freezer display case holding the lovely green pistachio confection, the nut-dotted hazelnut, the licorice, and the blood or-ange–almond milk. On the handsome wooden tables and chairs, diners slurp up the Sicilian classic—bucatina with sardines, raisins, and cauliflower—and crunch on the small fried polpettes that Maria taught Gino how to make, in salt cod or squash-and-pista-chio versions. Actually, Maria still likes to putter around, and some-times takes the bus from Bensonhurst to fry up cartocci (fried shells), which Gino fills with shrimp and mascarpone.

I wished Gino luck as I headed out the door—and meant it. He replied that business was "beautiful." "You should see the Verrazano Bridge at night!" he exclaimed. "It's kinky!" Silence. "Not kinky! What do you say? Funky! It's funky!"

WILL WORK NIGHTS

By Jason Sheehan

From *Cooking Dirty: A Story of Life, Sex, Love and Death in the Kitchen*

Reviewing restaurants for Denver's *WestWord* magazine, and
now for *Seattle Weekly*, Jason Sheehan doesn't just describe a
meal, he somehow divines the inner life of a restaurant. As
this flamboyant, picaresque memoir reveals, it's an insight
bred from his former life as a chef.

Eleven P.M. Sixty minutes before the first rush.

On the line, they're lighting everything. Fryers are being
super-heated, burners roaring. The four front flattops and the two
in the back—the cake grills—are being cleared and wiped clean of
oil. Sheet pans are being laid over the grills, double-stacked, and
even the ancient gas four-burner is being coaxed to life. Usually it
remains covered with a thick, custom-fitted plastic cutting board,
used for storage, as a shelf on the already overcrowded line. There's
nothing on the menu we can't do on the grills, in the fryers, in the
two nukers bracketed to the wall above the cold table. It's faster
not to use burners.

Only now, the cover is popped and all four rings are blazing
merrily away, bleeding flames across the grated top because the
gaskets are worn and the gas lines leaky.

"Why are we eighty-six?"

I get icy, pissed-off stares; quiet wrath. Nothing. I'm going to
kill Lucy. I figure this is all Wendy's fault somehow; you don't just
bring someone new into the family without asking.

"Look, guys. If this is about *him*"—pointing—"I had nothing to
do with it. I just—"

Freddy kicks the front of one of the fryers. "It's Friday, dude. What the fuck?"

"I know, Freddy. That's what I told Lucy."

"This isn't about him," James says.

"Dude, fish. *Fish!*" Freddy is shouting now. "It's fucking Friday. Where's all the fucking fish?"

I stand stunned. And then I fold as if punched, right up around the impact point of the sudden realization of what I'd forgotten. I close my eyes. Brace my elbows on my knees. Pinch the bridge of my nose between my fingers. Try not to scream. Shit, shit, shit . . . .

Behind me, James is muttering, talking to himself. Freddy's still yelling. Hero, laughing, slapping the board with his spatula. "You suck, wheel!"

It's Friday night. And this being Friday night in upstate New York (all full of Catholics—Irish Catholics and Italian Catholics and Polish Catholics, Catholics who've come here from every-where that Catholics have fled)—that means fish fry. Fish dinners with fries and a monkey disk of milky-sweet coleslaw, fish sand-wiches going the same way, both battered and dumped in a fryer sequestered just for this foul, noxious, evil duty. Not just a tradi-tion, an edict. God's law. Friday fish fry.

How had I forgotten to check on the fucking fish? Favorite trick of the dinner crew: not pulling the tubs of cheap, rock-hard haddock fillets out of the coffin freezer in the back for their slow thaw. In a water bath they take two hours or more. Dumped out on a prep table and allowed to collect bacteria, even longer. The fish would've been on special all night, written up on the board by the front door, put on a menu insert, programmed into the servers' POS system: SPEC FRY or SPEC SANDY. They'd probably served two hundred fish dinners earlier, would've gambled on how few cases to pull to leave us maximally screwed.

From my wounded hunker, I ask Freddy, "How many fillets we have?"

"Six, man. And they all stink."

I try to think. We'll only do half as many orders tonight—it technically being Saturday for most of the shift—but I can't have the fish pulled from the menu. Friday fucking fish fry is pure heaven on any restaurant's books—a fast mover with low food cost, high menu price and customers commanded by God to eat it or else they'll go to hell. I blame the Pope, the dinner shift, the management, everyone. But the last, best curses I save for myself.

Then I stand up straight. I look around at my guys, at Wendy. Briefly, I wonder if there's still some way I can blame this on him.

"All right. Wheel sucks. I forgot to check the fish. My fault."

Mutiny in the eyes of the crew.

"But we know what to do," I continue. "We can do this. Freddy, whatever fish is in the coolers, bury it. James, set the pans. Hero, get the hose. Freddy, on me when you're done. Wendy, on James." I step up to the pass, lean across the gleaming, hot aluminum, ducking my head under the glowing heat lamps, looking for Lucy. I call her over, tell her where we're at. "How's the floor?"

The floor is mercifully empty, servers rolling silver, slicing lemons, preening, staring dumbly at the walls—whatever servers do when there are no customers to pester. I tell Lucy to stall any new tables that come in as long as possible, then we break.

THERE ARE TWO WAYS to do a fish fry at a short-order restaurant.

The first is to slow-thaw a bunch of haddock fillets in a forty-two-degree prep cooler or under cold tap water in a clean sink. Once thawed, the fillets then need to be individually inspected; trimmed, if necessary, of excess skin or blood-dark belly meat left attached by the fishmonger; laid out on clean paper towels and stacked three deep in a clean, dry fish tub. The tubs are then stacked Lincoln Log-style in an upright ready cooler or lowboy. As soon as an order comes in, a single fillet is delicately lifted from its bedding and the company of its friends, dusted with flour and gently, lovingly dredged through a pan of room-temp beer batter made sweet and strong with buttermilk and a good stout. The gummy fish must then be thinned by running it between the index and middle fingers—surplus batter scraped back into the pan—and only after all this can the jacketed haddock be placed carefully into a hot fryer using a swirling motion: introducing it to the heat slowly to keep the fillet from curling as the batter tightens and to keep the batter itself from just bubbling away. There's a motion to it. A grace. Work one Friday night on fryer station in Catholic country and you will never forget it.

A couple minutes in the oil and voilà: perfect fried haddock, golden brown and puffy, religiously satisfactory and ready to be plated alongside crisp french fries and cold coleslaw. That's the way to do it right.

Then there's the way we do it in a hurry (the way we do it tonight):

1. Collect from the freezer the eighty pounds of frozen haddock fillets that the dinner crew neglected to pull. The fish is already separated into ten-pound consignments—each batch a solid block of chunky gray ice inside a stiff-sided but flimsy plastic box. The boxes are heavy, slippery, annoyingly hard to handle. They'll take the skin right off your hands if your hands aren't bone-dry. When the crew is hurrying, the odds of a broken toe from a dropped box go up dramatically. Doesn't happen tonight, though.

2. Take those boxes out the back door, pull off the locking lids, set them up inside empty bread racks braced at an angle against the back wall, and let Hero open up with the power sprayer we use for cleaning the floors and the grease out of the hood vents. With the hose screwed into the hot water tap and the sprayer turned against ice, it might as well be a flamethrower.

3. Power-wash the shit out of the fish tubs until the steam stops and the ice starts to crumble, stopping periodically to set back up the racks that have been pushed over or to retrieve the icy fish bricks that have slipped from their boxes and gone skittering off into the gravel. During these interludes, the chances of the sprayer "getting away from" Hero and "accidentally" soaking either Freddy or me are 100 percent. Tonight, Hero gets Freddy while Freddy is lighting a cigarette, his timing perfect, catching him just as he bends to cup the flame of his lighter against the wind. Freddy jumps, sputters, charges and takes a running swing at Hero. This just gets him another shot with the hose. The two

of them need to be separated briefly. I shove Hero aside, tell Freddy to go back inside, and he does, shaking water out of his long, ratty blond hair.

4. Bring the partially thawed cases into the prep kitchen, dump them out on the tables, and split the disintegrating fish-cicles length-wise into twenty portions, preserving as many whole fillets as possible. Place each chunk of fish ice into a long, shallow metal baking pan called a hotel.

5. Walk twenty laden hotel pans onto the line where James (with Wendy's bewildered assistance) will have set up deep bains★ on every available hot surface, each filled with a few inches of (hopefully already boiling) water.

6. Set hotel pans on top of bains, making twenty scratch double boilers, and cover hotels with plastic wrap, now making twenty jerry-rigged pressure cookers.

7. Wait. Smoke cigarettes. Bicker angrily with crew. Freddy is off in his corner by the fryers (standing post for the absent Juan), muttering under his breath and staring death rays at Hero. Hero just keeps laughing. This is going to come to a head soon, but not yet.

8. After ten minutes or so, pull the plastic wrap off the hotels, and what you have is eighty pounds (give or take) of surface-poached, center-frozen, limp gray haddock fillets and a god-awful stink. To get rid of the stink faster, pop the filters out of the ventilation hood and just let that baby roar. Hero does this, climbing up between the grills and pulling the greasy filters out of their tracks. The suction immediately snuffs the flames on the four-burner. This is going to come back to haunt us, too. But not yet.

★ A bain, or bain-marie, being any vessel capable of both holding water and having another pan set on top of it or into it.

9. Because they are now half-cooked, the fillets will flake to pieces at the least prompting. Look at one wrong and it's likely to dissolve into fish mush and ice. Owing to this physical instability, they can no longer take the pressure of being dredged in batter so must be casseroled. In assembly-line fashion, bring in a new set of hotels. Layer each one with batter, ease in as many fillets as it can hold using a long spatula, then cover with more batter. Stack the pans back in the freezer for a few minutes to firm up the batter and shock the fillets, then remove to the ready cooler. As orders come in, shovel fillets gracelessly into the oil. Fry long and hard. Carefully remove to plate for service.

10. Pray to whatever god might be listening that no one catches you.

Oddly, the fish actually tastes pretty good this way.

Well, maybe not *good*, but less bad than you'd think. Flaky and slightly oily outside, mid-rare in the middle. In texture it's not unlike a poached fillet of sole, and in flavor only as bad as frozen haddock ever is—which is pretty bad even under the best circumstances.

The real problem is, going into the oil cold (and often still frozen in the center), the fillets will drop the temperature of the fryer oil precipitously. This screws with the fry cook's timing, and when cooking for drunks—especially *lots* of drunks—the fry cook's timing is of paramount importance to the synchronization of the rest of the kitchen. It also makes a terrible mess, pisses off the dishwashers, breaks about a dozen different health codes.

And it's just wrong.

You probably think that wouldn't matter to a bunch of guys like us. But it does. It matters a lot. If you've ever worked in a kitchen, you understand what I'm talking about. You know that little catch you get in your chest when you're doing something you know is wrong. And if you haven't worked in a kitchen, you'll just have to take my word for it. All the bullshit, the punching, the posturing, the macho crap; all the bad behavior and criminal impulses; all the hard talk and pleasure-seeking and shameless conduct—that's all true. That's The Life, the atmosphere in which so much food is created every day. But it's also true that we want to be *good*.

Not good people. Not good citizens. Not good in any general way. A lot of us (and I'm talking about all cooks here, not just the four guys standing with me on this line) prefer the opposite of good so long as we can get away with it.

But we want to be good at what we do because being good at what we do is what saves us—balancing out all the rest, at least in our minds, at least in *my* mind. Someday, when the heat comes down, when they finally slap on the leg irons and the Hannibal Lecter mask and lead me off to come-what-may, I want my guys to be able to say, "He was a good cook. Sure, he was a reprobate, a degenerate animal. Always broke. Always borrowing money. He was a foulmouthed, bad-tempered, cross-eyed, snaggletoothed, brain-damaged, tail-chasing fuckup and a total wreck of a human being. But man, Sheehan could really cook."

That would be enough, I think. Mitigation—that's all I'm after. And I'm not alone in that. I've known chefs who'd scream and curse and throw pans and torture cooks for any little slight. I've known guys who went to jail for stealing food stamps from old ladies, for sticking up convenience stores; guys who would work any angle, screw their friends over for a buck, behave in ways that are just unimaginably bad. But I've seen these same knuckleheads quit good jobs rather than do wrong by the food. I've watched them take pride in the perfect placement of scallops in a pan, in cutting a microscopic *brunoise*, in standing up under fire on a Friday night with a bunch of other like-minded bastards, throat-cutters and fuckups without blowing it for the team.

Cooking can be a miserable gig sometimes. Gouge-out-your-own-eyeballs awful. But when you sign on to a kitchen crew, what you're doing at the simplest level is indenturing yourself to the service of others. You're feeding people, providing for one of their basic needs, and that is—all else aside—a noble thing. And I have long held to the conviction that at every station, behind every burner, in all the professional kitchens in the world, is a guy who wants to walk out the door at the end of the night, into whatever personal hell or weirdness is waiting for him, knowing that, if nothing else, he did one thing real well.

But tonight, we have done wrong and are duly ashamed. Still, that's how you set up eighty pounds of fish fast—freezer to line in just a little over twenty minutes. It's a nice trick. Jesus is satisfied. The Pope is satisfied. Management will be satisfied. All our masters are pleased. Everyone is still pulling sheets and bains off their stations, yelling for the dishwashers, when I holler out to Lucy, "Luz! Galley up! Bring it on."

The printer starts chattering immediately.

RUSS & DAUGHTERS

By Rachel Wharton

From *Edible Manhattan*

Deputy editor of *Edible Manhattan* and *Edible Brooklyn*—just
two of a growing chain of regional *Edible* food magazines—
Rachel Wharton recently won a James Beard award for her
Back of the House columns. This profile brings fresh color to
a Lower East Side institution.

There are many signs on the clean white walls of Russ &
Daughters—the Lower East Side landmark that's been
serving smoked sable, pickled herring and slices of salmon so thin
you can read the paper through them, since 1914—but the one
that tells you all you need to know isn't the jokey *Lox et Veritas* (a
pun on Yale's motto of light and truth); or the old-fashioned hand-
painted signs that promote "Genuine Sturgeon, Imported Nuts
and Caviar"; or even the one reading *De gustibus non est disputan-
dum*, which is Latin for "of taste there is no dispute" and Russ-ese
for "we don't decide which fish is best, you do."

Instead, the sign that sums the salmon-slicers' superiority is the
one that boasts a quote from Anthony Bourdain, a man known
more for his barbs than his bubbly blurbs. "Russ & Daughters," it
reads, "occupies that rare and tiny place on the mountaintop reserved for those who are not just the oldest and the last—but also
the best."

Bourdain is no dummy. Russ & Daughters isn't the only 100-
year-old, fourth-generation family-owned business in town, not by
a long shot, but it's one of the very few places in that category
where the word on the street, instead of "Meh, it was better way

back when," whenever when might have been, is still that the hour-long, out-the-door weekend line is worth the wait and that yes, you really do have to eat here before you die.

This is that rarity in the New York food world: The purveyor beloved by everyone from street thugs and city politicians to chefs like locavore Peter Hoffman and lion Marco Pierre White. ("It was the finest quality fish!" White enthused by recent letter.) Russ & Daughters has been profiled by PBS, canonized by Martha, lauded at length by Calvin Trillin in nearly everything he writes and even immortalized in a 2008 J. Crew catalog, all for good reason. Because the hand-whipped, eat-it-by-the-spoonful scallion-cream cheese, the chocolate-covered jelly rings, the egg creams spritzed with real bottles of Brooklyn seltzer, that salmon—each bite an alchemy of smoke and fat—the tins of caviar and trays of whitefish salad and luscious chopped liver and latkes (those last few made from scratch in the back) at Russ & Daughters are just as good as when Joel Russ first handed over the title of the shop to Ida, Hattie and Anne in 1933. Adding them into the now neon-lit name, by the way, way before women's lib.

Heck, now that there's more herring (with cream, with onions, with curry sauce), and even more salmon (thick-cut Scottish loins, gravlax, pastrami-style, organic double-smoked Danish), and even sandwiches like the now-famous Super Heebster (whitefish and baked salmon salad, horseradish cream cheese, wasabi-roe), you could argue Russ & Daughters keeps getting better. Especially for those who shopped for 40 years before the place started toasting the bagels. ("Yes, we toast!" says the sign.)

Actually, those bagels—chewy and legit, they're made by a local baker—weren't around at the start either. Neither were the flatter, carb-conscious "flagels" or the mini-bagels, which oldtimers argue are actually the size a bagel should be. What was there was herring.

Like so many Jews in New York City, Joel Russ emigrated from Eastern Europe, arriving in 1907 to help his sister "with her little herring business." They sold the Jewish staple from one of many pushcarts on the streets of the Lower East Side until Mayor Fiorello LaGuardia decided to "clean up" the city streets, pushing those carts into new indoor markets like the nearby Essex. Luckily Russ had saved his pennies, and in 1914 he opened the tiny J. R.

Russ National Appetizing at 187 Orchard Street, expanding his stock to include other smoked and cured fish, plus accoutrements like cream cheese, and then moving, by 1920, to the current home at 179 East Houston Street.

Those foods are what the second line on the neon sign means by "appetizers." To Jews of a certain age in New York City—and their offspring, no doubt—appetizing is a noun, not an adjective. Traditionally New York's Jewish delis sold meat, while "appetizing shops" sold smoked sturgeon, hand-packed tins of caviar, cured salmon, pickles, whitefish salad, cream cheeses, chocolates and "all the stuff," says Mark Russ Federman—the third-generation owner who recently handed over the business to his daughter Niki and her cousin Josh Russ Tupper—"that goes with bagels."

Russ & Daughters is now just one of a handful of appetizing shops in the city—there's a counter at Zabar's and a few out in Brooklyn's Jewish enclaves—but back in the day, they were in nearly every Jewish neighborhood, with scores on the Lower East Side alone, says Mark, who inherited the business from his mother Anne after working as a lawyer. But even with stiff competition, Russ & Daughters always held their own; Jews and gentiles from across the city made the trip for the city's best smoked fish. (And from the city's most beautiful servers: Joel Russ, never subtle, proudly called his daughters the Queens of Lake Sturgeon, putting the moniker on both the shopping bags and the letterhead.)

In the 1940s the shop expanded to include the space next door and added dried fruits, chocolates, nuts and sweets. Photos of a party archived in the office upstairs—a far cry from that early push-cart, the family now owns the building—show jazz trumpeters and guests in finery and feathered hats where today you order choco-late-caramel-covered matzo, some of the world's best dried fruit and hand-cut hunks of halvah. Of course other things have changed since then, too: The customer base is now only 50 percent Jewish, there's an espresso machine, electronic scales, online ordering, a blog cleverly called Lox Populi, and the major shift, instituted back in the 1970s but regarded by regulars as a recent revolution, of making customers take a number before being served.

And if you think the place can be chaotic now, the old way was not for passive newbies: Customers would jockey for a space in front of their favorite slicers, who would yell out "I see you! Who's next?" Then the customer next in line would yell, "my next!" The ins and outs of calling the queue weren't the only ropes to know: Eastern European custom calls for haggling, for jabs and barbs, explains Mark. "It's a whole other way of interacting," says Niki, of the old-school ways the old-timers conduct business. "I like the way the customers feel like they have ownership."

Because they do: A vast majority are multigenerational too. "I fed her Russ & Daughters in the womb," crows one second-generation customer of her daughter when Niki stops by her stroller to say hello.

Kibbitzing with the community is as much a part of the job as stocking herring. On a recent Saturday, the crowd includes an older lady who points to a bulging basket of bread and says, "That bagel in the middle there. Is it soft?" There's the slew of old guys who come in to buy fish for the family and eat a half pound of chocolate-covered jelly rings while they wait. There's Mr. Abe, who comes in nearly every Saturday afternoon; as he leaves, everyone in the shop calls out: "Goodbye Mr. Abe!" And there's Eric: Brought first by his parents, Iraqi Jews who adopted the Ashkenazi appetizing tradition when they moved to the States, he's about to relocate west himself, to California. "Russ & Daughters," he jokes, "are the two things I'm gonna miss most."

Many of these people watched Josh and Niki grow up, and saw them ride big bags of sweet onions destined for herring back to the storeroom, years before they donned the same long white coats their grandparents did. Now the cousins and co-owners work under paintings of first-generation owner Joel ("He brought in a big leather armchair and would sit under his own portrait," says Niki) and third-generation owner Mark (who still occasionally works the store).

But it wasn't inevitable that the fourth-generation Russes would end up slicing salmon and schmearing cream cheese: Josh was an engineer while Niki worked in international relations, but when Mark wanted to retire and sell the shop, both decided to quit their day jobs. "I didn't want it to leave the family," says Josh, a lefty who has since learned to slice fish with his right hand beautifully.

If Niki and Josh are somewhat new to the counter—both have a few years under their belts, hardly the blink of an eye in this storied institution—much of the rest of the staff has worked there for decades, like Herman Vargas, a master-slicer with dedicated fans who started out cutting up those bags of onions in 1980. Most of them still remember the 1970s when the Lower East Side was littered with drunks and muggers instead of designers and mixologists, and on weekends the shop shuttered by nightfall. (It's a sight yet to be seen by Anne and Hattie, who now live in Florida and are amazed to hear stories of the rebirth of their neighborhood.)

No matter the decade, however, the crowds have always been four-thick on Saturday afternoons, every head turned to the counter awaiting their turn and watching the zen-like hand-slicing, each transparent piece of salmon sliced with one smooth left-to-right move of a super slender knife, the little bit of fat at the center deftly trimmed just at the end. (Everybody here makes it look easy, but a recent reality show episode where chefs Chris Cosentino and Aaron Sanchez butchered a few pounds prove it's not.)

"There's something about slicing," allows Niki, who has also worked as a yoga instructor. "It's very meditative. It puts you in this zone." Especially on Saturdays, when the entire crowd of white-coated servers stands at the wood counters that run the length of the shop, every inch made a silky golden-brown thanks to decades of a daily dose of fish oil.

Yet slicing, while critical, isn't the only thing a Russketeer must know. There's the fish itself: which salmon is smokier (Scottish over Irish) or the difference between true belly lox ("real lox is not smoked, it's salt-cured," explains Niki) and cold-smoked Gaspé Nova ("the quintessential New York salmon," says Niki, "thanks to its combination of the fattiness of the fish and the mild smokiness").

They also have to know what a smoked or cured fish looks like when prepared to perfection: Russ & Daughters works with a carefully curated collection of smokehouses that works to hit the freshness and flavor marks the specialty shop wants. "We pick every fish we sell, and we reject a lot," says Niki. "After being a lawyer for nine years," she adds, "my father thought, 'Oh, this will be so easy.' So he asked my grandfather, 'How do you tell a good fish from a bad fish?" He answered, 'You feel for a certain taste, shine, all these things, and then maybe in 15 years, you'll be able to tell.'"

It's exactly that year-in and year-out routine—tasting, touching, slicing, bantering—that has kept Russes and customers alike coming back for generations. But there's also the meaning of the food itself. Something Niki says people get even if they don't know exactly what they're getting.

She means appetizing: "One of my missions," she says, "is to reeducate people about that. Appetizing is a food tradition that is quintessentially New York." Take their schmaltz herring, fishy fillets that are barrel-cured and salt-brined, beloved on the Lower East Side ever since the Old World moved into the New. "You're tapping into something, a primal experience," says Niki. "You're tasting history."

And at Russ & Daughters, Anthony Bourdain would probably tell you, history always tastes pretty damn good.

PIG, SMOKE, PIT:
THIS FOOD IS SERIOUSLY SLOW

By John T. Edge

From *The New York Times*

Director of the Southern Foodways Alliance, food editor for
the *The Oxford American*, and author of the guide *Southern
Belly*, John T. Edge delights in the details that make regional
foods distinct—like this idiosyncratic barbecue set-up.

At 3:45 on a recent Saturday morning—as frogs croaked into the void and a mufflerless pickup downshifted onto Cow Head Road—Rodney Scott, 37, pitmaster here at Scott's Variety Store and Bar-B-Q, gave the order.

"Flip the pigs," he said, his voice calm and measured. "Let's go. Some char is good—too much and we lose him."

A. J. Shaw, a college student home for the summer, and Thomas Lewis, a onetime farmer, left their seats and joined Mr. Scott in the pit room, a rectangular shed dominated by two waist-high concrete banks, burnished ebony by wood smoke, ash and grease.

Ten butterflied pig carcasses—taut bellies gone slack, pink flesh gone cordovan—were in the pits when Mr. Lewis reached for the sheet of wire fencing on which one of the pigs had been roasting since 4 the previous afternoon. In lockstep, Mr. Shaw topped that same pig with a second sheet of fencing, reached his gloved fingers into the netting, and grabbed hold.

As the men struggled, the 150 pounds of dead weight torqued the makeshift wire cage. When the carcass landed, skin-side down, on the metal grid of a recently fired pit, skeins of grease trailed down the pig's flanks, and the smoldering oak and hickory coals beneath hissed and flared.

"I cooked my first one when I was 11," Mr. Scott said, as he seasoned the pig with lashings of salt, red pepper, black pepper and Accent, a flavor enhancer made with MSG.

Working a long-handled mop, he drenched the pig in a vinegar sauce of a similar peppery composition. "You've got to always be on point, when you're cooking this way," he said.

Cooking this way isn't done much any more. This place, a couple of hours northwest of Charleston, as well as the Scott family approach to slow-smoking whole hogs over hardwood coals, appears to be vestigial.

For aficionados in search of ever-elusive authenticity, Scott's offers all the rural tropes of a signal American barbecue joint. The main building is tin-roofed and time-worn. Dogs loll in the parking lot, where old shopping carts are stacked with watermelons in the summer, sweet potatoes in the fall. On church pews under the eave, locals visit with neighbors and barbecue pilgrims commune with foam clamshells stuffed with pulled pork, $8 a pound.

The cookery is simple, but the processes used by the Scott family are not.

In the manner now expected of the nation's white-tablecloth chefs, the Scotts shop local, whenever possible. They buy pigs from farms in three nearby counties. And they turn to Mel's Meat Market, in the nearby town of Aynor, for butcher work and delivery.

That commitment to local sources extends to the tools of their trade. A local welder constructs the burn barrels, where wood burns down into coals, from salvaged industrial piping and junked truck axles, the latter from a mechanic just down the road.

And then there's the issue of the wood itself. Barbecue, as it's traditionally defined in the South, requires loads of it. Some North Carolina restaurants buy surplus oak flooring from planing mills. Some Tennessee pitmasters bargain for hickory off-cuts from ax-handle manufacturers.

The Scotts take matters into their own hands. They trade labor and chainsaw expertise for oak, hickory and, occasionally, pecan.

"If you have a tree down, we oblige," Rodney Scott said that afternoon, following the all-night pit vigil. As he talked, his father, Roosevelt Scott, 67, founder of Scott's, stood on the highway, negotiating with a man who had arrived with a limb from a live oak and the promise of two to three truckloads of pit fuel.

"We keep our own wood in reserve," the younger Mr. Scott said. "We've got 100 acres. But most of it comes walking in. Everybody knows we'll bring some boys and cut your tree for you, so long as we can get to it and it's not hanging over your house or your garage."

The crowd that Saturday afternoon was typical: Half black and half white, half locals and half pilgrims.

Locals, many of whom work at the Tupperware plant, on the other end of Cow Head Road, came to pick up half-pound orders, pulled from various quadrants of the pig and tossed with sauce in the manner of a meat salad. They knew to ask Virginia Washington—Rodney Scott's cousin, the woman behind the high-top order counter—for a cook's treat of fried pig skin, still smoky from the pit, still crisp from the deep fryer.

DeeDee Gammage planned to eat her barbecue between slices of white bread, in the car, on the way home. Lou Esther Black told Mrs. Washington that she would serve her take-away atop bowls of grits on Sunday morning. "I let the grease from the meat be my sauce," Ms. Black said. "You don't need butter."

Locals knew that if they dawdled until the serving table ran low, Jackie Gordon, Rodney Scott's aunt, would break down another pig on the bone table. They knew that, with a little luck, they might score a rack of spareribs, wrenched hot from a carcass.

Pilgrims lacked the locals' foresight, but made up for it in appetite. The average out-of-town order was two pounds.

In addition to pork, day-trippers bought sauce by the gallon, hot or mild. (They were probably not aware that the sole difference is how far Mrs. Washington dips her ladle into the jug and whether she stirs, to loosen the pepper sediment.)

At the register, out-of-towners bought quart jars of locally grown and ground cane syrup from Ella Scott, the 67-year-old mother of Rodney Scott, and wondered aloud whether any of that syrup made it into the family's sauce. (When asked, all the Scotts will say is that it has "a little sugar.")

Visitors took side trips to the smoke-shrouded pit house where pigs lay splayed and sauce-puddled. They stared down into the mop sauce bucket, where sliced lemons bobbed.

They ogled the five-foot-tall burn barrels, where hunks of wood the size of footstools flame, then smolder, then break down into the coals that Mr. Scott and his colleagues shovel into the pits. They traded theories about the barrels' construction, about how the coal grates within are formed by piercing the steel barrels with a crisscross of truck axles.

"Back home they've just about gone to gas for cooking," said David Hewitt of Florence, S.C., as he waited for his order. "And they serve on buffet lines. This place is the last of a breed. If you like history, this place is full of it."

At Scott's, pilgrims like Mr. Hewitt don't often notice the bits of vernacular engineering that have become family signatures, like the two-burner hot plate, set on a milk crate, beneath the metal table where Mrs. Washington doles out barbecue orders. (Those burners keep the barbecue at a temperature preferred by regular customers—and the health department.)

Similarly, the flattened cardboard boxes scattered about the cement floors may seem to be just a part of the ambient mess. But that corrugated carpet, stretching from bone table to the serving table, soaks up the grease that trails from pigs in transport and cushions Mrs. Washington's feet.

The Scotts take pride in the traditions they uphold—and the innovations they have introduced.

"I started out working on cars in the front and pigs in the back," Roosevelt Scott said, as crowds began to dwindle after the eighth pig of the day was hauled to the bone table. "We had a pool hall and, next door, a garage." For a while, barbecue was secondary. The primary family business was what the elder Mr. Scott calls a "one door store," stocked with dry goods, and that pool hall, which opened in 1972.

"This is a business for us," he said. "We don't do it the old way. We do it the best way we know how. That means a lot of oak. That means a lean pig, which means less grease and less a chance of grease fires. No matter which way you do it, though, some folks don't want you to go nowhere."

His son echoed his feelings. "People keep talking about how old-fashioned what we do is," he said. "Old-fashioned was working the farm as a boy. I hated those long hours, that hot sun. Compared to that, this is a slow roll."

Stocking the Pantry

Avocado Heaven

By Rowan Jacobsen

From *Eating Well*

Author of *A Geography of Oysters*, *Fruitless Fall*, and the recent *American Terroir*, Jacobsen has carved out his niche covering the intersection between food and the environment. Coming from that angle, even a simple avocado can be a fascinating case study.

On a jade-tinted hillside in the lush southwestern Mexican state of Michoacán, Chef Rick Bayless held up an avocado as if it were sacred. He halved the avocado around its equator with a penknife, which is how growers check for ripeness, and discovered that this particular specimen was spot on. He could tell by the way the bright-green flesh near the skin paled to yolk-yellow near the pit. An avocado that is green to the pit will taste grassy, he told me. If it's yellow at the core, it'll be creamy as custard, rich as ricotta.

The avocado looked like a snowglobe-size model of its surroundings: green hills, yellow fields and dark-domed peaks. This fruit, here in its native land, was one with its environment. Which might have explained the look on Bayless's face. Bayless is, among other things, the chef responsible for introducing many Americans to authentic Mexican cuisine, as well as one of the strongest voices in the sustainable-food movement. As executive chef of Frontera Grill, Topolobampo and the recently opened Xoco in Chicago, some of the top Mexican restaurants in the U.S., Bayless has seen a lot of avocados in his life, which means he has seen all too many bad avocados. But he was staring at this one with something passingly close to love. And I admit, I was starting to feel it too. Because I had traveled here, with him, to find out why Hass avocados from this little corner of the world are so damn good.

The answer was all around us. Avocados in this valley are so rich because they are born to wealth. The highlands of Michoacán, 200 miles west of Mexico City, are rimmed by towering, flat-topped volcanoes—1,350 in all. Millions of years of eruptions filled the valley with sweet, productive, mineral-rich soil, and the avocado tree pumps all those nutrients into its fruit. Most fruits are primarily sugar, but an avocado is mostly fat—heart-healthy, monounsaturated fat. A fully ripened Michoacán avocado can have a fat content of 30 percent.

Such production takes tremendous quantities of water, which isn't a problem in this semitropical paradise. From May to October, the mountains are drenched in rain. What doesn't get sucked up by the trees trickles into the porous aquifer, resurfacing in the sparkling rivers that lace the region. Cisterns in the orchards catch the water to supply the trees during the dry season.

Unlike any other avocado region in the world, avocado trees in Michoacán bloom twice, and it's not unusual to see fruit and flowers on the same tree. With temperatures softly oscillating between 50° and 80°F, trees can choose their schedule; there's no killer frost hanging over the day planner. It takes an avocado about 12 months to mature, but it won't soften until picked; if left on the tree, it will continue to put on fat for an additional six months. It doesn't just stay good; it gets better. Mountainous Michoacán, whose orchards range in altitude from 3,000 to 8,000 feet, also benefits from a multitude of microclimates. Any given week of the year, some orchard here is at the peak of ripeness. This unique flexibility allows Michoacán to ship premium, fresh-picked fruit year-round.

Due to the drought, recent California avocado harvests have been barely large enough to supply the West Coast. Michoacán supplies most of the rest of the country. In fact, Michoacán supplies nearly half the world's avocados. More than 200,000 acres of verdant avocado orchards blanket every hill in the region. It's the kind of success you have when you grow a crop where it wants to grow—indeed, where it has grown for thousands of years. And it's a vital support for a state that in the past four decades has sent millions of people to the U.S. in search of work. Today 300,000 Michoacáns are directly or indirectly employed in the avocado industry. The graceful, colonial-era cities bustle with shops and shoppers, and the tables in the street markets groan under the weight of freshly harvested fruits, vegetables, herbs and fish.

After a day spent shopping those markets, Chef Bayless was inspired to make me a batch of guacamole. It's hard to improve on the Aztecs' original ahuaca-mulli, or "avocado sauce," made of mashed avocados, chiles, tomatoes and onions, but Bayless may have done it with his roasted garlic guacamole topped with tasty garnishes like crisp bacon and toasted pumpkin seeds. The avocados he used had lovely hints of pine nuts and fennel. "Avocados don't have a bold taste, but they have a complex one," he explained. "It can be really fun to play around with different ingredients and see how they bring out different aspects of that complexity."

Bayless's comment stuck with me as I watched him cook. He used avocados to thicken salsa verde and to add richness to sopa de tortilla, a staple of Mexican cuisine. Later, when he concocted a sweet and luscious avocado ice cream it struck me that the avocado is nature's emulsifier par excellence. Thousands of years before the invention of margarine or mayonnaise, the avocado tree had already figured out how to whip healthy unsaturated oil into a stable and spreadable paste. From creamy soups to decadent desserts, it has excelled in that role ever since, allowing all of us to savor the fat of the land.

Roasted Garlic Guacamole with Help-Yourself Garnishes

Rick Bayless's new book is all about how to throw a great fiesta, or party, and a key part of any great fiesta is the food. "I like to welcome guests with this guacamole bar," he says. "I start off with a basic guacamole made with roasted garlic and set out bowls of toppings so everyone can customize each bite." (Recipe from "Fiesta at Rick's" by Rick Bayless; W.W. Norton and Company, July 2010.)

4 cups guacamole, for 16 servings

Active Time: 30 minutes
Total Time: 30 minutes

Ingredients : Guacamole

6 large cloves garlic, unpeeled
6 ripe medium avocados
½ cup coarsely chopped fresh cilantro, loosely packed
2 tablespoons fresh lime juice, plus more if desired
1 teaspoon salt

Ingredients: Garnishes

¾ cup Mexican queso fresco, queso añejo, salted pressed farmer's cheese, firm goat cheese, mild feta or romano, finely crumbled or grated
¾ cup toasted pumpkin seeds (see Tip)
¾ cup sliced pickled jalapeños
½ cup crumbled crisp-fried bacon or ¾ cup coarsely crumbled chicharrón (Mexican crisp-fried pork rind)
1 16-ounce bag large, sturdy tortilla chips

Preparation

1.To prepare guacamole: Place unpeeled garlic in a small dry skillet over medium heat; cook, turning occasionally, until soft and blackened in spots, 10 to 15 minutes. Cool, then slip off the skins; finely chop. Scoop avocado flesh into a large bowl. Add the garlic, cilantro and lime juice to taste. Coarsely mash everything together. Season with salt. Transfer to a serving bowl and place plastic wrap directly on the surface of the guacamole. Refrigerate until ready to serve.

2. To set up the guacamole bar: Scoop garnishes into small serving bowls and put the chips in a large basket or bowl. Encourage guests to spoon a little guacamole on a chip and top with garnishes that appeal.

The Kimchi Fix

By Jane Black

From the *Washington Post*

Jane Black's superb food reportage for this D.C. daily paper is
a major factor in keeping food policy ranked high on the
nation's agenda. In this article, she blends international
politics, recipe deconstruction, and restaurant reviewing—
and whets our appetite.

I made my first batch of kimchi the first week of October.
Since then, there has been only a single 13-day period
when I haven't had some in the fridge. Thirteen very long days.

What started out as a neat addition to a dinner party menu—
"Let's try something from the new Momofuku cookbook"—
turned into an all-out obsession with funky, spicy Korean fermented cabbage. It was terrific with the hanger steak at dinner and
maybe better with steamed rice or poached eggs after a few more
days in the fridge. Soon, I began to crave it, the same way most
people yearn for chocolate cake. That's when I realized that kimchi
also tastes pretty darn good right out of the jar.

"It's like cabbage crack," I told my fiance as we polished off one
of our early batches for a mid-morning snack. Then we both burst
into hyena-like laughter. We were in trouble.

My kimchi habit will no doubt be a great relief to the government of South Korea, which has made spreading the word about
the country's national dish an official policy. The Korea Food Research Institute has a traditional-foods division charged with the
"scientific research of Korean fermented foods such as sauces, alcohols, and kimchi for their globalization," according to its Web site.

At first, such a policy might seem odd; Americans have a fierce love affair with hamburgers, but I'm unaware of any government program to evangelize them. We've left that job to McDonald's. But in Korea, kimchi is a national obsession. Seoul has a kimchi museum with a vast collection of cookbooks, cooking utensils and storage jars. Families around the country own special refrigerators designed to maintain the optimal temperature for the stinky vegetables' fermentation and preservation. Perhaps the most famous example of the nation's kimchi fever is that South Korean scientists spent years developing a recipe for a bacteria-free "space kimchi" to accompany their first citizen's visit to the international space station.

"This will greatly help my mission," Ko San, then a 30-year-old computer scientist, said in a statement quoted by the *New York Times* before he was to blast off in 2008. "Since I am taking kimchi with me, this will help with cultural exchanges in space."

Kimchi has been an integral part of Korean culture for thousands of years. The first record of it dates to the 7th century, according to Cecilia Hae-Jin Lee, author of "Quick and Easy Korean Cooking" (Chronicle Books, 2009), though it is believed that Koreans have eaten it for far longer. Modern versions didn't arise until the 15th century, when the first chili peppers arrived from the new world. About that time, cooks also began to add salted seafood, which gives the dish its pungent perfume.

Traditional kimchi, the kind I've been making, uses Napa cabbage. But there are seemingly infinite varieties. In Seoul, you might find baby ginseng kimchi, while north and south of the city, eggplant and pumpkin varieties are common. Historically, kimchi was made in late fall and buried in earthen jars to preserve it during the winter. Today, it is made year-round and varies with the season, incorporating Asian radishes in winter and cucumbers in summer.

Rice-based (and occupying) cultures such as Japan took a shine to kimchi long ago. The food's recent entrance into the American mainstream is driven by two larger trends. The first is a new fixation on all things fermented: pickles, dilly beans, sauerkraut and chowchow are now standard at gourmet groceries and farmers markets. Why not stinky pickled cabbage?

The second is broader awareness of, and familiarity with, Korean cuisine. Over the past 30 years, Americans have embraced sushi, pad Thai and the Vietnamese noodle soup pho. But Korean food has been a harder sell. In part, it's because the cuisine is newer to America. The largest wave of Korean immigrants arrived here in the 1970s and '80s. And it is only recently that a second, more assimilated generation has taken over.

I see the change at Korean restaurants. Eight years ago, when I worked near Koreatown in New York, I was relentlessly steered to the "safe" bibimbap despite my pleas for something else. Today, Korean chefs are willing to walk a newbie through a traditional menu (see: Honey Pig in Annandale). Hot young chefs, such as Momofuku's David Chang in New York and Kogi's Roy Choi in Los Angeles, are experimenting with using classic ingredients in new ways. "When chefs put kimchi in a quesadilla, they start to get the flavor out, and both Koreans' and Americans' impression that it's just too spicy starts to dissipate," said Debra Samuels, co-author of "The Korean Table" (Tuttle, 2008).

Once I fell for kimchi, I started to see it everywhere. This week the Source by Wolfgang Puck is launching a new Asian menu in its lounge including a dish of Korean short ribs with cabbage and radish kimchi. At the Bethesda Central Farm Market, Eric Johnson, who made his name as a chocolatier, turned up this month selling vegan kimchi: cabbage pickled with garlic, ginger and cayenne. (A strong believer in whole and raw foods, Johnson won't add fish sauce or salted shrimp unless he can make the ingredient himself.) Oh Pickles, a vendor at several Washington area markets, also plans to add kimchi to its line of pickled cucumbers and tomatoes soon.

"People really recognize it and love it," said the Source's executive chef, Scott Drewno. In summer, he said, when he serves it alongside a soft-shell crab sandwich, people always ask for an extra bowl of kimchi on the side.

These days, most Koreans buy their kimchi, says author Lee. But making it is cheap and easy—plus, you can avoid the commercial brands that add MSG.

First, salt the cabbage and let it sit overnight. That will flavor the leaves and draw out the moisture. Next, add any other vegetables:

Scallions, chopped radish and mustard greens are traditional, but I like ribbons of carrots, too. Then, mix in garlic, ginger, Korean chili pepper, salted shrimp and/or fish sauce and a touch of sugar.

The amounts of each ingredient vary. I believe Chang's recipe, which calls for 20 cloves of garlic, might be addictive. But the quantity of garlic makes it awkward to talk to anyone who hasn't also been eating it. (That's why many Korean restaurants offer you strong peppermint gum after your meal.) Lesson: Make your kimchi to taste.

Many recipes make a gallon or more of kimchi. So once it's ready, there's the question of how to use it all. A Korean proverb says: If you have kimchi and rice, you have a meal. And that's certainly true. Other traditional dishes include kimchi pancakes, very fermented kimchi mixed with ground pork, scallions, flour and egg, then sauteed; and kimchi soup, which adds a few clams and fish stock or even water to chopped kimchi.

As part of its effort to globalize kimchi, the South Korean government collaborated with the Cordon Bleu to develop more Western-friendly recipes that are available at the Food in Korea web site. Some, such as sesame kimchi twists and Camembert-and-sesame kimchi fritters, sound promising. The chocolate cake with kimchi and the napoleons filled with kimchi pastry cream? Not so much.

The best fusion idea I've heard yet is Lee's Thanksgiving kimchi stuffing. Add old, very fermented kimchi to her usual bread, celery, onions and walnuts, and use kimchi juice as the liquid to bind it all together. "We used to make a traditional stuffing and the kimchi version, and after a while we thought, why bother with the regular one?" Lee said.

Step aside, bacon. Everything is better with kimchi.

Sardines!

By Jeff Koehler

From *Tin House*

Author of *Rice Pasta Couscous* and *La Paella*,
writer/photographer Jeff Koehler discourses on food and
travel from his adopted home base of Barcelona. This
ruminative essay from the literary magazine *Tin House* traces
how he ended up there, with some fishy detours.

Few things travel as well as canned sardines. The familiar flat tins end up on shop shelves in every dusty nook and far-flung cranny across the globe, as I discovered as a young, itinerate backpacker in some of Africa's dustiest and Asia's furthest-flung spots. During this period of discovery in tastes when food made as big an impact on me as the places and people, I feasted on sardines regularly. They tended to be strong in taste, mealy in texture, and soggy with the oil, tomato sauce, mustard, or seasoned vinegar in which they had been packed. But they were new and exotic to me, cheap, and readily available.

Many of these meals—made simply of moments spent drawing the headless and tailless fish from their packed clusters—remain unforgettable: on an empty, dilapidated cargo ship, traveling up the isolate west coast of Madagascar; in Kassala, Sudan, before joining Eritrean refugees on the week-long road to Asmara to vote for the country's independence from Ethiopia; on a local bus from Phnom Penh to the Vietnam border, hurrying to reach Ho Chi Minh City in time for the Tet celebrations; in a remote northern tribal area along the Pakistan-Afghanistan border one brisk early spring.

After four years on the road, I settled into the penurious existence of a London grad student and bought my sardine supply
from a Kashmiri corner shop. I ate them for lunch in my cramped
residence-hall room with fat purple olives, salty Bulgarian feta, and
Iranian flatbread, while studying broken-spined copies of Lorca,
Gorky, and Pinter. Sure, I ate them for their low cost, but also because they carried with them the familiar light of the African and
Asian roads that, especially during those dusky winter London afternoons, I dearly missed.

But it wasn't until I impetuously followed a woman from London and settled in Barcelona that I was initiated into the glories of
fresh sardines.

Sardines have been popular since antiquity. The ancient Egyptians, Greeks, and Romans all enjoyed them, often preserved in salt.
In the King James Bible, the fish that Jesus multiplied to feed the
multitude are referred to as "little" (Matthew 15:34) and "small"
(Mark 8:7, John 6:9), almost certainly sardines. Preserving sardines
was the main industry in Mary Magdalene's village of Magdala on
the Sea of Galilee; the town's Greek name, Tarichaeae, means "the
place where fish are salted." These days Yonah brand preserves
kosher "Sea of Galilee" sardines by packing them in oval tins.

The practice of canning sardines began in Nantes, France, in
1834. By 1860, there was a lively import market for them in the
United States. When the Franco-Prussian War (1871–1872) im-
peded the trade, a savvy New York importer named Julius Wolff
went north to scout out a local source. In Eastport, Maine, on Pas-
samaquoddy Bay, he opened the country's first sardine factory, using the immature herring that swam off the state's coast. The first
American "sardines" were sealed in cans on February 2, 1876, and
in a year, sixty thousand cans had been packed and sold. The boom
spread quickly. Within five years, factories dotted the coasts of
Maine and nearby Canada, and, in 1896, the first factory opened
on the West Coast.

Monterey, 120 miles south of San Francisco, was the center of
California's industry. John Steinbeck set his novel Cannery Row
among its Depression-era sardine canneries. The beginning of the
book draws a lively portrait of the times:

In the morning when the sardine fleet has made a catch, the purse-seiners waddle heavily into the bay blowing their whistles. The deep-laden boats pull in against the coast where the canneries dip their tails into the bay. . . . Then cannery whistles scream and all over the town men and women scramble into their clothes and come running down to the Row . . . to clean and cut and pack and cook and can the fish. The whole street rumbles and groans and screams and rattles while the boats rise higher and higher in the water until they are empty. The canneries rumble and rattle and squeak until the last fish is cleaned and cut and cooked and canned and then the whistles scream again and the dripping, smelly, tired . . . men and women straggle out and droop their ways up the hill into the town and Cannery Row becomes itself again—quiet and magical.

Monterey's production peaked with 234,000 tons of processed sardines in 1944, the same year that Steinbeck wrote his novel. But, whether through over-fishing and exploitation or consecutive years of failed spawning, the industry collapsed as quickly as it rose, and the last Monterey cannery shuttered its doors in 1973. Today, sardines are fished in American waters almost exclusively for fish-meal, cat food, and bait for Japanese tuna or Maine lobster fisheries.

It's no surprise, then, that while imported canned sardines are easy to buy in the United States, it's almost impossible to find fresh ones. During a visit this summer, I found tips sprinkled throughout online chatrooms and heard rumors about one place in New Jersey, which imports them once a week from Portugal, another in Rhode Island, and a Korean place in the San Fernando Valley that sometimes carries them.

Such deep searching isn't necessary around the Mediterranean. These slender, dense packets of nutrients, rich in calcium, protein, and omega-3 fatty acids, and—thanks to being far down on the food chain—low in mercury, are eaten with great gusto not just for their healthfulness but their sublime flavor. Under international trade laws, "sardine" covers almost two dozen species of fish (for U.S. products it exclusively means young herring), though the true sardine, from Portugal, Spain, France, Morocco, and Algeria, refers to the young pilchard (*Sardina pilchardus*) caught in Mediterranean or Atlantic waters. They have green backs, yellowish sides, silver bellies, and ruddy-brown meat. (Atlantic sardines tend to be larger, with smaller heads and bulkier bodies.) Though commercially fished all year round, they are most abundant in markets from July to November.

I spent much of the past two years traveling around the Mediterranean, researching a new cookbook, and feasted on sardines nearly everywhere: grilled sardine sandwiches heaped with raw onion, tomato, and chopped parsley in Istanbul; liberally dusted with cumin and fried in Cairo; char-grilled and dashed with lemon and salt in Morocco. In Sicily I sampled the island's famous pasta con le sarde—bucatini with sardines, wild fennel, raisins, and pine nuts—at least half a dozen times, though I preferred sarde imbottite—sardines butterflied, stuffed with breadcrumbs and pine nuts, and baked. Sardines are equally beloved in Algeria. One cookbook I bought in Algiers this winter includes nine different ways of preparing them, from simply baked with bay leaves to prepared in a vinegar and oil marinade called escabeche.

Recipes for escabeche appear in two medieval Catalan cookbooks—the anonymous 1324 Libre de Sent Sovi and Ruperto de Nola's 1477 Libre de Coch. Introduced into Spain during the Moorish rule of the region that began in the eighth century, escabeche has long been a popular preparation of everything from small birds to eggplant. De Nola, rightly, indicates that the marinade is best for fish. While any type of fish can be preserved escabechado, sardines—for their size, firm meat, and bold flavor—are the traditional choice. Quickly pan-fried, the sardines are layered into a rectangular clay cazuela and covered with a hot marinade of olive oil, wine vinegar, unpeeled cloves of garlic, sprigs of thyme, pimentón (smoky, sweet paprika), bay leaves, and peppercorns. It takes a day for the fish to sing with the infused flavors, and it can be kept and enjoyed for weeks.

This was one of the first dishes I tried to work out in my kitchen by repetitiously imitating versions I had eaten in smoke-stained, tile-walled bars. Reveling in having my own kitchen again, I tried to recreate certain tastes using skills that were more logical than sophisticated. I hadn't yet developed a vocabulary to name the flavors I was trying to achieve, nor the spices I needed in order to do so. I was, I can see now, a dozen years later, teaching myself to cook by taste—by working backwards from taste—just as others learn the piano by ear. Some of these dishes were good (and they tended to get repeated), others passable. But it didn't matter. I was cooking only for myself and the Catalan woman I had followed (and then married). I had time; there would be plenty of meals.

Sardinas en escabeche became part of my repertoire, and I still enjoy it in autumn when the hues and scents of the dish feel right for the cool, clear days. Eventually, I learned to prepare sardines in many different ways. At home we like them pan-grilled and eaten with plump grapes. Or grilled and crowning a slice of toasted country bread piled with strips of roasted red peppers, eggplant, and onions. Or batter-dipped and fried with slices of acidic apple. These days, my two girls love it when I bury a mess of sardines whole under a mound of coarse sea salt, and then bake the lot in a hot oven for 15 minutes. They enthusiastically take turns breaking open the salt crust with a wooden mallet while my wife and I scramble to dig out the succulent fish—moist and completely cooked in their own juices—before the girls crush them.

But, without a doubt, the most pleasurable way to eat fresh sardines is a la brasa, grilled outside in the open air over hot embers. The flavors are at their robust finest, the flesh sparkling and briny, shaded with smoky oils. Inside, that distinct smell of searing sardines is overpowering, even pungent (and immediately alerts every neighbor as to what's on the stove), but outside, among green leaves and dusty loam, or on a sandy beach with sea breezes, it's evocatively, stirringly aromatic.

Food in Catalonia is frequently celebrated simply for itself and a sardinada is a celebration of sardines. Abundant and inexpensive, sardines make a perfect centerpiece for large gatherings of friends, extended families, even village feasts. The peak of the sardinada season is de Virgen a Virgen ("from Virgin to Virgin"), between the feast days of Carmen—July 16th, when maritime parades and watery blessings of the seaman's protectress marks summer's start—and of the Assumption of the Virgin Mary into Heaven—August

15th. This is the hottest period of the year, when meals are served especially late and preferably out-of-doors, and, more importantly, when sardines gorge themselves on the warm sea's abundant plankton and fatten to their most flavorful.

My first summer in Barcelona, I joined a group for a sardinada along the coast south of the city. As cuttings of orange trees burned down to embers, the group assembled, bearing aperitivos, bottles of wine, desserts. Freshly caught sardines were brought out, kilos of them, at a calculation of eight or so per person (though some of our friends have been known to put away two or three times that many). When the embers were ready, the sardines were laid whole—neither head nor tail trimmed, nor innards removed—in a double-handled grill rack. Set just a few inches above the embers, the fish cooked for a couple of minutes on each side until the skin turned crispy gold and the eyes went white. We sprinkled the fish with a pinch of coarse sea salt and a drizzle of olive oil, then devoured them, picking them up with our fingers as fast as they were cool enough to handle. Sublime.

I've eaten plenty of grilled sardines since, and the distinctive, rustic flavor always brings me back to that first summer—plucking sardines from a hot grill, fingers blackened and greasy, surrounded by a growing pile of sucked-clean spines (and empty wine bottles). I may not have yet been able to understand much of the conversations swirling around me, but I already knew that I had arrived in the place where I would settle.

And if I want to take myself back further, back to my cramped room in London as an impressionable student, or, more potently, to some distant and dusty place as an eager, unsure wanderer, all I need to do is peel back the lid of a sardine tin and extract a single silvery fish from the packed cluster.

Sardines in Escabeche

Serves 4

1 pound fresh, whole medium sardines (about 16)
1½ cups virgin olive oil
Salt

Flour for dusting

½ cup white wine vinegar

6 garlic cloves, unpeeled with loose outer white paper re-
    moved

3 sprigs thyme

1 teaspoon Spanish *pimentón dulce* (sweet paprika)

3 bay leaves

12 whole peppercorns

Gently scale the sardines with a knife. Remove the head
and guts in the following manner: hold the sardine with one
hand and with the other rock the head first upwards, breaking the neck, then downwards, and finally firmly pulling it
toward you, drawing out the guts. Run a finger through the
cavity to make sure it is clean. Rinse well with cool, running
water and pat dry.

In a large skillet, heat 3 tablespoons of the oil over
medium heat. Salt and dust the sardines with flour and fry
until the skin is golden brown, 2 to 3 minutes. Turn gently to
avoid breaking the skin, and fry the other side until golden,
about 2 minutes. Transfer to a rectangular earthenware, ceramic, or glass dish. Lay in the sardines side by side, alternating head-tail directions so that they fit snugly together.

In a non-reactive saucepan, bring the rest of the oil, the
vinegar, garlic, thyme, paprika, bay leaves, and peppercorns to
a boil. Remove from the heat and let cool slightly.

Gently pour the marinade (including the herbs) over the
fish. The fish should be mostly covered.

Let cool. Cover with plastic wrap and refrigerate for at
least 1 day and as many as 10.

Remove 1 hour before serving and serve at room
temperature.

Rare Breed

By Molly O'Neill

From *Saveur*

Cookbook author, memoirist, and former *New York Times* food columnist Molly O'Neill has lately made a deep excursion into American food history, researching her new book *One Big Table*. Who better to hang out with a heritage poultry breeder?

Beyond the town of Lindsborg, with its church steeples and 2,000 or so houses, the Kansas prairie is a flat forever. There's nothing to absorb wind or sound. The whinny of gears in a pickup; the bullish snort of a combine harvester turning frosty dirt—the noises of a winter afternoon seemed bigger than anything mortal. Standing in a field on Frank Reese Jr.'s farm outside town as the shadows grew longer, I felt truly alone.

I pictured Reese, a poultry breeder who was born near here, shepherding his turkeys across this same, endless horizon as a boy and wondered whether he too had felt alone. From an early age, he had the job of ushering birds on his family's farm from the barn to the open range so that they could peck for insects. He took to the role, and to the birds. When the other children in his first-grade class wrote adoring sonnets to their cats and dogs, Reese crafted a personal essay titled "Me and My Turkeys."

He was surprised by the looks he got. In his young mind, love was love, and he has no memory of ever not loving turkeys. That is the only way he can explain having devoted his life to preserving the traditional American breeds that were once common on dinner tables across the country. After all, though Reese is a perfectly good cook, he's not the sort of fanatic who'd spend decades chasing the Platonic ideal of an ingredient. He also doesn't seem like the type of person who'd take up the banner against industrial farming.

In fact, Reese, who is 61 years old, would prefer to spend his evenings reading antique poultry magazines or the spiritual writings of Saint Augustine and Saint Teresa. He is solidly built and speaks in measured tones. In his well-pressed flannel shirt, he looks as if he might have stepped off a page of the 1954 Sears, Roebuck catalogue.

And yet, to food lovers, animal lovers, and many family farmers, this fourth-generation farmer from Kansas is more than just a turkey breeder with old-fashioned ways. He is a saint. Reese is the man who saved American poultry.

From the outside, the farmhouse at the Good Shepherd Turkey Ranch, which is what Reese calls his farm, looks like a monument to a vanished way of life. Set on a corner of the 160-acre spread, the three-story home has Victorian trim and a fresh coat of white paint. It is framed by two red barns and a venerable elm tree, the kind you'd expect to see a swing hanging from. A pie should be cooling on the sill of the kitchen window. Kids should be chasing around the yard.

But Reese is a bachelor. Instead of family portraits and Norman Rockwell prints, turkey-related art hangs on the walls alongside his collection of religious art and blue ribbons from poultry shows. The house is well tended—Reese restored the white pine woodwork and ordered burgundy-colored Victorian-style wallpaper from the designer wallpaper company Bradbury & Bradbury for the dining room and sitting room—but the scent of diesel fuel and turkey coop from Reese's work clothes laces the air. Feed catalogues, fan letters, tax forms, utility bills, and photographs of turkeys are arranged in neat piles on the dining-room table. I'd spent the day visiting the farm with Reese, and he'd invited me in from the cold. The house was utterly quiet but for the sound of the farmer riffling through the papers on the table. Finally, finding what he was after, he waved a black-and-white portrait of a handsome Bronze turkey. "Charlie!" he exclaimed.

"Out of a thousand turkeys," Reese said, "there is always one who wants to be with you all the time. Charlie was my first. When

I was a kid, the neighbor's dog got his tail. The vet took one look and said, 'You better just butcher him.' I went nuts and said, 'You *fix* him!' So he sewed his tail back on, and Charlie and I hung out for the next ten years."

For decades, Reese assumed that he'd gotten so friendly with turkeys when he was a kid merely to make the best of a frustrating situation. "I was the youngest and too little to drive the tractor or handle the cattle or pigs," he said, "so I got sent to the poultry house." Eventually, though, he came to the awareness that there had to be more to it than that. "My father once said that he took me to the state fair when I was three and that all I wanted to do was drag him through the turkey exhibits," Reese told me. "So maybe I was just born this way."

Until he'd grown enough to manage turkeys on his own, Reese showed chickens. He took his first blue ribbon at the Saline County Fair when he was eight years old and won every year for the next decade. Starting at the age of ten, he showed turkeys too.

"I got beat a lot," he said. "Back then, there was no kids' division, and I was up there showing with all the old, legendary turkey breeders: Norman Kardosh and his Narragansetts, Sadie Lloyd and her Bourbon Reds, Cecil Moore and his Bronzes." The older turkey breeders may have taken home the blue ribbons, but they also took note of Reese's talent. These farmers and enthusiasts had spent lifetimes preserving American barnyard breeds, some of whose bloodlines could be traced to the 1890s. Until Frank Reese appeared, none of those breeders had anointed an heir to continue their legacy. Each knew the clock was ticking.

Growing up, Reese was never more in his element than he was at poultry shows. These bustling events, which took place across rural America throughout the 20th century (and still do, in some areas), culminated in big annual national competitions, where farmers and hobbyists displayed prized birds that they'd bred for hardiness, meat quality, reproductive prowess, and physical beauty. Held in vast exhibition halls, the juried contests were similar to dog shows, a *Best in Show* milieu in which hair dryers were aimed at feathers rather than fur. "If you won the national show, you were set because everybody wanted to buy your birds," said Reese.

The shows were also where older breeders mentored potential successors. "They taught me the breed history," Reese remembered. "They had me sitting on the ground with my standards book, studying each bird." Reese was talking about *Standard of Perfection*, a guide published by the American Poultry Association that recognizes eight distinct varieties of turkey that are considered to be the purest farm breeds and describes the ideal physical characteristics of each one. The book, first published in 1874, harks back to an era when the differences between common breeds of chickens and turkeys were as dramatic as the differences between, say, a Great Dane and a Dachshund. These varieties were raised for different uses: big roasters for Sunday dinners, tough and flavorful stewers for soup, plump-legged fryers, and so on.

Norman Kardosh, a breeder from Alton, Kansas, was Reese's most influential teacher. "Norman taught me about the importance of fine breeding, how it ensures the survival of the best bloodlines and how that, in turn, ensures biodiversity among the species. Without those two things, any creature is doomed to extinction."

At some point in the late 1970s, after earning a nursing degree and finishing a stint in the army in Texas, Reese realized that standard bred birds—as the types of poultry recognized in *Standard of Perfection* are called—were in trouble. He was raising turkeys at his home south of San Antonio and competing on the side. "I'd always competed against 50 to 100 birds at every show. Suddenly it was just me," he recalled.

American farmers just weren't raising standard bred birds anymore, at least not in significant numbers. "The commercial industry had developed a couple varieties that cost less to feed, fattened up faster, and sold well, and farmers raised these to the exclusion of all others," Reese explained to me. "This means that one flu could wipe out every bird in this country." To make matters worse, he said, commercial birds—a broad-breasted white variety developed in the 1950s—all tend to taste the same. "They have no flavor! No individuality!" he lamented.

Reese began expanding his flock. Meanwhile, he worked as a nurse at a hospital in San Antonio and eked out additional money by taking odd jobs and even modeling. In his early 30s, Reese looked every inch the Marlboro Man, whom he once portrayed in an advertising campaign.

Texas was fun, said Reese, "but it was no place to raise a turkey." So, in 1989, he moved back to Kansas, bought a farm outside Lindsborg that he called Good Shepherd Turkey Ranch, and ramped up his breeding program. He was more worried than ever about American poultry. "The bloodlines were dying out. Norman didn't want to believe me," Reese recalled. "He was in his late 70s, but he got in his truck and went looking for his birds. He went to every farm he'd sold to, and he didn't find one Norman Kardosh Narragansett." Reese's other mentors were beginning to pass away. "Norman was the last to go," Reese said. "I promised him that I would not let these birds die off the face of the Earth."

By 2002, Reese had increased the national population of standard bred turkeys to such an extent that he was able to sell to some restaurants and individuals. "The only way to save these birds is to get people to eat them," he said. Reese created a cooperative of several farmers in Kansas and sold 800 heritage turkeys—as the farmers branded their standard bred birds—that first year. Two years later, Reese took on a business partner, a young poultry farmer named Brian Anselmo, whom Reese considered to be the next heir to the old-breed poultry legacy. In 2007, the number of farmers in the Good Shepherd co-op grew to a dozen; they sold 10,000 old-breed turkeys that Thanksgiving. It wasn't much compared with the 46 million industrially raised turkeys sold during that holiday each year, but it was a milestone nonetheless.

In 2008, Anselmo died suddenly of complications of asthma at the age of 28. Reese, recognized by then as the premier source of old-breed birds in the nation, became even more focused on selling his breeding stock. "I'm all these birds have now," Reese said. Nowadays, he's pouring his energy into plans for the Standard Bred Poultry Institute, a place where farmers will learn how to breed, raise, preserve, and cook these birds. He is building the facility, using his own savings and, he hopes, donor money, on the ridge just beyond his barns. "I'm leaving it all to them," Reese said.

We'd been sitting in his dining room for a long while. Outside, the wind was keening around the house. Reese pushed back from the table, and I followed him as he walked to the kitchen, zipped a barn jacket over his flannel shirt, pulled on a stocking cap, and walked out his back door.

We headed toward the pasture next to the larger of the two red barns. There, under a darkening sky, hundreds of turkeys were already crowding at the fence, strutting excitedly, puffing their feathers, and craning their wobbly-skinned necks. The birds mobbed Reese as he pushed through the gate. At the center of this shiny, feathery universe, Reese chattered and scolded. Bending down, he scooped up a huge Bronze and cradled it in the crook of his arm.

"This is Norman," he said, beaming. The bird had bright eyes and copper-colored feathers with black edges. He put Norman down, and the animal spread its lush tail feathers in an impressive rainbow. "Isn't he something?" said Reese. "We've been hanging out for a few years. Norman isn't going anywhere. Norman's staying right here."

The Charcuterie Underground

By Mike Sula

From *Chicago Reader*

Reporting and blogging about the Chicago food scene, Mike
Sula immerses himself in the Windy City—its restaurants,
food carts, markets, bars, local color, and politics. The best
way to change intrusive meat-curing regulations? Sula goes
undercover with a sympathetic gang of illicit sausage makers.

Every Tuesday morning a refrigerated white truck with
an anthropomorphic pig painted on its side pulls up in
front of a house on a tree-lined street in a North Shore suburb. A
Wisconsin farmer emerges and unloads three to four boxes filled
with pork shoulders and bellies butchered from naturally raised
pigs. He walks across the lawn and hands them off through the
front door before driving on to the city to make his regular deliveries at the likes of North Pond and Frontera Grill.

Inside, a 37-year-old apron-clad stay-at-home dad and furniture
maker named Erik prepares his preschool daughter's lunch box in
the kitchen. Then he joins his business partner, Ehran, in prepping
for the day's bacon curing and sausage stuffing.

Erik and Ehran, also a stay-at-home dad, are the principals of
E & P Meats, a budding underground charcuterie business with an
e-mail list of more than 200 customers. Once a month they drive
into the city and surrounding suburbs to drop off vacuum-sealed
packages ordered from a rotating menu of about 15 meats they've
stuffed, cured, and smoked entirely on the premises of Erik's handsome home. The deliveries are about half of the 40–60 orders they

fill—the other half are collected by customers who show up at the door.

When I visited last month they were rubbing down a few pork bellies with rosemary sprigs and a salt cure and experimenting with a new Italian sausage recipe. On the back porch, alongside the potted rosemary, three smokers issued thin white plumes that filled the neighborhood with a sweet, meaty perfume. Two contained slabs of bacon and the third—a ceramic tile Big Green Egg—held half a dozen of the paprika-and-mustard-rubbed chickens that Erik periodically smokes for favored mothers of his daughter's classmates.

"We end up giving away probably, I don't know, 60 pounds of meat a month or more," says Erik. "Keeps all the neighbors happy if they don't like the smoke smell." They haven't made a profit yet.

Because they sell meats that aren't prepared in a licensed commercial facility, Erik and Ehran are operating outside the law. But some laws, they fervently believe, were made to be broken. "It's one of those things that's kind of overregulated," says Erik. "People have been canning and curing forever. It was invented to preserve food and keep things healthy."

The charcuterie resistance is growing. Professional restaurant chefs without legal licensing or dedicated facilities cure their own meats out of view of the health inspectors all the time. And Erik and Ehran aren't the only ones making and selling outside of those professional kitchens: A former restaurant chef is currently curing two dozen duck breasts in a south-side warehouse; they'll end up on restaurant menus sometime around the holidays. Personal chef Helge Pedersen cures and ages lamb legs for the Norwegian salted meat fennelar, along with guanciale, soppressata, and pancetta, in a dedicated refrigerator in his Humboldt Park apartment and another in a garage space on Western Avenue. He sells them to friends as he hones his craft in anticipation of the day he opens his own retail space.

Laurence Mate is an amateur charcuterie maker downstate who documents his projects on the blog This Little Piggy. To make an end run around the government regulations governing the production and sale of charcuterie, Mate—another furniture maker—had a law student help him figure out how to set up a private club for members, who must register on his Web site in order to make "donations" by the pound for his terrines, sausage, pulled pork, and the spicy Calabrian salami paté nduja. He hasn't been challenged so far. Like Erik and Ehran, he makes no money and does it for the love of the craft. But if he had to cut through all the red tape required to produce and sell his products like a retailer, he says, it wouldn't be worth the effort.

"The regulations are written for industrial food operations," says Mate. "And if you apply them to small-scale local producers, no one's gonna do it. It's legislating local food out of the market. Unfortunately, the health departments don't appreciate that. But that food is actually safer. It's easier for someone on that small scale to move things more quickly and be more careful. Local markets are self-regulating. If there's anything wrong with your products and someone gets sick from it, then you're out of business."

Not surprisingly, the Chicago Department of Public Health disagrees. "That person's comment reminds me of the criticisms leveled at Upton Sinclair and others a century ago who advocated for a safer food supply," e-mailed spokesman Tim Hadac. "True, the local market 'self-regulates'—but it does so sometimes at the expense of consumers' health and even lives. Every year in the U.S. foodborne illness causes an estimated 300,000 hospitalizations and 5,000 deaths. We in public health prefer commonsense, science-based regulation that focuses on prevention of food-borne illness before it occurs."

Of course plenty of those illnesses were borne by regulated food. "The revival of local food economies is being hobbled by a tangle of regulations originally designed to check abuses by the very largest food producers," wrote locavore-in-chief Michael Pollan in his open letter to whoever would be president in the *New York Times* last fall. "Farmers should be able to smoke a ham and sell it to their neighbors without making a huge investment in federally approved facilities. Food-safety regulations must be made sensitive to scale and marketplace, so that a small producer selling direct off the farm or at a farmers' market is not regulated as onerously as a multinational food manufacturer. This is not because local food won't ever have food-safety problems—it will—only that its problems will be less catastrophic and easier to manage because local food is inherently more traceable and accountable."

When you know who made your food, Erik and Ehran add, you know what you're eating. "A friend came to me and said 'I love your sausages—don't tell me what you put in there,'" recalls Ehran. "I said, 'No, I will tell you. Ask me, and I will tell you, because it's not leftover scraps.'"

"It's no longer scary to know what's in your sausage," says Erik. "It's just pork shoulder and about five spices."

E & P Meats was born a little over two years ago after a wine-fueled soul-searching conversation between Erik and his wife, who produces TV commercials. "We were getting kind of drunk and talking about what we could do so she could quit her job," he says. "And I said, 'Oh, maybe we can make sausage.' So I went the next day and bought the best grinder I could find at the kitchen store."

Guided by Susan Mahnke Peery and Charles G. Reavis's Home Sausage Making, Erik and a friend, Phillip (the p in E & P), began grinding out bangers, brats, and Italian sausages. They hosted parties in Erik's backyard, catered an outside event, and even made a few sales before Phillip's wife was transferred to Michigan, taking him out of the picture.

Enter Ehran, an Israeli-born ex-cinematographer and frequent guest at Erik and Phillip's sausage parties. "I've been cooking all my life," he says. "I think part of me getting to cooking was coming here and not having food as I'm used to—food that is made more at home, by hand."

The pair began studying recipes from a number of published sources along with developing their own—particularly for bacon. Ehran assisted with an informal sausage-making workshop given by a friend who teaches at Kendall College. "All the Jewish people here say, 'Oh, what is an Israeli boy doing making bacon?' says Ehran. "I grew up eating pork."

"It took us like six months to get our formulas right," Erik says. Willing guinea pigs tested varieties such as maple and applewood smoked, an unsmoked Irish bacon, and more obscure recipes like a hammy French salt pork commonly used in the lentil dish petit sale. Free samples of paprika-rubbed turkey breast, pistachio-truffle sausage, and sage breakfast links were doled out to friends, neighbors, teachers, and their children's schoolmates. Ehran even flipped a vegetarian acquaintance with their pastrami.

"Having to pay for them was just a natural transition," says Ehran. "They didn't complain."

In May they each took a 15-hour course from their local health department and subsequently received state licensing for food service sanitation—the first step in going legit. That same month they released their first menu, consisting of four bacons, and thus began what has since become known as the monthly ritual of Meat Week.

Near the beginning of each month they release a menu—now usually several bacons, a sausage, and maybe a deli meat—and orders begin popping up in their in-box. Then they spend a frenzied few days putting up the bacon and grinding and stuffing the sausage. "We work like crazy," says Ehran. "Usually we'll go four nights past midnight. The kids are asleep."

As word spread and they began taking on customers outside their immediate circle of friends, the demand began to take a toll on the equipment. A few months ago Erik's Waring sausage grinder, bought at Sur la Table, caught on fire in the midst of processing 40 pounds of meat.

E & P may not yet be profitable, but they do make enough money to afford some professional equipment upgrades they find on Craigslist, "usually from some giant guy with a beard," says Erik. "And they're always disgruntled. The guy we bought the refrigerator from—I told him what I was doing and he's like, 'Stay small.'"

"I think that once we got the slicer there was no way back," says Ehran. "I also realized that I don't know how I lived without one all my life."

Their recently released holiday menu offers pistachio bacon brittle, cold-smoked Scottish salmon, and a membership in a six-month-long bacon-of-the-month club for $50. But they have yet to delve into the more complicated production of aged hams and long-cured and fermented meats like salamis. They'll need to jump over many more regulatory hurdles to get legal for that, but they're getting ready to start practicing, converting a storage room in Erik's basement into a cedar-lined temperature-and-humidity-controlled curing room.

And they're not planning on being outlaws forever. Early next year Erik will be taking a course on the FDA's food safety management system, the Hazard Analysis and Critical Control Points. He'll need to do that as well as submit a plan for approval to inspectors from his city's health department before E & P can open its own dedicated and fully licensed production and retail space. It's a notoriously difficult and expensive process, but something has to be done soon. Their wives are losing patience with the chaos of Meat Week, which keeps getting longer and longer.

"We're definitely looking to move into a place where we can have Meat Week every week," says Ehran.

Wines for Drinking, Not Overthinking

By Salma Abdelnour

From *Food & Wine*

Author of the upcoming *Jasmine and Fire*, a culinary memoir
about Lebanon, freelance food/travel writer Salma Abdelnour
has a knack for capturing the essence of a destination through
its food. Here, she matches the spirit of certain comfort foods
with the right wine.

Ever since I was too short to reach the checkout counter
at the supermarket, I've had an insatiable curiosity about
food. The less I know about a certain ingredient, the more I want
to taste it and talk about it—whether it's Galician *berberechos* clams
or white-boar soppressata. But when it comes to wine, I tend to
keep my mouth shut. I drink wine nearly every day, and I enjoy
learning about varietals and regions and producers. But wine lingo
and wine trends intimidate me, and I second-guess my tastes and
instincts. I'd be mortified to be overheard gushing about something totally passé, like White Zinfandel. Let's be clear here: I hate
White Zinfandel. (I'm supposed to hate it, right? Or is it coming
back in style?)

To get over my wine anxiety, I decided to conduct an experiment: What if I took wine off its pedestal and treated it the same
way I treat everything else I eat and drink? I would talk to some of
the world's most respected experts and compare wine to foods and
beverages I'm comfortable with—namely, burgers, bacon and coffee. Maybe then I could finally overcome my insecurities.

The White Castle Burger of Wine

My first question to the experts: What's the White Castle burger of wine? Just as chefs like to boost their street cred by admitting to certain lowbrow tastes—from fast-food fries to RC Cola—I wondered if sommeliers had guilty pleasures, too. I had two goals: One, to make them fess up some embarrassing secrets. And two, to feel less mortified if I happen to enjoy a wine that's unfashionable, even trashy—because if professionals privately drink déclassé wines, then the world is safer for the rest of us.

Some experts, like David Lynch, the wine director at San Francisco's Quince, told me that wine geeks who are slumming it will drink beer or certain "disgusting" cult spirits, like *amaro*. Others, like Berkeley–based wine importer Kermit Lynch (no relation), begged off the question. One famous expert I spoke to sniffed, "A lot of wine professionals would admit, privately, that they like Silver Oak. But please, that's off the record." (Silver Oak is a popular California Cabernet that's considered outmoded by snobs.)

The most convincing answer came from Laura Maniec, the wine director for B.R. Guest Restaurants (which includes Las Vegas's Fiamma Trattoria and Manhattan's Blue Fin). "Ask most sommeliers, 'Do you drink Pinot Grigio?' and no one says yes," Maniec told me. "But if you blind-taste them, you'd be surprised how many guess it's a very young Grüner Veltliner Federspiel, Chablis or Albariño. They don't admit that they like Pinot Grigio, but they do like it in blind tastings."

I asked her to point me toward a really good Pinot Grigio, and for fun, we agreed to meet at a White Castle to conduct a tasting. I think we both just wanted to eat some sliders. So as not to get arrested, we brown-bagged the bottle, a 2006 Schiopetto Pinot Grigio from the Italian region of Friuli ($30), and poured it into Riedel glasses masked by Styrofoam cups.

The wine was, indeed, refreshing. "I like the ripe honeydew, apple, tangerine and Meyer lemon flavors in here," Maniec said. "It has a rocky minerality and a long finish. How can anyone say they don't like this?" We were pleased with how well the wine complemented the french fries, too. "Usually fries are best with Champagne," Maniec said. "But the saltiness works well with any acidic wine." For my future french-fry cravings, Maniec recommended another, less expensive Pinot Grigio that she's a fan of, the 2008 Tiefenbrunner delle Venezie from northeastern Italy ($15).

She then brought out a surprise bottle: Zinfandel. Many wine pros don't admit to drinking New World wines like Zinfandel, Maniec explained. "We tend to drink high-acid, earthy wines that take us to the place they're from. New World wines don't tend to have as much terroir. But Zinfandel is always true to its colors. It tastes like ripe, cooked fruit." We tasted one of her favorite Zinfandels, a 2007 Kunin from California's Paso Robles region ($24), and it was, quite frankly, sublime with the White Castle burgers. "Saying you don't like this," Maniec said, "is like saying you don't like chocolate."

The Bacon of Wine

My next challenge: to discover the bacon of wine. Whether I'm tasting fried Jimmy Dean at a diner or slow-braised Berkshire pork belly at the swankiest restaurant in town, I'm eating bacon—and I'm probably pretty happy about it. There had to be a wine equivalent, a varietal so fundamentally delicious that I'd love it without having to think too hard about it, whether the bottle cost $10 or $400.

A few experts I talked to chose Pinot Noir. "The acid is soft, the tannins aren't aggressive; it's drinkable juice," said Paul Grieco, the wine director and a partner at Manhattan's Terroir, Hearth and Insieme. Kermit Lynch gave a very specific suggestion: "White Burgundy from a sunny year, from a good winemaker. It will please those who are into terroir and those who just like the taste of Chardonnay."

But, unexpectedly, the most popular pick was Merlot. "It's an easy wine to drink, for the most part. And some of the world's best wines, like Bordeaux's Château Pétrus, are made with Merlot," said Eduard Seitan, the wine director and a partner at Chicago's Blackbird, Avec and the Publican. Matt Skinner, the Australian sommelier who works with London-based chef Jamie Oliver, also chose Merlot: "When I started learning about wine, I read a description of Merlot as plush, round, inky, sweet, full. I thought, I want to drink that. It's like a bear hug from your grandma. It's safe and warm. It puts its arms around you and says, 'It's OK. I'm not here to challenge you, I'm just here for you to enjoy.'"

A wine that's pure, uncomplicated joy: That's what I was look-ing for. I asked Skinner to recommend two bottles, one under $15, the other over $30. Then I enlisted F&W wine editor Ray Isle to try them with me at my Manhattan apartment. "Merlot is one of the great grapes of the world," Ray explained as we opened Skin-ner's first recommendation, a 2007 Errazuriz Merlot Estate from Chile that sells for $13. "It's more plush and forgiving than Caber-net Sauvignon, although that can be both a virtue and a drawback. But when it got so popular in the 1990s, farmers started overpro-ducing it and the wine quality fell. Merlot itself is not the problem; the problem is what people did with it."

We poured two glasses of the Errazuriz, and I took a sip. The wine had loads of dark fruit, a lush and velvety feel, and then still more fruit. "This wine hits one note—but it's a nice note," Ray said. I didn't have to pay close attention to catch the nuances; there weren't many. Then again, when I'm eating a BLT, I'm not exactly focused on the nuances of the bacon in the sandwich, either.

Next we opened Skinner's second recommendation, a 2005 Chateau d'Aiguilhe Côtes de Castillon from Bordeaux, which is mostly Merlot blended with some Cabernet Franc. "For $35, that's a really pretty wine," Ray observed. "It has what Merlot wants to have, that deep, dark fruit. The Chilean bottle was more one-note, but this Bordeaux is more like a chord."

Half an hour later, after the Errazuriz had opened up a bit more, it became more subtle and beguiling. Now it was inching closer to pork belly instead of a diner BLT—not that I was quibbling either way.

The Coffee of Wine

For my last experiment, I wanted to find a wine that was as versa-tile as it was reliable—a wine that I could happily drink every day. I was looking for the coffee of wine.

Again, I got a range of answers from the experts I queried, from Riesling to Champagne to Syrah. But the response that seemed to really nail it came from Alpana Singh, wine director at Lettuce En-tertain You Restaurants, which includes Everest and L20 in Chicago: "For me, Sauvignon Blanc fits that bill. For the most part it's reliable, zippy, goes with a wide variety of foods—spicy dishes, sushi, lots of things. The acidity perks up your palate."

It's also her fallback pick at restaurants, Singh says. "If I don't know how the wine has been stored, I'll order Sauvignon Blanc. At least it has been refrigerated and will have some acidity to preserve it. There's a big difference between good and bad coffee, but if you really need caffeine, you'll drink bad coffee. It's the same with Sauvignon Blanc."

I decided to test her theory by drinking Sauvignon Blanc every day for a week. On the first night, I had just returned from a week of joyful overeating in New Orleans when I was invited to dinner with friends. They served a 2005 Sincerity from Chile, and the acidity made me salivate in a way I didn't think I could muster post-Louisiana-gluttony. It wasn't the best Sauvignon Blanc I'd ever had, but it worked well with the braised artichokes, roasted asparagus and buttery, pine-nut-studded rice—even though artichokes and asparagus are notoriously tough to pair with wine. Score one for Sauvignon Blanc. Night two: I met a friend at a terrific Bosnian hole-in-the-wall in Queens, and afterward, I brought home a sugar-syrup-drenched spongy cookie called hurmasice. I ate it with a glass of 2008 Te Muna Road Sauvignon Blanc from New Zealand's Craggy Range ($20), one of the wines Singh recommended, and together they made a splendid nightcap.

On subsequent days, Sauvignon Blanc was a fantastic utility player, pairing well with everything from a Bibb lettuce salad with olive-oil-packed tuna to spicy pulled-pork tacos and grilled-eel sushi. I alternated between the Craggy Range and another wine Singh likes, the 2007 Westerly Vineyards from California's Santa Ynez Valley ($20).

The only time Sauvignon Blanc failed me: One night, after talking a friend through a bad breakup, I went home and poured a glass of the Craggy Range. But the acidity wasn't quite the soothing sensation I was looking for just then. I needed something a little rounder, warmer and more instantly uplifting. An espresso, perhaps, or a glass of Merlot. Or maybe what I really needed was one of my favorite new guilty pleasures: a White Castle burger, paired with a big fat Zin. But this time, hold the guilt.

Moxie: A Flavor for the Few

By Robert Dickinson

From *Gastronomica*

The quarterly journal *Gastronomica* is a mix of scholarly
articles and essays by passionate amateurs—like this account
by Nashville-based writer and public administrator Robert
Dickinson, who just had to satisfy his curiosity about a vintage
soda pop.

If you grew up anywhere but New England, you've probably never heard of a drink called Moxie, yet it is the oldest
continually produced soda in America—and quite possibly the
worst tasting, as well. Moxie inspires fierce devotion in its fans,
which have included presidents, baseball stars, and a Pulitzer Prize
winner, and confused disbelief among its detractors, who just can't
fathom what anyone would see in the stuff. I discovered Moxie
while doing a little routine Web browsing, and after reading its illustrious history, I knew that I had to have a taste. I was particularly
curious as to why, if Moxie really does taste like a telephone pole,
as one Web site claims—or dirt, or battery acid—the drink has
such a passionate following.

Unfortunately, Moxie isn't sold in the Southeast where I live, so
I turned to the Internet to try to track down a can. Several Web
sites actually specialize in regional sodas and can ship you a case of
Moxie or Cheerwine or Boylan Grape any time you get a hanker-
ing. The problem was that these specialty stores don't just give
away the Moxie, and being thrifty on the best of days, and given
the high probability that I wouldn't actually like Moxie, I was

hesitant to place the thirty- to forty-dollar minimum order that the online soda merchants require. It occurred to me, though, that the folks who actually make Moxie must be quite proud of a soda that can produce such varied and extreme reactions among its drinkers; since only a few companies currently bottle Moxie, it stood to reason that one of them might be happy to send a can or two to a benighted, Moxieless southerner if he asked in just the right way.

A Proposition

So, on a cold Nashville day in the winter of 2007, I composed the following letter and mailed it to the Catawissa Bottling Company of Catawissa, Pennsylvania, and to the Coca-Cola Bottling Company of Northern New England, Inc., both of which bottle and distribute the beverage in question:

Dear Sir/Madam:

As a southerner, I'm no stranger to the charms of a nice, cold soda pop, although we often just call it "coke," no matter what the brand. Until a few days ago, however, I was completely unaware of the existence of one of your products. It started innocently enough. A friend wanted to know what the state dog of Tennessee was (there isn't one). A few clicks on the Internet later, and we learned that the state drink of Maine is a mysterious brew called Moxie. Now, like everyone who's seen a gangster movie, I was familiar with the term, but not, as I've said, with the drink.

Not content to let it rest at that, and not anxious to go back to work, we dug deeper and uncovered a whole subculture of Moxie lore—stories, memorabilia, rumors, testimonials. A sample:

"They say it takes nerve to drink a Moxie. I learned you can throw all of your normal conceptions of soda out the window when it comes to the taste of Moxie." [*]

---

[*] www.amazon.com/Moxie-Soda/dp/B0002BQLIM (accessed 11 May 2008; not currently posted).

"History has known only a few standards that cleanly divide Earth's population into irreconcilable camps. Moxie is one of these. No one is apathetic in the matter." *

"I grew up in mid-coast Maine where Moxie was more beloved than mother's milk . . . and more widely consumed." **

It's clear that Moxie is more than a drink, more than the longest continually produced soda in our great nation's history, more than the source of a great word for nerve, spunk, chutzpah. Moxie is the fluidic substance of the collective memory of a people, the taste of childhood, the pride of New Englanders, who know that not just anyone can suck down a Moxie and stick around to tell the tale.

Which brings me to my point. I would like to try my first Moxie—to be an initiate, to take a side. But, as you may know, none of the stores in my town of Nashville, TN, sell Moxie. I propose a trade—regional treat for regional treat. I will send you a box of Goo Goo Clusters (delicious blend of caramel, marshmallow, peanuts, and chocolate—my friends from New York City always ask for a box when I visit), a picture of Elvis, AND a bag of pork rinds, for a 6-pack of your finest Moxie.

Please consider my offer and respond via post or email. I hope you'll find my terms acceptable, but in any case, please keep doing what you do, and remember. . . . If you've got Moxie, you've got taste. I look forward to hearing from you.

Sincerely,
Robert T. Dickinson

Since 1876

While I waited to see whether anything would come of my proposal, I went back to the Internet to conduct more research and

---

* www.amazon.com/gp/cdp/member-reviews/ARN08JJ0DXOAK (accessed 11 May 2008).
** Ibid.

found references to Moxie lurking in sources ranging from the *New York Times* to etymology blogs such as www.word -detective.com. Americans have been drinking Moxie since 1884, although a similar drink first appeared in 1876 as a patent medicine called "Moxie Nerve Food." We're all familiar with *moxie* as a slang term for nerve or spunk (e.g., "Say what you will about that Al Capone, the man's got moxie"), and when I discovered the drink, I could only assume that slang preceded soda, that Moxie's name was the result of a slick young marketing man bathing his product in the allure of the speakeasy. Surprisingly, however, it was the drink that was apparently so chockfull of bubbly refreshment that its name was later used to describe that indefinable quality of folks who just seem to know the score. *

Until the early 1920s Moxie was one of the most popular soft drinks in America and was enjoyed by some of our finest citizens. The story goes that Vice-President Calvin Coolidge toasted his ascendance to the presidency with a glass of Moxie. E.B. White, Pulitzer Prize winner and author of *Charlotte's Web*, had high praise for the soda as well. "Moxie contains gentian root," White said, "which is the path to the good life." ** Even Boston Red Sox legend Ted Williams, the Splendid Splinter, got into the act as a Moxie pitchman in the 1950s. †

Despite such an impressive history, however, people in most areas of the country have never heard of Moxie, let alone tasted it. Moxie was once nationally distributed, but due to the vagaries of free-market economics, including competition with Coca-Cola, the soda took a smaller and smaller share of the soft-drink market over the years until it became a regional curiosity, unknown to Tennesseans, even ones who are pretty well traveled. These days

---

* Paul Lukas, "Surviving By Fizzy Logic," *New York Times*, 23 July 2003, at www.nytimes.com/2003/07/23/dining/23SODA.html?pagewanted=all (accessed 19 October 2009).

** Scott Elledge, *E.B. White: A Biography* (New York: W.W. Norton and Co., 1986), viii.

† Jenn Abelson, "Can A Bitter Taste Find Sweet Life Again?" *Boston Globe*, http://www.boston.com/business/articles/2007/08/05/can_a_bitter_taste_find_ sweet_life_again (accessed 11 May 2008).

Moxie distribution is concentrated in New England, although Cornucopia Beverages, a wholly owned subsidiary of the Coca-Cola Bottling Company of Northern New England (itself a subsidiary of Japan's Kirin Brewing Company), began selling Moxie in Florida through Sweetbay Supermarkets in October 2007. *

As unknown as it is in most of the United States, Moxie has developed a fiercely devoted following in the areas where it is sold. Case in point: the Moxie World Web site (www.moxieworld.us). Here, devotees can find a detailed listing of retail outlets and restaurants that carry Moxie, links to collectors' sites, and lists of Moxie-related events, such as the twenty-sixth annual Moxie Days Festival held in July 2009 in Lisbon Falls, Maine. Fans even have a governing body of sorts in the Moxie Congress, a group of memorabilia collectors and Moxie connoisseurs whose mission is to promote and celebrate their favorite soft drink. Moxie displayed its real-life political clout as well when the Maine legislature made Moxie the state's official drink in 2005. **

Curiously enough, however, a large contingent of naysayers holds the equally strong opinion that Moxie is, well, not very good. To wit:

"The taste of Moxie is hard to describe, but if you have some really old sarsaparilla or birch beer around the house, mix it with a little battery acid and you'll get the general idea." †

"Have you ever licked a telephone pole or railroad tie? That is about what Moxie tastes like." ‡

The phrase "acquired taste" also appears quite frequently. But for every slur against Moxie, you'll find a glowing tribute, a paean to Moxie's wholesomeness, a fierce defense of its good name:

---

* Personal e-mail correspondence with Justin Conroy, marketing analyst, Coca-Cola Bottling Company of Northern New England, Inc., 17 December 2007.

** Abelson, "Can a Bitter Taste Find Sweet Life Again?"

† www.word-detective.com/111097.html (accessed 11 May 2008).

‡ www.roadfood.com/Forums/tm.aspx?high=&m=10927&mpage=1#10943 (accessed 19 October 2009).

"It's not a syrupy fruit or cola, and it's not a trendy California dill flavored monstrosity—it's the grandpappy of all of those! It's been marketed as a health elixir, it is the reason we say 'that kid's got Moxie!' and it's history in a bottle. And I adore it!" *

"There is nothing finer than smoking a fine cigar and having a snifter of Cognac, aged Scotch, a Tawny Port Wine, dry red wine, a harsh warm Guinness Stout or a cold glass of Moxie." **

If nothing more, my research had shown that Moxie refuses to be lumped in with the ubiquitous carbonated sugar waters that fill our grocery stores and vending machines, and I was even more anxious to take my first sip.

Contact

Less than a week after I made my offer, I received my first response from Paula at Catawissa:

Hello Robert,

I really appreciated the letter you sent. I had to pass it around the office. I hope you don't mind. Our company has been in business since 1926 and often the barter system was used. So sure, I'll send a couple of bottles and cans of diet and regular.

We also make our own line of soft drink flavors and are known for our famous Big Ben's Blue Birch Beer, along with 16 other flavors. Samples will be included.

Respectfully,
Paula Clark
Catawissa Bottling Company
Since 1926

True to her word, Paula sent the following to my apartment in Nashville:

---

* www.exoticsoda.com/moxie.html (accessed 19 October 2009).
** www.moxie.info/editoral.htm (accessed 11 May 2008).

1 can Moxie
1 can diet Moxie
1 bottle Moxie
1 bottle Big Ben's Sarsaparilla
1 bottle Big Ben's Birch Beer
1 bottle Big Ben's Cream Soda
1 bottle Big Ben's Ginger Beer

Judging by my shipment, Catawissa seems to specialize in the quaint sodas of yesteryear—drinks that evoke first dates at the soda shop, zoot-suited gangsters, or old West gunslingers. Put another way, many Catawissa products are drinks that have little chance of grabbing a very large share of most markets. According to *Beverage Digest*, a beverage industry trade journal, the Coca-Cola and Pepsi-Cola companies controlled a 75 percent share of the carbonated soft drink market in 2005, selling over 7.6 billion cases of soda. In the same year the Atlanta-based Monarch Beverage Company, which owned Moxie before selling the brand to Cornucopia in early 2007, commanded a 0.1 percent market share and sold approximately 9.8 million cases of all of its products combined.* Nonetheless, Catawissa was clearly proud of its own carbonated wares, even if many of its products don't generate the same eye-popping sales figures as the corporate behemoths that it competes with for shelf space.

The Coca-Cola Bottling Company of Northern New England also came through with a shipment of Moxie. The following letter was enclosed:

Dear Mr. Dickinson,

We are well aware of the regional distribution of Moxie and the pride this product instills in Maine. We are also well aware of the problems finding Moxie south of the Mason-Dixon line. Snowbirds commonly complain about missing Moxie during their winter pilgrimages down South.

---

* *Beverage Digest* 48:7 (8 March 2006), at www.beverage-digest.com/pdf/top-10_2006.pdf (accessed 11 May 2008).

Enclosed you will find not six cans of Moxie as requested, but twelve cans in a convenient "fridge pack" designed to help better fit in your refrigerator and enjoy this beverage ice cold. In return, we are interested in trying your favorite regional treat—if you want to send the mentioned Goo Goo Clusters, that would be outstanding.

Please let us know what you think of Moxie and thank you for your interest in our hidden gem!

Sincerely,
Justin J. Conroy
Coca-Cola Bottling Company of Northern New England

Of course, a good southerner isn't one to back out on a deal. I had promised an assortment of Tennessee treats and was ready to make good on that promise. In the spirit of regional goodwill, I sent not one but two boxes of Goo Goo Clusters to the Catawissa staff—one regular (with peanuts) and one "deluxe," which replaces the peanut with the slightly more upscale pecan. I also enclosed a bag of Golden Flake pork rinds and a postcard of Elvis circa 1970 with full muttonchops, taken during a recording session in Vegas. Finally, the Catawissa folks got Polaroids of myself and two friends—one smiling, and one grimacing in pain after taking a sip of Moxie. To the Coca-Cola Bottling people I sent the same two boxes of Goo Goos and a photo of a young Elvis astride a motorcycle. I had had a change of heart about the pork rinds. They are, after all, pretty unhealthy. I'll have to hope that the younger, better-looking Elvis made up the difference.

The Tasting

The moment of truth took place on Tuesday, January 23, 2007. At first sip, Moxie is reminiscent of a weak root beer. Not bad, but not memorable either. Then the bitterness takes hold. Like medicine. Like the tar on a telephone pole. Like the sludge at the bottom of the barrel that you're supposed to just throw away. But Moxie is a complex beast, and once the initial shock wears away, the bitterness mellows, and one is left with a bittersweet taste that isn't so bad and may even qualify as, dare I say it . . . pleasant. In the spirit of scientific inquiry, however, I was eager to get a more representative sample than just myself, so I decided to share a little ice-cold Moxie with my friends. Here are a few opinions:

DON: "It was like nothing I have ever sipped before. That says it all. It was OK, but that aftertaste was . . ." [he trails off here]

LAURA: "BLECH!"

JEFF: "Since I was a young man, I've tried to live my life the 'right' way, set my goals and life expectations on the straight and narrow path. Moxie was not the 'right' way."

PHILIP: "It's different, but I didn't think it was too bitter. I'd definitely buy a case occasionally if they sold it around here."

ELIZABETH: "It was awful. At first, you're like, this is fine, but then the aftertaste kicks in."

MATT: "I like the bitterness. It's good."

VICTORIA: "I don't think I'll be drinking the rest of this."

Overall, Moxie wasn't the biggest hit in my study group, but comparisons with battery acid and railroad ties may not be quite fair either; some of the group, after all, did enjoy it. My final assessment, therefore, is that Moxie is a soda, and, like other sodas, some people like the taste and some people don't. The cult of Moxie, however, isn't so much about taste as it is about history and place. In other words, drinking a soda isn't just about quenching your thirst and getting a caffeine fix. Just as much as an accent, what a person drinks is a badge of identity. For someone raised on it, sipping a Moxie is a symbolic act, a performance of one's "Maineness." It's the Louisianian sucking the head of a crawfish. The debate over the relative merits of Memphis, Texas, and Carolina barbecues. The Tennessean passing on an iced tea in a chain restaurant because it's not "sweet tea." I suspect that my trades with these companies were so satisfying because, in addition to swapping Goo Goo for Moxie, sweet for bitter, they were an exchange of two cultures and a recognition that these traditions have an intrinsic value that transcends the monetary values attached to a soda and a candy bar. Paula and Justin had mailed me a small piece of New England, I had offered a taste of my own heritage, and we had found the deal mutually agreeable.

Home Cooking

POTLUCKY

By Sam Sifton

From *The New York Times Magazine*

Recently anointed as the *Times'* new chief restaurant critic,
Sam Sifton also contributes this occasional food column for
the Sunday magazine section—a frank, funny, down-to-earth
dissection of one recipe and how to tweak it.

I was invited to cook dinner for Nora Ephron. This is what happens if you hang around New York long enough, writing about food and editing about movies. You end up at ground zero. The invitation was to a potluck. Guests were meant to bring food inspired by Ephron's career or by the woman herself. It was essentially high-stakes food charades. My draw was meatloaf. Ruh-roh.

Ephron is famous for her meatloaf, a version of which is on the menu of Graydon Carter's new restaurant and clubhouse, the Monkey Bar. And cooking plays no small role in her new film, "Julie & Julia," which opens on Aug. 7. The movie, which Ephron wrote and directed, is an adaptation of Julia Child's memoir of learning to cook in France and then writing "Mastering the Art of French Cooking"—as well as of Julie Powell's memoir of learning to cook in Queens and then blogging her way through every recipe in "Mastering the Art of French Cooking."

Opinions about movies are for film critics; I hazard them at great personal risk. (I work closely with film critics.) But I can say that the food in "Julie & Julia" is beautiful. (Can't I?) The aesthetic of Ephron's sole is perfect. She may be to food as Scorsese is to bar fights. Just thinking about cooking for her, I felt sick and wondered if bringing a few bottles of cold Pellegrino or Laurent-Perrier Champagne would do instead. I've read widely in the literature. Nora Ephron loves Champagne.

But I got down to cooking. I started to grind. What was borne out by my experience I pass along as gospel: Do not make Nora Ephron's meatloaf for Nora Ephron. This is a sucker's play and remains true even if you're cooking for someone's aunt on a Saturday night in Fort Myers, Fla.: Don't make a person's signature recipe for that person, ever. Instead, take it as a starting point. Move the ball along.

And practice. A couple of years ago, Ruth Reichl edited a huge cookbook that was built out of the recipe files of *Gourmet*, the magazine she has edited since stepping down as the restaurant critic of *The New York Times* in 1999. (How'd you like to cook eggs for her?) In it is a meatloaf recipe that combines beef and veal, pancetta and Parmesan, brightened with lemon zest and white wine. It's a luxurious feed, and I'd run versions through the oven before deciding to take it on the road.

I made one additional change for Ephron. Instead of chopping a fine dice of pancetta as I generally do, I went to the store and asked for thin-sliced pancetta that I would roll and cut into chiffonade at home. Pancetta-studded meatloaf is delicious, of course. But I wanted the bacon really to melt into the meats; I was aiming for an ethereal loaf.

And I was working fast. So it wasn't until the meatloaf came out of the oven that I realized the nice fellow who was manning the meat slicer at my local market was also a dangerous and psychotic meal killer who had not removed the plastic wrap from the pancetta before slicing it into paper-thin rounds. I'd cut these rounds into fine ribbons that had cooked into the meat perfectly, except for the plastic parts, which didn't melt into the meat at all. There was a kind of stubble on my finished loaf—plastic pin bones.

I had two hours until dinner with Ephron. I felt a blaze of panic, the sort that awakens you from that dream in which you're forced to take an exam in a subject you've never studied. I stared at the fuzzy meatloaf for 10 seconds. Then I fed it to the children and started all over again. (It's all right. I gave them each a set of tweezers for the plastic. It was like a game to them.)

Two new meatloaves resulted from this challenge round of cooking. The *Gourmet* recipe, which I'd come to think of as fancy, was now unlucky, and I thought it wise to have a backup. So in addition to a new, nonplastic version of that, I cooked a huge meatball, drawn from a dish that Mark Ladner used to offer at Lupa, in Greenwich Village, before he went off to be the executive chef at Del Posto: turkey and Italian sausage, cut through with pepper flakes and rosemary, baked in a kind of soffrito. You could make the argument that it's perhaps more beautiful as a dozen meatballs. But it's a marvelous single loaf as well: a fine-textured, surprisingly light dinner that pairs excellently with sautéed greens and the smallest portion of fresh pasta in butter and mint.

With 30 minutes on the clock, I put my meats into serving pans and headed north to the Upper West Side, which is obviously where you'd have dinner with Nora Ephron if such a thing were on the docket.

"This is remarkable," she said in the end, brightly. I went to the hostess's study to enter the words in my notebook. She might just have easily given a small smile and patted me on the arm. That would have been devastating. But I don't believe it was that close. These are both excellent dishes to serve friends, and they make for good leftovers. Add a salad, some decent bread, a lot of red wine. Sometimes New York is the greatest city in the world.

Fancy Meatloaf

Adapted from Gourmet.

Serves 6 to 8

½ loaf Italian bread, crust removed, torn into small pieces
    (about 2 cups)
1 cup whole milk
1 pound ground beef
1 pound ground veal
2 large eggs, scrambled
4 ounces thinly sliced pancetta, chopped
¾ cup grated Parmesan
1 bunch parsley, cleaned and finely chopped (about 1 cup)
2 teaspoons grated lemon zest

Kosher salt and freshly ground black pepper
¼ cup extra-virgin olive oil
¼ cup butter
1 cup dry white wine.

1. Preheat the oven to 375 degrees. Soak the bread in the milk for 10 minutes.

2. Mix the beef, veal, eggs, pancetta, Parmesan, parsley and lemon zest in a large bowl. Season liberally with salt and pepper. Squeeze the bread to remove excess milk, then chop and add it to the meat. Mix gently until well combined, but do not overmix. Transfer onto a board and shape into a fine meatloaf, shy of a foot in length and 4 inches across. Loosely cover and refrigerate for 15 minutes.

3. Heat the oil and butter in a large, ovenproof skillet over medium-high heat. Add the meatloaf and sear without moving it until it is browned, about 5 minutes. Carefully slide a spatula under the meatloaf, then gently use another spatula to help turn it and brown the second side, again without moving it for 5 minutes. Transfer to a plate.

4. Pour out all but 2 tablespoons of the fat, return the skillet to the stove and raise the heat to high. Add the wine and deglaze the pan, scraping up the browned bits stuck to it with a wooden spoon. Return the meatloaf to the skillet and then transfer to the oven, basting occasionally with the pan juices, until a meat thermometer inserted into the center of the loaf reads 150 degrees, about 25 minutes.

5. Transfer the meatloaf to a platter and let stand, tented with foil, 10 minutes. Slice, pour the pan juices over the top and serve.

Turkey Meatloaf

Adapted from Mark Ladner

Serves 6 to 8

8 cloves garlic, minced
1 tablespoon finely chopped fresh rosemary
Red pepper flakes
1 cup fresh bread crumbs of any provenance

Kosher salt and freshly ground black pepper

¼ cup whole milk

1 pound ground turkey

1 pound sweet Italian pork sausage, casing removed, crumbled

¼ cup extra-virgin olive oil

4 ounces bacon, chopped

1 medium red onion, finely chopped

1 28-ounce can whole tomatoes, preferably San Marzano, seeds removed

1 cup red wine

¼ bunch mint

1. Preheat the oven to 450 degrees. Combine 2⁄3 of the garlic, the rosemary, pepper flakes, bread crumbs and liberal amounts of salt and pepper. Add the milk and mix. Add the meats and mix once more to combine; don't overmix. Transfer onto a board and shape into a fine meatloaf, about 9 inches long and 4 inches wide.

2. Place in a baking pan with high sides, drizzle with about 2 tablespoons of olive oil and bake for 25 minutes, turning halfway through to brown evenly. Remove from the oven and reduce the heat to 325 degrees.

3. Meanwhile, fry the bacon in the remaining 2 tablespoons of oil until it starts to curl and its fat is rendered. Add the onions and remaining garlic, cooking until the onions are translucent, about 4 minutes. Add the tomatoes and wine and bring to a boil.

4. Pour the sauce over the meatloaf, cover tightly with foil and bake until a meat thermometer inserted at the center reads 150 degrees, 20 to 30 minutes.

5. Transfer the meatloaf to a platter and let stand, tented with foil, for 10 minutes. Cut into thick slices, spoon tomato sauce over the top and scatter with torn mint leaves.

ALL THAT GLITTERS

By Janet A. Zimmerman

From egullet.com

Thanks to the internet, a superb cook like Janet Zimmerman—
a culinary instructor based in Atlanta, Georgia—can also be
one of the mainstays of the eGullet culinary society, providing
a constant lifeline of cooking technique to readers. There's
more than one way to roast a chicken . . .

Students of philosophy (of which I was one) rarely get through school without a class on the ancients, which often includes a day or so on the alchemists. If you're not familiar with these guys, here's what you need to know: they spent all their time looking for a magic element that would turn base metals to gold. Seriously. Sometimes this element is referred to as "elixir" but mostly it's known as the philosopher's stone. Today, this seems like a fruitless and frivolous pursuit, but for hundreds of years the best minds in science were certain that it was only a matter of time before the philosopher's stone would be discovered. Midas would be real.

I started thinking about the philosopher's stone after reading a post on Michael Ruhlman's blog about roasting a chicken. The subject of the post was that American commercial enterprise is conspiring to convince us all that it's too hard to cook from scratch so that food manufacturers can sell us processed food. He chose roasted chicken as proof that it's not hard to cook. With tongue ensconced in cheek, he wrote a set of instructions called "The World's Most Difficult Roasted Chicken Recipe."

"Turn your oven on high (450 if you have ventilation, 425 if not). Coat a 3- or 4-pound chicken with coarse kosher salt so that you have an appealing crust of salt (a tablespoon or so). Put the chicken in a pan, stick a lemon or some onion or any fruit or vegetable you have on hand into the cavity. Put the chicken in the oven. Go away for an hour. . . . When an hour has passed, take the chicken out of the oven and put it on the stove top or on a trivet for 15 more minutes. Finito."

Ruhlman is not the only one to champion roasted chicken as the quintessential easy meal. In the *Les Halles Cookbook*, Anthony Bourdain says: " . . . if you can't properly roast a damn chicken then you are one helpless, hopeless, sorry-ass bivalve in an apron. Take that apron off, wrap it around your neck and hang yourself. You do not deserve to wear the proud garment of generations of hard-working, dedicated cooks."

Bourdain's recipe for roasted chicken is, however, by no means easy. To start with, he has you lie down on the floor, bend your knees and bring your legs up, so you know how to position the chicken. Then, keeping that position in mind, you cut holes in your chicken and place the ends of the drumsticks in them (this so you don't have to truss). You smear herb butter under the skin of the breast, and fill the cavity with herbs, onions and lemon pieces. Place the giblets and some more onion in the bottom of a roasting pan and pour some wine over it. Finally, the chicken goes on top of that and into the oven. But wait! You have to turn the temperature up halfway through cooking. Oh, and you baste, and then you have to make a pan sauce. Now, I'm sure all that work produces a decent roasted chicken, but easy? Call me a sorry-ass bivalve if you want, Tony, but I am damn sure not going to lie down on the floor imitating a dead chicken. Not in this lifetime. I went back to Ruhlman.

I don't know if Ruhlman thought anyone would follow his directions; they seemed to be an afterthought to his post. But despite big gaps and some questionable instructions, I gave it a whirl and did exactly what he said, pretending that I knew nothing about chicken roasting. An hour and 15 minutes later I had a roasted chicken that was edible, so in that sense, it worked. It wasn't good: it was overcooked, the skin was too salty, and the thighs were soaked in chicken grease. It yielded a hot scorched lemon, which I threw away. However, it was easy. (It would have been even easier without having to find fruits and vegetables for the cavity. What is it about lemons that makes people want to abuse them so tragically? Here's a better use for a lemon: make a Sidecar and drink it while the fruit-free chicken cooks.)

I understand why Ruhlman says it's easy to roast a chicken, why he wants—even needs—it to be easy. He's taken it upon himself to prove that cooking isn't hard. Chicken seems like a slam dunk. I also understand why Bourdain goes to such lengths in preparation. He thinks that all of those things make for a better bird, and since he starts out by ridiculing anyone who can't produce a good roasted chicken, he'd be in serious trouble if he couldn't deliver.

Other authors and chefs are not so quick to call roasted chicken easy, but neither will they come right out and call it difficult. They tend to be coy. In *Mastering the Art of French Cooking*, Julia Child and Simone Beck say, "You can always judge the quality of a cook or a restaurant by roast chicken." Like those two dames de cuisine, most authors agree that a "perfectly roasted chicken" is a crown jewel of the kitchen, a feather in the cap of any serious cook. But no one admits the bare truth: you can't have it both ways. If it's easy, it can't be the hallmark of a successful chef. If it makes or breaks the reputation of a restaurant or cook, then—news flash—it's not going to be easy.

Paul Simon could just as easily have sung about 50 ways to roast a chicken (just slit it up the back, Jack; throw it in a pan, Stan; learn how to truss, Gus). Before you get that bird anywhere near an oven, you have to make decisions. Do you brine it? Salt it? Rub, butter or marinate it? If you butter, does it go on the outside, or under the skin? Plain or herbed? What, if anything, goes inside the chicken? Then comes trussing: you can tie the legs together loosely or you can draw them up tightly so they almost cover the breast. (Or do nothing.) Even putting the poor chicken in a pan is problematic. Deep or shallow pan? Rack or no rack? Vegetables under it, or not? Next, when you get it to the oven, what temperature do you use? Not only can you roast at high temperature or low, but you can start out low and turn it to high, or start out high and turn it to low. But you're not done yet: baste? Don't baste?

Whew.

You might think you'll get definitive answers if you turn to the experts, but agreement among them is as elusive as phlogiston. The recipe in *Mastering the Art of French Cooking* has you salt the inside of the bird, butter the inside and outside, place the bird on a bed of vegetables, start it out at a high temperature, turning and basting for 15 minutes. Turn the oven down and continue to baste and turn. Somewhere in there, you salt the outside of the chicken. James Beard has a similar method of turning and basting, but before cooking, he has you rub the inside of the chicken with lemon juice, seal a chunk of butter inside, and sew the chicken shut.

Alton Brown suggests building a "stone oven" from fire-safe tiles inside your real oven, heating it up with the oven cleaning setting, then enclosing the chicken in the tile box to roast it. (Yeah, right after I get up off the floor from my chicken-yoga exercise, Alton.)

The lemons-in-the-cavity idea originates with Marcella Hazan. In her recipe, however, you don't toss the fruit in haphazardly. You must roll a pair of lemons on the counter and prick their skins all over with a skewer, then pack them into the cavity as tightly as commuters on the 5:25 train. As the chicken cooks, the lemons heat up and spray the inside of the bird with hot lemon juice. Apparently, this is a good thing.

Heston Blumenthal trumps all others for length and complexity. He has you brine the bird for six hours, then rinse and soak for an hour, changing the water every fifteen minutes. You bring a pot of water to a boil and prepare an ice bath. Dunk the chicken into the boiling water for 30 seconds, then into the ice water. Repeat, as if you're trying to sober up a drunken sailor. Put your recovering bird to bed on a rack and cover it with muslin, letting it dry out in the refrigerator overnight. The next day, preheat the oven to 140°F and cook the bird for four to six hours, or until a thermometer in the meat reaches 140 degrees (by some accounts this can take even longer—there are tales of cooking for twelve hours). Let it sit for an hour. Then brown the chicken all over in oil in a heavy skillet. Meanwhile, you've chopped up and cooked the wing tips in 100 grams of butter. The final step is to inject this chicken-flavored butter into the bird in several places.

Every cookbook author in the world, it seems, has a special way with roasted chickens. Some have more than one—Thomas Keller is on record with at least four methods, from "salt it, truss it, throw it in a hot oven" (wherein he says, "I don't baste it, I don't add butter; you can if you wish, but I feel this creates steam, which I don't want"), to the *Ad Hoc* version of roasting the bird on a bed of vegetables—after rubbing it with oil. What? If Keller can't make up his mind about how to roast a chicken, what hope do we mere mortals have?

In the *French Laundry Cookbook*, Keller says, " . . . even a perfectly roasted chicken will inevitably result in a breast that's a little less moist than one you would roast separately, which is why I always want a sauce with roast chicken. . . . " Had he ever taken a logic class, he would have recognized the inherent contradiction in that sentence. For what he's said is this: "even a perfectly roasted chicken is not perfect."

And there we have it: there is no method that results in perfect roasted chicken. It's the philosopher's stone of the modern kitchen. All the lemon-stuffing, trussing, turning, basting, and temperature manipulation in the world won't change that. Blumenthal spends two days brining, rinsing, boiling, chilling, drying, cooking, and searing—and he still has to inject butter into the chicken meat. Lie down on the floor and become one with your chicken, build a citrus Jacuzzi inside your bird, or massage it with butter like a pampered spa client. At the end of the day, you still won't have gold.

All those chefs know the reasons why. First, chicken thighs and breasts need different treatment, and any method that cooks them the same way, at the same temperature, for the same time, risks overcooking and thus drying out the breast by the time the thighs are done. Second, treatments designed to keep the breast meat moist, such as brining or cooking at lower temperatures, result in disappointing skin. And of course, the main point of roasted chicken is the crisp, brown skin. But you need to achieve it without ruining the rest of the chicken.

They know this and we do too, if we've put much effort into roasting chickens. Yet we persist. We keep trying to roast these birds whole, trussing and turning, brining and basting. Why?

It's the size. Chickens are small. Along with turkeys, they're the only whole animal most of us will ever cook in a modern kitchen.

If cows were the size of chickens, would we roast them whole, wondering all the while why those legs are so tough and the loins all dried out? Maybe so; maybe if cows were chicken-sized, we'd find a familiar myriad of misdirection: stuffing them with lemons, trussing them up, starting them on their stomachs, then flipping them udder-side up, swerving from high to low heat and careening back. But cows are not the convenient two- to four-pound size of chickens, so we cut them up and treat the parts appropriately.

On the other hand, if chickens were the size of cows, we'd know how to handle them. We'd butcher them and cook the various parts the way they deserve. We wouldn't roast a whole one. We'd put that search for the poultry philosopher's stone behind us.

I know what you're saying. "But a perfect roasted chicken is not impossible. I had one in 1997." I myself have had two roasted chickens that—if not perfect—were so close to perfection as to be indistinguishable from it. One was at Alain Ducasse's Essex House restaurant in New York. It was one of the special French chickens with blue feet (or so it said on the menu; it arrived at the table footless). It had shaved black truffles under the skin. It was breathtaking. The second I actually made myself. A friend showed me how to use the charcoal grill that had been abandoned in the backyard of my rental flat, and also showed me how to cut out the backbone to spatchcock the bird. Brined and grilled, it was flawless.

But a major scientific principle is that results have to be replicable to count. If you can't get the same results from an experiment after the first time, then—scientifically speaking—your results might as well have never happened. And that's where all these philosopher-stone attempts fail. Yes, that first chicken I spatchcocked and grilled was awe-inspiring. But the next time? It was good, but there was no comparison. I kept trying, but I never again reached that pinnacle. Anyone who's had a roasted chicken that neared perfection knows what I mean.

Oh, sure. You can fool yourself that because the chicken you had back in 1997 was perfect, it must have been the cooking method, and you can religiously follow that method for the rest of your life.

You can pretend that all the subsequent chickens cooked by that method are as good as that first one. But you'd be lying. Perfect roasted chicken is more than the bird itself. It depends on a confluence of elements that only happens once. My ADNY chicken was perfect not just because of the quality of the bird and the truffles under the skin; it was perfect because I had it at my first visit to a really high-end restaurant, because I was with wonderful friends, because we stayed at the table for four hours while servers doted on us. My grilled chicken was perfect because for the first time in my life, I mastered a charcoal fire and spatchcocked a chicken by myself.

So, maybe you have had a perfect roasted chicken. Dream about it and count your blessings, but don't ever expect it to happen again.

We live in the real world. Perfect roasted chicken moments may happen, but rarely more than once, and not to all of us. What are the rest of us supposed to do if we want roasted chicken?

Paul Simon said it best: The answer is easy if you take it logically.

Think of a chicken as a four-pound cow with wings. Get over the idea that roasting a whole chicken is a worthwhile pursuit and recognize it for the philosopher's stone that it is. Save your time and sanity: roast thighs, which really are easy, or breasts, which take a little more care and preparation but are still not difficult. Before you try lemons, trussing, butter, fire bricks, or a two-day brining-dunking-drying-cooking-searing-injecting binge, take a deep breath. Cut that chicken up and don't look back.

Get yourself free.

And yet.

That ADNY bird was incredible. So was my first grilled chicken. They weren't figments of my imagination. What's more, I made one of them. Why shouldn't I be able to do it again? It wasn't that difficult, really. Just brine, then remove the backbone. Start a fire.

Yes, I know what I said. The second time the magic was gone. But what if I'm just forgetting something, or what if one little change would elevate my next chicken to those heights? I'm sure I can do it. Maybe I could buy a blue-footed chicken and a truffle.

No. I won't get obsessed. Besides, simpler is better. I know that. I'll do what I did before, but I'll pay more attention to the temperature and the time, and that's it. If that doesn't work, I'll go back to roasting thighs.

Wait, I know—I could rub some butter under the skin. Everyone swears by that. But that's all I'll do. I'm not going to get insane over this.

But maybe I could dry it overnight so the skin stays crisp. What if I put some butter and herbs inside the chicken and then trussed it?

I have some lemons . . .

The Juicy Secret
to Seasoning Meat

By Oliver Strand
From *Food & Wine*

Like many professional cooks turned freelance food writers,
New-York-based Oliver Strand has an impressive reservoir of
technical know-how—but he also knows that it doesn't always
translate to the home kitchen.

When I started working in restaurants more than 10 years ago, I was taught to season meat with salt and pepper well before cooking. Ideally, a whole chicken would be seasoned a full 24 hours before it was roasted, because salting so far ahead of time, I was told, gives the meat more flavor.

I took the practice as gospel, because that's what you do in a professional kitchen, especially if it's one staffed by talented cooks (which it was) who are making good food (which, in all modesty, we were). When you work in a restaurant, you learn by watching carefully, asking the right questions and following instructions. That's also how you avoid being confronted with the most dreaded question the chef or sous chef could level at you, in front of the rest of the staff: "What do you think you're doing?"

So I felt spun around when I worked in another restaurant where the meat was always seasoned with salt and pepper right before cooking. Salting meat ahead of time, I was now told, dries it out.

Chefs disagree all the time, but rarely about basic technique—and there are few things more basic than sprinkling salt and pepper on steak or short ribs. But after surveying some notable chefs around the country, I discovered a dispute so divisive it's almost ideological. Not only are there two camps, but each side thinks it is categorically right, and the other, painfully wrong. On one side you have New York City chefs Tom Colicchio, of Craft and Top Chef fame, and Jean François Bruel of Daniel, both of whom assert that meat should never be seasoned until just before cooking. (Bruel goes even further with steaks, which he finishes seasoning only after they have been seared or grilled.) And on the other side you have David Tanis of Chez Panisse in Berkeley, California, and San Francisco's Judy Rodgers, whose *The Zuni Café Cookbook* contains an entire section on the art of salting meat ahead of time. There's no geographic pattern. Mario Batali of New York City's Babbo seasons duck legs for confit the day before. Suzanne Goin of Los Angeles's Lucques doesn't.

I have had knockout meals in the restaurants of all these chefs, and I have never thought that the Berkshire pork at Craft needed more flavor, or that the grilled quail at Chez Panisse was dry. Chefs at these culinary heights don't make such obvious mistakes.

But surely there's a correct method, or at least one that's more right than the other. And one that makes more sense for home cooks. In their search for succulence, chefs often turn to practices like brining (almost all the meat dishes are brined—soaked for hours in a saltwater solution—at Paul Kahan's pork-centric The Publican, in Chicago), or sous-vide, which calls for using some fairly expensive equipment to slow-cook food in a low-temperature water bath. But I wanted to know what was practical and reasonable when making everyday meals at home. Buying and seasoning a chicken the day before you plan to roast it couldn't be easier. But the question remained: Is it tastier?

Before I conducted my own experiments, I decided to consult with scientist Harold McGee, the author of *On Food and Cooking* and a columnist for the *New York Times*, where he unravels—and often debunks—assumptions about cooking. Even though McGee hasn't done controlled tests on the timing of seasoning, he is decidedly in favor of salting meat ahead of time. (He's particularly fond of grinding his own hamburger with seasoned chunks of beef, a recipe from *The Zuni Café Cookbook*.) He explained that while a high concentration of salt has a desiccating effect, which is helpful for curing meat, the small amount of salt used to season food has a hydrating effect: Salt helps the cells hold on to water.

That was the theory I wanted to test. I bought a sampling of meats, two pieces of different kinds of cuts—one of which I would season 24 hours ahead of time, the other just one hour before cooking. (Some recipes call for seasoning 48 or even 72 hours in advance; McGee explained that the further ahead of time the meat is seasoned, the more even the distribution of salt. But having to prepare a chicken on Sunday in order to roast it on Wednesday is asking a lot.) I would use the same amount of salt on each piece of meat—three quarters of a teaspoon per pound. I'd also weigh the meat both before salting and just before cooking, to see if seasoning ahead of time drew out juices. (McGee was right: None of the cuts lost water weight from salting.) And I decided to try a variety of cooking techniques. I would roast whole chickens and racks of pork, sear dry-aged rib eyes and braise lamb shanks.

I invited over some opinionated friends for this meal of multiple meat courses, all of which we tasted blind—we were a table of good eaters, people who knew their way around a well-marbled steak and a well-timed critique. But before I started cooking, I realized that I had to prepare myself to be wrong. If I learned that my training was off the mark, and that all these years I'd been making one horrible mistake after another by salting meat the day before cooking it, then I had to be willing to change my methods. The truth? I can handle the truth.

And I can easily handle two chickens. I roasted both for about 45 minutes at 475 degrees, which is in line with what professional kitchens do. I didn't add any ingredients to enhance the flavor (butter, olive oil, spices or herbs), just salt and pepper.

The skins of both birds became crispy and golden in the oven, the breasts juicy and delicious. But the skin of the chicken that was seasoned just before roasting tasted saltier than the meat, and while I'm not sure I'd have noticed it on its own, when I sampled it next to the other chicken it seemed clumsy, an amateur effort. The chicken that had been seasoned the day before was more flavorful, but more than that, it tasted more balanced. And just as McGee had theorized, it was more succulent.

Next were the dry-aged rib eyes. I was careful to use good technique, letting the meat come to room temperature before searing it in a cast-iron pan and letting it rest afterward. Both Tom Colicchio and Suzanne Goin had stressed the importance of these fundamentals. "There are so many factors you need to pay attention to, and salt is just one of them," Colicchio had said.

When I served the two steaks at a bloody medium-rare, everybody could immediately tell which rib eye was seasoned when. But there was no consensus on which one was better. Rob, a chef, said he liked how the salt flavored the fat of the steak that was seasoned the day before, and Christine, my wife, thought it tasted more aged. But Kerry, who eats out more than anybody I know, leaned toward the brighter flavor of the steak salted right before cooking. That was also the preference of Mark (though he might be biased: His wife is from Argentina, where steaks are seasoned with coarse salt just before grilling).

I didn't feel strongly either way—which was its own judgment. To me, both steaks were equally juicy and tasty. As a matter of practicality, picking up a good steak after work and cooking it that night is just fine.

But then I served the two pork racks. This time, there was a strong consensus: The one salted just before roasting was clearly moister and more delicious. The pork seasoned the day before was so dry, it was the most disappointing thing we ate.

And we were just as unanimous when it came to the braised lamb shanks: The lamb seasoned the day before was exquisite, dramatically better than the other. If the pork was the evening's least inspired dish, this was the most delicious. It had less to do with a discernible saltiness than the overall composition of flavors. It tasted richer, fuller, meatier. Simply put, it tasted more like lamb. The shanks were as close to a revelation as you'll find in an enameled cocotte. "I never thought salting ahead would have this profound an effect," Rob said. "Braising is so forgiving, it's low and slow, and there's all the flavor from the other ingredients, but this lamb is amazing. There's no comparison."

It was a conclusive end to an eye-opening evening. I had expected to arrive at a hard-and-fast, one-size-fits-all principle, and instead, I arrived at a series of answers weighted by the most practical concern of all: What's worth the effort? Some of cooking is art, and some of it is skill, but much of it is logistics, a question of timing and space and making sure you have enough parsnips, say, to feed your guests, but not so many that they crowd the pan and steam instead of roast. What's true at home is also true in a professional kitchen, though we go out to restaurants precisely because they do things we wouldn't or couldn't do ourselves. I couldn't help but think that some chefs don't season in advance because it's a bother.

But really, it takes no extra effort, just some forethought. And so I will always season lamb shanks the day before they go into the braise. I will try to season chickens the day before, but if I don't have the chance, I won't sweat it; and I will season steaks and pork roasts right before searing. Not only can I handle the truth, I can handle several truths.

FEED IT OR IT DIES

By William Alexander

From *52 Loaves*

Sure, he has a full-time day job in a research lab in upstate
New York—but that didn't prevent William Alexander (also
author of *The $64 Tomato*) from plunging into a quixotic
quest to bake the perfect loaf of bread—and then writing a
tremendously entertaining book about it.

Week 20

"Feed the bitch!" said the voice on the phone.
    "Feed the bitch or she'll die!"
    —ANTHONY BOURDAIN, *Kitchen Confidential*, 2000

I was as nervous as a sinner in the first pew, which may have
partly explained the undersized, dense, and misshapen loaf
I'd just baked, the least attractive one I'd made in months of bread
making.

Zach took one look at it and winced. "Ooh. Doorstop."

Even worse, one of the four crosshatch slashes had blown out as
if a hand grenade had gone off inside, leaving a large tumor on that
side of the loaf, while the other three cuts were mere scratches that
hadn't opened up at all. This had happened because my fancy ten-
dollar *lame* was already dull and ready to be tossed in the garbage.
If ever I wanted a loaf to turn out well, it was this one, for I was on
my way to a weekend with Charles van Over, bread authority and
author. I was hoping that van Over could diagnose my airless and
tight-crumbed peasant loaf.

I kissed Katie good-bye.

"Dad, what if he tells you your 'lousy' bread is great? That'd be pretty embarrassing. What do you say then?"

"I guess I'd feel pretty foolish." But the odds of that happening were about nil. I eyed the loaf, so sorry-looking I had seriously considered "forgetting" it to save face. But, I reasoned, if you're going to the proctologist, you'd better be prepared to drop your pants, so, loaf and overnighter in hand, Anne and I headed out to van Over's home overlooking the Connecticut River.

Charlie greeted us warmly and went right for the bread knife.

"This is very good bread," he said, chewing on a lopsided slice. "Better than what you'll get in most bakeries."

Huh?

"But there are no air holes," I protested.

He held it up to the window to better see the texture. "Nice. You don't want air holes in bread like this. A peasant loaf is sandwich bread."

Oh. I hadn't known that.

"But it's too moist inside," I protested again.

"Leave it in the oven a half hour after baking. It'll dry out. Bill, I'm serious, this is really good bread."

I could see Katie smirking in our kitchen a hundred miles away.

"I'm not happy with the spongy texture. I want a much more open, webbed crumb, an *alveolar* crumb," I argued, using the wonderfully evocative word I'd swiped from Steven Kaplan—"the Professor" (as Charlie called him)—who'd hooked us up.

"You're not going to get that with this bread. You've gone about as far with this bread as you can go, but now you need to go to the next level. Have you ever used a starter?"

Oh, jeez, a starter. No way.

A starter is a batter or dough of flour, water, wild yeast, and bacteria (in other words, a sourdough, or in French a *levain**) that you maintain with regular "feedings" of flour and water for years or even generations. It can be used either in place of or with commercial

---

* Although the terms are synonymous, bakers tend to stay away from the term *sourdough* because of its connotation of San Francisco sourdough, which is a unique, rather sour variety of sourdough and is not representative of most starters.

yeast. I had thought about it a couple of times but had been frightened off by the demands of caring for it. The celebrity chef Anthony Bourdain described his baker's *levain* this way:

> A massive, foaming, barely contained heap . . . which even now was pushing up the weighted-down lid of a 35-gallon Lexan container and spilling over the work table where it was stored.

Then there were worried posts like this to a professional bakers' Internet forum:

> I am wondering what one does during holidays to feed their levain—besides the obvious going in to feed it. We feed ours 2 times a day. The levain is going to miss 2 feedings. I will be sleeping and it can die before I go in to feed it.

Feed it twice a day, every day, or it *dies*? I don't always manage to feed my kids twice a day! Who needed this hassle?

"I don't know, Charlie. It seems like a lot of work."

"Not if you keep it in the refrigerator." He pulled a one-gallon recycled plastic container marked "Crème Fraîche" out of his fridge.

"You only have to feed it once a week. I got this from a friend in Alaska who asked me to take care of it while he did some traveling."

He opened it up. It had an acrid, but not particularly unpleasant or sour, smell.

"How long ago was that?"

"Twelve years."

I gulped. My neighbors wouldn't trust me to water their houseplants for a week while they're away. "I don't know. . . ."

"I'll give you some to take home. It's the only way you're going to bake the kind of bread you're after." We had a delicious lunch on Charlie's patio and returned to the kitchen to make bread (using Charlie's twelve-year-old *levain*, of course) in, of all things, a food processor.

"You ever make bread in a food processor?" Charlie asked.

I was tempted to answer in my W.C. Fields voice, "No, and if I did, I wouldn't admit it." Food processor? What kind of baker was this?

"WHAT EXACTLY DOES HE DO?" I asked Charlie's baker, Skip, at five o'clock the next morning while he formed baguettes in the kitchen of the Copper Beech Inn in Ivoryton. In the early mornings the inn's kitchen became, under Charlie's auspices, a small commercial bakery, doing one thing but doing it extremely well, baking a single type of bread (baguettes) for a single client (the inn). Having spent a full day with Charlie, I still couldn't quite figure out exactly who he was or what he did. Former restaurateur and baker, occasional food industry consultant, author, inventor of the folding bread knife and the HearthKit oven insert (a three-sided baking stone meant to simulate baking in a brick oven), proselytizer, bon vivant, chef, bread authority, tinkerer, Jacques Pépin's *boules* partner—none of these really captured the essence of this youthful seventy-year-old who, above all, was passionate about bread.

"Charlie's a concept person," Skip said, a smile crossing his face. "He likes ideas. Big ideas."

His biggest idea to date is that the best way to knead bread, whether at home or in a bakery, is in a food processor, a method he discovered practically by accident when asked to prepare bread for a party honoring the president of Cuisinart. Van Over was so impressed with the result—and the ease of preparation—that he patented the process for commercial bakeries. One would not expect dough subjected to a razor-sharp metal blade whirring at over 1,300 rpm to make good bread or anything else, but I had sampled a baguette the previous night at dinner and thought it among the best I'd ever eaten.

Charlie attributes the technique's success partly to the fact that the kneading time is short—forty-five seconds—and does not whip air into the dough the way a commercial dough hook does as it lifts and stretches—and aerates—the dough over a ten- or fifteen-minute kneading.

"I thought flour needed oxygen," I'd asked in his kitchen. "Isn't that why it has to age for several weeks after milling?"

True, but once the flour is mixed with water and becomes dough, oxygenation destroys the beta-carotenes in flour and can cause the flour to break down, Charlie had said. His explanation echoed the words of the French bread authority Raymond Calvel, the scientist who'd come up with the technique he dubbed auto-lyse, letting the dough rest and condition before kneading.

In the kitchen, Skip now added instant yeast, water, and salt to the flour and processed it for just forty-five seconds, then went home to have breakfast while the dough fermented. He'd return at eight to make the bread. Later that morning, the baking finished, Charlie came in with a tub of starter for me. He mentioned that he and his wife, Priscilla, were on their way to France in a few weeks.

"Oh, really?" I said. "You wouldn't happen to know of any ancient monasteries over there that still bake bread, would you?" Brother Boniface, the ancient baker at Mepkin Abbey, might be deceased, but the appeal of his ancientness had stayed with me. "I like old things," I explained as we stood in the inn's gleaming, modern stainless steel kitchen. "I think it'd be neat to make bread in a place where they've been baking for a really long time, you know, to get in touch with the tradition."

"I suspect you'll have a hard time finding one," Charlie said, adding that, as an atheist, he wasn't really in touch with that world. "That's a dying tradition. But I'll ask around. Do you know Peter Reinhart? He's written a couple of books on bread, and he's a former monk or something. He might know."

Charlie handed over the *levain*. "Just feed it at least once a week with equal parts flour and water." By weight, he meant. "Leave it out for a few hours after each feeding, then keep it in the fridge. It's like having an undemanding pet."

During the long drive home, Anne kept glancing nervously into the backseat at the starter. I asked her what she was so jittery about.

"Remember friendship bread?"

I almost drove off the road.

Week 21
With Friendships Like This . . .

> Friendship is not so simple.
> —ALBERT CAMUS

"Eeek!" Anne had screamed that fateful day as she opened the refrigerator door. She jumped clear across the room, fulfilling the foreboding I always have upon returning home after a vacation. As I approach our street, I often think I smell smoke, confirming the vague dread I've had all week that the electrical wiring I did without a permit in 1992 has shorted and the house is now a charred wreck. Or the water pipes have burst. Or I left the back door wide open and a family of deer has taken possession of our living room. Not that my neurosis is totally unfounded. We have in fact returned after a week away to find the unreliable front door blown wide open (but no deer or burglars present—the house was apparently too cold for either) and water dripping from the light fixtures. But none of my worries had ever included the refrigerator.

"Calm down," I said, assuming that the milk jug had leaked again. I have an amazing skill for buying the one jug out of sixty that has a pinhole leak in the bottom. I opened the refrigerator.

"Yow!" I cried, jumping backward and slamming the door. "What is that?"

"I don't know," Anne said, "but we're going to need a bigger boat."

"Or Steve McQueen. It looks like the Blob."

Having exhausted our Hollywood analogies, we cautiously approached the refrigerator like a couple of timid explorers entering a cave.

"You go first," Anne said.

I cracked open the door. Slime rolled out onto the floor. What a mess. A glutinous, beige gook was draped over everything on the top two shelves and the inside of the door. Some of it had hardened onto the walls of the refrigerator, creeping into every crevice, coating every surface. In other places it was still fresh and very much alive. Anne spotted the culprit—a one-quart plastic container with the words "Friendship Bread" written on it. The lid had blown off and was nowhere in sight. Anne gingerly picked up the container even as ooze continued to flow over the top, like an active volcano, and dropped it into the garbage.

"Martha's friendship bread," she muttered with disgust as we started mopping up the mess. Several weeks earlier, our babysitter had given us this mysterious container of friendship bread starter, onto which was taped an index card with the recipe for baking friendship bread, plus instructions on passing the starter along.

Apparently it was a well-established tradition in town. Of Amish origin (so the story goes), the idea is to pass this container of bread starter from neighbor to neighbor. If you're lucky enough to have it find you, the instructions call for letting this yeast culture ferment at room temperature for four days before adding equal parts flour, sugar(!), and milk(!!). After letting it sit another five days at room temperature(!!!), you use one-third of it to make your "bread" and pass on the other two-thirds, along with feeding instructions and the bread recipe, to not one but two unsuspecting neighbors.

Rather than being appreciative of this gift, we found ourselves faced with an unplanned project that we had to deal with, ready or not. "My people," Anne noted dryly—meaning the Irish—"bake the bread before giving it away."

"Sounds like a gastronomic chain letter," I mused, rather wary of ingesting this substance that had been sitting on countless counter-tops around town for who knows how many weeks, months, or even years. What really caught my attention was the warning, "DO NOT USE METAL SPOON OR BOWL!" Why? Was it corrosive?

"We're terrible people, aren't we?" Anne said. "It is a nice way for a community to bond."

"That's what Jim Jones said as he was serving up the Kool-Aid. Look at this recipe. A cup of oil, a cup of sugar, and . . . vanilla pudding? This isn't bread, it's a Twinkie." Still, we couldn't very well just throw it out. So until we could figure out exactly what to do with it, we stuck it in the fridge. And promptly forgot about it and went on vacation. But it didn't forget about us. While we were lounging on a North Carolina beach, growing fat on Carbon's Golden Malted waffles, the Blob was growing fat on sugar and spoiled milk, growing and growing and growing and finally bursting from the confines of its plastic Chinese-soup-container prison.

"I'm never going to get this refrigerator clean," Anne muttered as we mopped, wiped, scraped, and rinsed for the next hour. This wasn't mere hyperbole. The hardened slime was more difficult to remove than old paint, and we would ultimately end up throwing out the refrigerator. It was due to be replaced soon, anyway.

In truth, friendship bread did sound like a nice tradition, and this is how bread had been sustained for thousands of years. The

Egyptians, you'll recall, didn't use yeast from a foil packet in the refrigerator; they saved a bit of the dough as a starter from each day's kneading to kick off the next day's bread. And I'm sure they passed a little starter along to family members and neighbors, though probably absent the warning about metal utensils.

Now, with Charlie's twelve-year-old starter from Alaska in the refrigerator, I had joined that tradition, and I was secretly rather happy and proud about it. Twelve years old. But would it give me the alveolar, netted crumb that Charlie had promised? I just hoped that I could keep the beast alive long enough to find out.

The next weekend I baked my first loaf of peasant bread using Charlie's *levain*. I was hooked. The naturally leavened dough rose slowly (even with the dash of instant yeast Charlie recommended to give the *levain* a little boost) and not as high as a commercial-yeast-risen dough—in fact, it hardly rose at all—but making bread this way felt pure and was immensely satisfying. The question was, how would it taste, and, more to the point, would the *levain* give me my gas holes?

At dinner, I sliced off the end piece and held it up for everyone to see.

"Holes!" Katie cried.

"Holes!" Anne yelled.

"Holy sh . . . ," I started to yell.

Charlie had been right. Switching to a *levain* was the key—but not to *every* door. The second slice had fewer holes than the first, and the one after that had none. In fact, the middle 80 percent of the *boule* was too dense and too moist. Still, it was the best loaf of bread I'd ever baked, and I was elated.

The crumb had a rich, natural flavor, a bit tangy but not nearly as strong as a San Francisco sourdough, a result not only of the wild yeast and bacteria in the *levain*, but of the long, cool fermentation, which allowed time for the production of various organic compounds such as alcohols, esters, ketones, and aldehydes—scientists have identified over two hundred such compounds in a fermented dough—which even in their minuscule amounts provide the signature taste and smell that we associate with freshly baked artisan bread.

The real treat, however, was the crust, extraordinarily sweet and bursting with flavor, and for once not rock-hard. If I could get the entire loaf to taste like the crust, I'd have the best bread on the planet. Of course, to make the crumb taste like the crust is physically impossible, for the crust—both its brown color and its unique, sweet flavor—is formed by a complex chemical process known as the Maillard reaction, which begins to take place at about 300 degrees Fahrenheit, a temperature that the surface of the bread can easily reach, but not the moist interior, which never rises above 212 degrees, the boiling point of water.

During the Maillard reaction, proteins under high heat break down (or "denature") and recombine with sugar molecules and all those wonderful products of fermentation to form dozens of new flavor compounds, which in turn break down to form even more compounds, hundreds in all, giving the crust a flavor as different from the crumb as toast (also a Maillard-reaction product) is to bread.

For the first time, I had baked a loaf of bread that I didn't feel I needed to apologize for. As I placed the replenished *levain* in the fridge, though, Anne pointedly asked, "What are you doing with that?"

"I'm putting it in the refrigerator. What does it look like I'm doing with it?"

"I mean next week. When we go on vacation. You're not leaving it here, are you?"

So it could creep out of the container and destroy another refrigerator?

"Of course not," I improvised, thinking this was like having a pet. "I'm bringing it with us. Got to make the bread."

Even on vacation.

How to Make Perfect Thin and Crispy French Fries

By J. Kenji Lopez-Alt

From seriouseats.com

With an M.I.T. degree and a cooking resumé from some of
Boston's finest restaurants, it's only natural that Kenji Lopez-
Alt's freelance food writing would focus on kitchen science,
producing features like the Food Lab for goodeater.org and
the Burger Lab for seriouseats.com.

N.B. I apologize in advance for the length of this post.
French fries are a pretty epic subject for me . . . .
I'm gonna come right out and say something that I'm sure you
won't all openly agree with: McDonald's french fries are great. At
their best, they are everything a french fry should be: salty, crisp,
light, and not greasy. Granted, you get the occasional odd franchise
that lets 'em sit under the heat lamp for a couple hours too long,
but on the whole, I find it remarkable that the bigwigs have discovered a way to create a frozen fry that even a one armed eyeless
chimp has trouble screwing up. And I know, because they've got
one working the fry station at the franchise on my corner.

To be absolutely honest, I've never been able to make fries as
good as theirs (shhhhh!). Sure, my thick-cut pub-style fries are su-
per-potatoey and fantastic, and when I'm in the mood for them,
my seasoned steak fries can't be beat, but for thin, super-crisp fries
(I'm talking the kind that only appear in fast food restaurants and
French bistros under the name frites)? I'm always better off running down to the take-out window than bothering to fry them
myself at home.

Until now.

I've been literally giddy with the quality of the fries that have been coming out of my kitchen for the last two days. My wife won't hear the end of it. Even my puppy is wondering why his owner keeps exclaiming "Holy s--t that's good!" every half hour from the kitchen. I've cooked over 43 batches of fries in the last three days, and I'm happy to report that I've finally found a way to consistently reach crisp, golden Nirvana.

The Anatomy of a Perfect Fry

There are a few factors that go into making a perfect fry:

Perfect Fry Factor #1: The exterior must be very crisp, but not tough.

In order to achieve this crispness, the surface structure of a fry must be riddled with micro-bubbles. It's these tiny crisp bubbles that increase the surface area of the fry, making it extra crunchy. Ideally, this layer should only be as thick as it needs to be to add crispness. Any thicker, and you start running into leathery territory.

Perfect Fry Factor #2: The interior must be intact, fluffy, and have a strong potato flavor.

Fries with a pasty, mealy, or gummy interior or even worse, the dreaded state known as "hollow-fry" (when the interior is missing entirely) are an automatic fail in my fry book.

Perfect Fry Factor #3: The fry must be an even, light golden blond.

Fries that are too dark or are spotty have an offputting burnt flavor that distracts from the potato. Light golden but perfectly crisp is how I want my fries to be.

Perfect Fry Factor #4: The fry must stay crisp and tasty for at least as long as it takes to eat a full serving.

Fries that comes straight out of the fryer are almost always perfectly crisp. The true test of a great fry is whether or not it remains crisp and edible a few minutes later after its been sitting on your plate. [. . .]

So how does one going about achieving these goals? The traditional double fry method (once at low temp, then again at high temp) works, but it's far from foolproof, and fails to meet all of the requirements I've set for a perfect fry. For one thing, the fries inevitably come out too brown—sometimes massively so. For another, they lose their crunch within a few minutes after coming out of the fryer. Clearly the method needs an overhaul. I suppose I could do what the McDonald's Corporation did and spend millions of dollars researching exactly how to accomplish fry perfection time after time anywhere around the world, but unfortunately Serious Eats doesn't pay me well enough to do that. I'm also understaffed, to say the least. So I decided to go with the next best alternative: steal their recipe.

That's much easier said than done.

Hamburgling

Anyone with a buck can get a batch of fully cooked McDonald's fries, but I was after something more. I wanted to get fries from the store in their fully frozen state so that I could examine their surface for clues on how they were parcooked, as well as attempt to fry them myself at home to discover if there is any secret in the fry oil in the shops.

I figured I'd just be able to walk into the store and order them straight from the cashier.

"Welcome to McDonald's, may I take your order?"

"Yes Ma'am. I'd like a large fries please, hold the cooking."

"Excuse me?"

I know she's already said no in her head, but I press on just the same: "Um . . . I'd just like the frozen fries please."

"I'm sorry sir, we just don't do that."

Time for some intimidation tactics: "Ok. Could I speak to the manager please?"

"I am the manager."

Sh–t. I bring out the really big guns: "Listen, the thing is, my wife is pregnant—like really pregnant—and she sent me on a quest for McDonald's french fries. But she only likes them really fresh, like straight out of the fryer fresh, so I figured I'd just get some frozen, and fry them for her at home. You know how it is. Women—no accounting for'em, right?"

She remains unimpressed, and needless to say, I go home fry-less, contemplating whether attempting to leverage an unborn, un-conceived son in exchange for a couple dozen frozen potato sticks is grounds for eternal damnation. Thank God I'm an atheist.

In a last ditch effort, I appeal to my Facebook fans for some as-sistance, promising cold hard cash and full credit in this story to anyone who could get me a stash of frozen McDonald's fries. Within 24 hours, I had received this email from a Grant Held:

Kenji, you put forth an excellent challenge; I enjoy both chal-lenges and your food writing immensely, so I came up with an ex-cellent plan that worked the first try.

Getting your frozen fries was simply a matter of finding the right fraternity man; one who had the ability to make up extem-poraneous bullsh-t and the all important "charm factor." Some would say possessing these attributes can help you get laid in col-lege, but I plead The Fifth. . . .

The plan involved me printing out a fake list of items needed for a Scavenger Hunt sponsored by "The Simplot Foundation." A "Mr. Simplot" had endowed an annual prize for the winning team of the scavenger hunt, which would be used to fund the "research projects of the members of the winning team each year." (Mem-bers also had to belong to the Harold McGee Society and Order of Brillat-Savarin.)

I walked into the McD's on xxxxxxx. (The exact location has been removed because we don't want to get the manager fired.)

I had pre-printed a list of items for said made up "Scavenger Hunt." (I basically Googled "Scavenger Hunt Lists" and added "Frozen McDonald's french fries.")

I walked in, asked for the manager and explained the scavenger hunt. I said I needed 25 fries, which I was willing to pay for, but they had to be frozen. Her English was not ideal, so I spoke Span-ish, and a young associate took kindly upon me and explained what I needed. The manager agreed, but thought I was asking for 25 FREE packages of cooked fries!!! And she was willing to give them to me!!! (She said my accent was great but my grammar was terrible . . . oh well . . .)

I said I needed FROZEN fries, which really perplexed her, but my young McD's associate friend explained the concept of a scavenger hunt and soon enough I was invited into the kitchen and she grabbed a handful of fries and placed them in the zip lock bag I brought with me.

Grant, you are a genius amongst men, and I am forever in your debt.

The handoff was made the next day, and I finally had a batch of frozen McDonald's fries on which to operate.

Deconstructing the Arches

The first thing I noticed was the surface texture of the fries. They seemed smooth, but on closer inspection, I noticed that they were dotted with tiny tiny bubbles, indicating that they had definitely been fried at least once prior to arriving at the store. I measured them with calipers and found that they were precisely ¼ of an inch thick. A good size for optimizing crust to interior ratio.

McDonald's used to fry their potatoes in beef tallow, giving them extra flavor and making them extra crisp, but they stopped doing that years ago. But perhaps there's still something magic about their oil? To test this, I fried up a batch of the frozen fries in 375°F peanut oil, letting them cook for about 3 minutes before draining, seasoning, and tasting.

They were just as perfect as the fries at the store. That answers the first question: there is no magic in the oil. Something must be done to those potatoes during the pre-processing that makes them unique.

For the next phase, I started doing some research and caught a lucky break by finding this article online, which essentially runs through the whole process of what goes on in a McDonald's potato processing plant as told by LeAron Plackett, a thirteen-year-long employee. The parts that interested me most were on the second page:

The fries are then flumed out of the A.D.R. room to the "blancher." The blancher is a large vessel filled with one hundred and seventy degree water. The trip through the blancher takes about fifteen minutes. . . . After the fries leave the blancher, they are dried and then it's off to the "fryer," which is filled with one hundred percent vegetable oil. The oil is heated to three hundred and sixty five degrees and the fries take a fifty second dip before being conveyed to the "de-oiler shaker," where excess oil is "shook off."

Bingo.

So McDonald's does indeed use a double fry method, but it's far from the traditional one. Rather than a slow low temperature fry for the first round, the fries get dunked into very hot oil for only 50 seconds (the second fry is then carried out at the actual location). In addition to this, the potatoes get a pre-fry blanching step in hot water. What could the purpose of this be?

To answer that question, it's important to understand exactly what happens when a french fry is cooked.

The Balance of Pectin, Starch, and Simple Sugars

Like all plants and animals, potatoes are composed of cells. These cells are held together by pectin, a form of sugar that acts as a type of glue. These cells also contain starch granules—tiny sacs that resemble water balloons, as well as simple sugars. When these starch granules are exposed to water and heat, they begin to swell, eventually bursting, and releasing a shower of swollen starch molecules. Now the problem is, in order to get the ideal crust, all three of these elements must be in the proper balance, and the proper state. Too many simple sugars, and your potato will brown long before it crisps. If pectin has broken down too much before the starch granules have had a chance to burst and release their sticky innards, your potatoes will either fail to form a crust, will fall apart before it gets a chance to, or in the worst case will cook up completely hollow [...]

That's not a good thing.

Pre-cooking the fries in a water bath the way McDonald's does accomplishes two goals. First, it rinses off excess simple sugars, helping the fries attain a light gold color, instead of a deep dark brown. Secondly, it activates an enzyme called pectin methylesterase (PME). According to an article in the *Journal of Agricultural and Food Chemistry*, PME induces calcium and magnesium to act as a sort of buttress for pectin. They strengthen the pectin's hold on the potato cell's walls, which helps the potatoes stay firmer and more intact when cooked to a higher temperature. That's why the surface of a

McDonald's fry looks the way it does: rather than blistering into large bubbles like a traditional double-fried french fry does, the reinforced walls form the super-tiny bubbles that give them their extra crunch.

Now, like most enzymes, PME is only active within a certain temperature range, acting faster and faster as the temperature gets higher until, like a switch, it shuts off completely once it reaches a certain level. 170°F is just under that cutoff point.

My objective just became much clearer: in order to get my fries ultra crisp, I'd need to find a way to strengthen their pectin before allowing their starch granules to burst.

Bringing Home the Gold

The most obvious way to do this is just to copy McDonald's exactly: cook the potatoes in a precisely maintained 170°F water bath for 15 minutes. I tried it using my Sous-Vide Supreme, followed by a fry at 360°F for 50 seconds, and a second fry at 375°F for 3 ½ minutes. It worked like a charm. The fries tasted nearly identical to those that come from McDonald's. Of course, now two new questions entered my head: What about for those poor souls who don't have a temperature-controlled water bath? And more importantly, now that I've got the fries down, could I make them even better? I mean, they taste fantastic now, but we all know that McDonald's fries get soggy pretty darn fast. If these fries were really going to be perfect, I'd have to address that issue.

To solve the first problem, my initial thought was to start the potatoes in cold water, and slowly bring it up to a simmer. My hope was that by doing this, they'd spend enough time under the 170°F cutoff point to improve their structure adequately. No dice. The potatoes were certainly better than ones dunked straight into the fryer, but they didn't come close to the originals. Next I tried adding a measured amount of boiling water to a pot containing the cut potatoes. I calculated exactly how much water I'd need in order for it to equilibrate to 170°F. It worked a little better, but the water temperature dropped off too quickly for it to be effective. Was I gonna have to break out the beer cooler for this one? There had to be another way.

That's when I thought—perhaps there is another way to strengthen pectin without having to rely on some fickle enzyme (I've never liked enzymes anyway), and it struck me: apple pie.

What's this got to do with french fries? Well everyone who's ever baked an apple pie knows that different apples cook differently. Some retain their shape, while others turn to mush. The difference largely has to do with their acidity. Thus super tart apples like Granny Smith will stay fully intact, while sweeter apples like a Macoun will almost completely dissolve. Just like a potato, apple cells are held together by pectin. Moral of the story: acid slows the breakdown of pectin.

What if rather than trying to fiddle with temperature, I just relied on the use of acid to help the potatoes keep their structure?

I tried bringing two pots of cut potatoes to a boil side by side, the first with plain water, and the second with water spiked with vinegar at a ratio of one tablespoon per quart. [. . .] The fries boiled in plain water disintegrated, making them nearly impossible to pick up. When I added them to the hot oil, they broke apart even further. On the other hand, those boiled in the vinegared water remained perfectly intact, even after boiling for a full ten minutes. When fried, they had fabulously crisp crusts with tiny, bubbly, blistered surfaces that stayed crisp even when they were completely cool. As for the flavor, if I tasted really hard, I could pick up a faint vinegary undertone, though I wouldn't have if I didn't know it was there. Even knowing it was there, it wasn't unpleasant at all. After all, I'm used to putting my fries in ketchup or mayo, both of which contain plenty of acid. [. . .]

Getting Inside the Fluffy Interior

Now that I'd perfected the crust, the final issue to deal with was that of the interior. One last question remained: how to maximize the flavor of the interior. In order to stay fluffy and not gummy, a lot of the interior moisture needs to be expelled in the cooking process, so my goal should be to make this evaporation as easy as possible. I figure that so far, by cooking it all the way to boiling point, I'm doing pretty much the right thing—the more cooked the potatoes are, the more the cell structure breaks down, and the easier it is for water to be expelled. To confirm this, I cooked three batches of potatoes, starting each in a pot of cold, vinegared water, and bringing them up to various final temperatures (170°F, 185°F, and 212°F) before draining and double-frying them. Not surprisingly, the boiled potatoes had the best internal structure. Luckily, they were the easiest to make as well.

But was there anything more I could do? I thought back to those McDonald's fries and realized a vital step that I had neglected to test: freezing. Every batch of McDonald's fries is frozen before being shipped out to the stores. I always figured this step was for purely economic reasons, but perhaps there was more to it?

I tried freezing half a batch of fries before frying them and tasted them side-by-side against the other half. [. . .] The improvement was undeniable. The frozen fries had a distinctly fluffier interior, while the unfrozen ones were still ever-so-slightly gummy. It makes perfect sense. Freezing the potatoes causes their moisture to convert to ice, forming sharp, jagged crystals. These crystals damage the cell structure of the potato, making it easier for them to be released once they are heated and convert to steam. The best part? Because freezing actually improves them, I can do the initial blanching and frying steps in large batches, freeze them, and have a constant supply of ready-to-fry potatoes right in my freezer just like Ronald himself!

I know it's bad form to toot your own horn, but I'm simply amazed that these fries have been coming out of my own kitchen. I've been eating fries in various shades of good or bad constantly for the past few days, and I'm absolutely sick of them, yet I am still eating them even as I sit here and type. I really hope my wife doesn't mind greasy keyboards. You never know what's gonna set her off.

For instance—she gets mad when I say things like that about her on completely public forums. Go figure.

Perfect French Fries

serves four
Note: Potatoes can be frozen after step 2. To freeze potatoes, place entire sheet tray in freezer. After fully frozen, place in Ziploc bags, press out air, and freeze for up to 2 months. If cooking straight from frozen, do not cook more than ¼ batch

at a time unless you have a large vessel for deep frying, as oil
temperature will drop too precipitously.

Ingredients

2 pounds russet potatoes (about 4 large), peeled and cut into
¼-inch by ¼-inch fries (keep potatoes stored in a bowl of
water)

2 tablespoons distilled white vinegar

Kosher salt

2 quarts peanut oil

Procedure

1. Place potatoes and vinegar in saucepan and add 2 quarts
of water and 2 tablespoons of salt. Bring to a boil over high
heat. Boil for 10 minutes. Potatoes should be fully tender, but
not falling apart. Drain and spread on paper towel-lined
rimmed baking sheet. Allow to dry for five minutes.

2. Meanwhile, heat oil in 5-quart Dutch oven or large
wok over high heat to 400°F. Add ⅓ of fries to oil (oil temperature should drop to around 360°F). Cook for 50 seconds,
agitating occasionally with wire mesh spider, then remove to
second paper-towel lined rimmed baking sheet. Repeat with
remaining potatoes (working in two more batches), allowing
oil to return to 400°F after each addition. Allow potatoes to
cool to room temperature, about 30 minutes. Continue with
step 3, or for best results, freeze potatoes at least over night, or
up to 2 months.

3. Return oil to 400°F over high heat. Fry half of potatoes
until crisp and light golden brown, about 3 ½ minutes, adjust-
ing heat to maintain at around 360°F. Drain in a bowl lined
with paper towels and season immediately with kosher salt.
Cooked fries can be kept hot and crisp on a wire rack set on
a sheet tray in a 200°F oven while second batch is cooked.
Serve immediately.

Rather Special and Strangely Popular: A Milk Toast Exemplary

By John Thorne

From *Rather Special and Strangely Popular: A Milk Toast Exemplary*

John Thorne generally practices his culinary archeology—
resurrecting old recipes while spinning a kitchen yarn or
two—in his homey newsletter Simple Cooking. This essay,
however, was published in an endearingly old-fashioned
format: a tiny hand-printed limited-edition booklet.

Elspeth's Milk Toast

This recipe is rather special and strangely popular. Toast a few
slices of very thinly cut bread. Butter lightly and dust with salt
and pepper. Put in a soup plate and keep hot. Add enough hot
milk to soften, but not to swamp. Serve at once.

—MOLLY KEAN'S *Nursery Cooking*

Molly Keane is a noted Irish novelist and playwright. I
had bought her book on nursery food for a lark, and
was leafing through it in that idle way one does, nodding to familiar friends and sizing up potential new ones, when my eyes fell on
"Elspeth's Milk Toast." I read the introductory sentence, then the
short recipe, then faltered as I moved to turn the page.

Whatever, I wondered, could she mean by "rather special" and,
more, by "strangely popular"? I had never eaten milk toast, but I
was aware of it—as one is, I guess, growing up in New England . . .
or, at least, spending time with old New England cookbooks. I

certainly understood enough to know that this recipe was exactly—no more, no less—what I would expect a milk toast recipe to be.

On the other hand, I had no reason to think that Molly Keane was deluded. Maybe, I thought, she was onto something that I was unaccountably missing. I put the book down and went over to the bookcase that holds our not insignificant collection of English, Scottish, and Irish cookbooks, to see what they had to say on the subject.

Then came my next surprise. I looked through old ones and new ones, books as magisterial as the original *Mrs. Beeton* and as specialized as *The English Breakfast*, Kaori O'Connor's fascinating collection of facsimile Victorian cookbooks on that subject, to find . . . *nothing*.

The closest I came was a recipe in Miss Allen's oddly conceived *Breakfast Dishes for Every Morning of Three Months* (1884).

Bread and Milk

Cut the bread into dice, put them into a basin; boil the milk, and when boiling pour it over the bread. Cover the cup up for five minutes, and then stand it by the fire for five more. Sugar to taste.

This recipe, unappealing as it is (not only doesn't it sound very good, but one gets the feeling it isn't meant to be so. Analeptic, maybe; tasty, not at all), gave me a hint, and some further searching confirmed it. The British have always eaten milk-sopped bread, and it doesn't need be so punishing. Samuel Pepys, for instance, writes in his diary about happily dining on "Creame and brown bread."* However, when it comes to milk *toast*, we are speaking pure American. **

---

* This is quoted in *Pepys at Table*, a collection of his diary entries concerning food. The book's editor, Christopher Driver—channeling our new pal, Miss Allen—opines that "few twentieth-century stomachs could handle so rich a dish," to which one can only reply, "Speak for yourself." As it turns out, a thick slice of really good whole-wheat bread soaked in warm cream is quite an epicurean delight.

milk toast n. U.S. Toast softened in milk. . . . Martin Amis, London
Fields: Milk toast, thought Guy. An American dish, served with
honey or syrup.
— *Oxford English Dictionary*

According to Stuart Berg Flexner in *I Hear America Talking*, his
popular history of our linguistic ways, the phrase "milk toast" is
American and began appearing in the 1820s. Our collection of old
American cookbooks doesn't really start until the mid-1800s, but
milk toast does turn up in those, and continues to do so with in-
creasing frequency right through the rest of the century.

Unfortunately, these recipes are uniformly nasty and would
have killed my interest in the dish permanently—had it not been
for Google Books and a bit of good luck. One of my early "milk
toast" searches there ferreted out a passage from *The Wabash: or Ad-
ventures of an English Gentleman's Family in the Interior of America*
(1855). In it, the author tells of encountering milk toast at a breakfast served at Congress Hall (a hotel) in Saratoga Springs.

Hot rolls of every description and numberless little dishes of
sausages covered the table, together with large platters of milk
toast. This delicacy is made of slices of toast, buttered and sprinkled with pepper and salt, and laid in a dish of warm milk, which
serves as a sauce to the rest: most of us were very fond of this
American toast.

Up until that moment I had associated milk toast with the nursery and sick bed of yesteryear. As a toast lover, I welcomed any dish
that put it to good use, but curiosity and appetite are only occasionally twins. When I set out on this search I had no intention of
trying milk toast, and certainly no plans to write about it.

** It eventually occurred to me to go back and remind myself who Elspeth,
provider of Molly Keane's recipe, actually was. She turned out to be from
Switzerland, which shifts the question of how milk toast appeared in an Irish
cookbook to how a Swiss au pair happened to make it for the Keane children.
Is it also a Swiss dish? I leave this mystery to be unraveled by more intrepid
investigators than myself.

However, there was both a contagious relish in the description of those platters of milk toast, as well as an element of complete surprise. Where we today would have expected this foreign visitor to fall into rapture about our griddle cakes or hoe cakes or flapjacks, here he was ecstatic over . . . milk toast?

This fascination was enough to not only make me want to try the dish myself but carry me through the profound disappointment of discovering that *all* the early "milk toast" recipes in those aforesaid old cookbooks were for toast sopped in *white sauce*—milk thickened with flour or cornstarch.

This is a *terrible* thing, and why it should be the case here, I simply don't know. I suspect the perpetual and tiresome gentility of most period cookbook authors, forever preferring the luscious thickness of a sauce, however faux, over honest plain milk or, more to the point, pricey and perishable sweet cream.

So it is that flour is added to the milk toast recipe in every edition of *The Fannie Farmer Cookbook* until Marion Cunningham, newly at the helm, removed it from the 12th edition. Years later, in her *Breakfast Book*, she would lament:

> Why in the world did we ever abandon milk toast? Although it sounds deceptively bland and dull, it isn't; and as the Victorians discovered, it can revive the peaked or sad. Nourishing and soul-satisfying, milk toast will banish the blues.

I suggest she turn around and point an accusatory finger at her predecessors—then give them a rap on the knuckles from me.

The earliest recipe I found for milk toast without this fiddling was in *Mrs. Rorer's New Cook Book* (1902). Her version is simple and to the point, and—see the caution—gives the dish the right sort of attentive respect.

> Milk Toast is made by pouring scalding hot milk over dry toast. A tablespoonful of butter may be added to each quart of milk. To prevent scorching, heat the milk in a double boiler. Caution.—The main point is to pour the milk over the crisp warm toast at the very last moment, and serve quickly.

If Fannie Farmer had been so wise, this American classic might not have become the forgotten dish it is today.

EVEN SO, real milk toast was never lost. Search the vernacular records and you will find such memories as those recorded by the Southern herbalist A. L. Tommie Bass, born in 1908. In *Plain Southern Food*, he recalls that when his father had "a bad stomach," he'd ask for some milk toast to soothe it.

> Mother would first brown the bread and then she would put it in a bowl or something, and pour the milk over it, and add the sugar. Now, the way they made it in the army, why, they toasted the bread and dipped it in honey and milk, and put it back in the stove and browned it, you know. They didn't add spice, but some folks does.

If you think about it, you can't imagine Tommie Bass's mother making a white sauce to cover the toast—not because it would be too much trouble, but because it would be frivolous and wrong, for the same reason that a child prefers a mug of chicken noodle to one of cream of chicken soup. There is comfort and pleasure even in canned noodles, but there is none in murk.

Consider, from that perspective, the version of milk toast that Tommie Bass remembers from the army: toast dipped in honey and milk, then crisped up in the oven. The recipient can relish each step of its making, as that slab of toast gets tastier and tastier. By the time you sit down to eat it, you're already half in a swoon.

When President James Garfield was shot by an assassin in 1881, he lingered on for months, for most of that time with a bullet lodged in his spine. He had a hard time keeping down solid food, so he was fed various meat broths, scraped raw beef, breast of woodcock, *koumiss* (fermented mare's milk), rum and other spirits, and, almost always, milk toast. At one point,

> the President said to Mrs. Garfield, who was sitting by his bedside, that he would like a piece of milk toast . . . Mrs. Garfield thereupon prepared the toast carefully herself, and the patient ate with

apparent relish and enjoyment a piece about half as large as a man's hand. . . .

Once you've shaken off that last odd image, let your mind step away from dish to the scene itself: the failing patient and the comforting wife who prepares for him a dish that is easily and quickly made, soothing to eat, and preceded by the primal aromas of hot milk and toast.

All this becomes more potent still, when the recipient is present during the ritual of actually making the dish. And this is especially so if that person is a sleepy, hungry child.

Small matters often seem great to children. Now, I would not willingly forget how, when I was a little girl, dear Grandma Wayne used to tempt my poor appetite, of mornings, with *such* milk-toast as no one else, I was very sure, could ever make. I have never, to this day, outgrown the taste thus cultivated for it, and often when I am feeling out of sorts, and nearly sick, my thoughts turn to the blessed time when "grandma" made milk-toast in a pint basin for me in the mornings of long ago. . . .
—*Arthur's Illustrated Home Magazine* (1874)

Even Mr. Toaster, who teaches the young heroine of Jane Eayre Fryer's *The Mary Frances Cook Book* (1912) to make milk toast for her ill mother, seems to have had the same childhood experience. When Mary Frances has the toast ready to bring upstairs, he exclaims, "That's right! That's the way my grandmother made it," and adds longingly, "That milk toast would taste awfully good." (She politely offers him a bite, but he declines, confessing that anything he puts in his mouth falls right out behind, which is why he is so thin.)

Maggie Waldron, in *Cold Spaghetti At Midnight*, a book devoted to all sorts of spell-casting food, captures the milk toast ritual from the mother's perspective.

The very name of milk toast brought comfort to my daughter Sara. Especially when I suggested it might hit the spot. She always had it in the same bowl, made exactly the same way. The bread had to be white and dense and nicely toasted, two slices for a serving, well buttered and sprinkled with cinnamon, with whole milk heated to simmering, and seasoned with salt and a generous grind of pepper. I watch in amazement as she goes through the same ritual with her own little girl.

For an experience to become a ritual, or at least possess the properties of one, the things involved must be few, so that their meaning is not diffused, and they must somehow assume a perceptible weight. They attain this partly from the reassurance that comes of being "just so," and partly by already possessing the solidity of the absolutely familiar.

As soon as I started to assemble the ingredients for my own first batch of milk toast, these same qualities began to assert themselves, starting with the loaf of bread. The artisan bakery where we get ours makes several wonderful loaves, but none of them seemed the thing for milk toast.

I had in mind the sort of old-fashioned loaf that grandma's grandma used to make, rectangular below and puffed out above, with a thin brown crust and a soft but chewy (and flavorful!) interior. This, of course, is what store-bought bread generally looks like, but never really is. Besides, it's all sliced, and I wanted to cut my own to just the right thickness.

I went to our local supermarket and, for the first time in years, moseyed down the bread aisle. The variety was simultaneously astonishing and depressing. What was once, all on its own, considered the staff of life was now scattered with flax seeds and sold as a nutritional supplement. Most of it was sheer fakery—but, even worse, a few dense and sprout-riddled loaves might have been exactly that.

Matt suggested that I try the other, more conventional bakery in town. There I found what they called a "French loaf," although I doubt any bakery in France offers anything like it. This was a lazy sort of *pain de mie,* baked like ordinary bread rather than in the traditional closed pan that produces a loaf with a perfect rectangular shape and very tender crust.

However, "mie" means "crumb"—*pain de mie* has an interior that is tasty, tender, and moist, yet firm enough for slicing—and so had this bread, too. It was, essentially, a loaf of good old-fashioned white bread, meant for slicing, not pulling apart with your fingers, and just the thing for making milk toast.

As to the milk, we live in an area that still has local dairies, including one with all Jersey cows. Getting first-rate milk is no problem at all (if we wanted, we could get it home delivered in glass bottles!)

It was time to fire up the toaster.

By now, of course, I had perused many, many milk toast recipes, all of them similar but few of them the same. There were those who sweetened their milk toast and those who salted and peppered it (or both). There were those who buttered their toast—some on one side and others on both sides—and those who buttered their toast *and* melted butter in the hot milk. There were a few who included a hot oven as part of their method, most elaborately by bake-toasting pullet-sized morsels of bread and then sopping them with the hot milk.

I decided, however, that being naturally fussy about my milk, my bread, and the method of toasting it was plenty enough without any fancy flourishes (although the careful reader will note that some tagged along anyway).

SETTING THE SCENE. I didn't invite Matt to join me when I made milk toast for the first time, fearing the whole exercise would teeter over into paralyzing self-consciousness. In the future, when she is in a blue mood, I can surprise her with a bowl of it. Or, even better, hint around that, when I'm in a similar condition, she might surprise *me* with it.

In any case, I made milk toast on a morning when she was away at work. I laid my place at the table, set out the (unsalted) butter and sliced some of it into pats so these could soften a bit while I made the toast. Next to it, I put a small bowl of coarse sea salt and the pepper grinder.

MAKING THE TOAST. I sliced the bread as thick as I could and still have it fit into the toaster slot. I then set the toaster at its lowest setting and pushed the toast down three or four times, rotating it a quarter turn before each descent. This got the slice toasted evenly all over, something no toaster seems capable of doing on its own.

HEATING THE MILK. I have bad luck heating milk on the stove. I close my eyes for *one second* to moisten my eyeballs and, when I open them, the milk has boiled over and burned on the stove into a plaque of unremovable scum. So I poured the milk (about one cup) into a small pitcher and heated it in the microwave in thirty-second increments. It was plenty hot after three rounds. To further things along, I put the pitcher into the shallow bowl in which I planned to eat the milk toast, and heated this as well.

ASSEMBLING THE DISH. I sat down at the table, put one of the pre-cut pats of butter onto the center of the piece of toast, and slowly poured the steaming milk over it, thus melting the butter and letting it spread over the top of the toast (and leaving a nice soft mass of it in the center, perfect for dipping). I did this a splash at a time, waiting until the toast had completely absorbed it. I wanted my milk toast to be sopped to perfection, but still capable of being eaten with a fork. The last thing I wanted was mush.

With pepper, I was prodigal; with salt, a miser. Despite the unsalted butter, I needed the merest pinch, sprinkled on each bite after I neatly cut it out with the edge of my fork.

THE EATING. It is tempting to become dewy-eyed at this moment—the steamy scent of the hot milk mingling with the toasty, wheaty aroma of the toast as the golden pat of butter liquifies, the fork tines slip into pulpy softness—tempting, because all these things are true.

But that would make milk toast seem like something you eat because it's delicious, and you don't, really. If you let the weight of the moment rest on that idea, you'll be disappointed. Milk toast is not a gourmet fantasy. It is about something else.

Usually, when I like what's set on my plate, I can't stop eating until it's all gone. I don't like that this is so, but there it is. Milk toast, however, is as nothing if eaten like this. You surrender to it and not the other way around. You don't step into a grove of cedars and huff and puff to get your lungs full of that vivifying resinous smell. Gasping spoils everything; the point is to just stand there and quietly breathe.

Milk toast is, at its best, quietly absorbing sustenance. It comforts; it gently sets you adrift in a pleasant, contemplative mist. In fact, it's like having a cat sleeping in your lap—you only really enjoy it when you're in the mood, but then there's nothing quite like it.

That, I think, is why the dish is "rather special"; it is "strangely popular" because those who aren't on its wavelength will never get what it's all about. We each have to find our own way to milk toast, and so no two recipes for it will ever be exactly the same.

Rôties À la Crème ou au Lait
Picayune Creole Cook Book (1901)

6 slices of Bread.
1 Pint of Hot Cream or Milk.
1 Tablespoonful of Butter.

Toast the bread nicely, and butter well on both sides. Lay in a dish, and pour over hot milk. Serve hot.

Or, heat one pint of cream, add one large tablespoonful of butter, and pour over the hot toast. Slightly stale bread may be utilized in this way. This is a great supper dish among the Creole plantation homes of Louisiana.

Milk Toast
Child Care Part 1. The Preschool Age, Mrs. Max West (1918)

Put on the table hot crisp toast or twice-baked bread (see below) and a pitcher of hot milk, slightly salted. One-fourth teaspoonful of salt to a cupful of milk is sufficient. Pour the milk over the toast as needed, using hot bowls or deep saucers for serving. This is the easiest way of serving milk toast, and, if care is taken to have all the dishes hot and to salt the milk, it is usually acceptable.

Twice-Baked Bread. Bread cut or torn into small pieces and heated in a very slow oven until thoroughly dried and very delicately browned is good food for children. . . . The advantage of tearing instead of cutting the bread is that it makes it lighter in texture and easier to eat. The crust should be torn into pieces about 2 inches wide. The inside of an ordinary loaf of bread will make 16 pieces of conventional size. Tear first across the loaf and then tear each half into eight pieces. . . . It is well to keep the crusts separate, as otherwise they are likely to get too brown.

Milk Toast

Stillmeadow Kitchen, Gladys Taber (1947)

I am one of those queer people who really like milk toast. Toast bread lightly, spread it with butter, and pour over it 1 cup of hot milk, add a big piece of butter, salt and pepper. Eat in a thoughtful mood. By tomorrow, you will want a poached egg dropped on it too.

Baked Milk Toast

Marion Harland's Complete Cook Book (1906)

Trim off the crust from slices nearly half an inch thick; toast to a uniform light brown. Have on the range a pan of boiling water, salted. As you remove each slice from the toaster dip quickly into the boiling water and lay in a well-buttered pudding dish, buttering the toast while smoking hot and salting each slice. When all the soaked toast is packed into place, cover with scalding milk in which has been melted a tablespoonful of butter. Cover closely and bake fifteen minutes.

This is so far superior to the usual insipid preparation of milk toast that no one who has eaten the first can enjoy the poor parody.

Corn Bread Milk Toast

Maggie Waldron, *Cold Spaghetti At Midnight*

When you have a stray piece of corn bread, and the world is too much with you.

Split 1 large square of corn bread or 1 corn muffin and toast under the broiler. Spread with 1 tablespoon of butter and place in the center of a big warm bowl. Add 1½ cups of hot milk and sprinkle with nutmeg. (Serves 1.)

Milk Toast

M.F.K. Fisher, "The Midnight Egg and Other Restorers," *Bon Appétit* (1978)

To make a restful, nourishing, delicious Milk Toast, on a cold night or any time at all when solitude seems indicated, warm a generous bowl while making two slices of toast. The bread should be firm and hearty, but not strongly flavored as is rye or pumpernickel.

Warm two cups of creamy milk, just to the simmer point. Butter the toast generously and cut into cubes. Season the milk with salt, pepper and paprika if desired. Put the bits of buttery toasted bread in the warm bowl, pour the seasoned milk over them, and walk gently to wherever you have decided to feel right in your skin.

Cream Toast

Margery Taylor and Frances McNaught, *The Early Canadian Galt Cook Book* (1898)

Cream toast is a delightful, old-fashioned supper dish, not at all like its modern substitute, milk toast. Heat the cream by setting the dish containing it in a dish of boiling water. When the cream is thoroughly heated, salt it and drop thin slices of delicate brown toast in it. When all the toast is dipped, serve what hot cream remains in a gravy boat. As the toast is served, pour a little cream from the boat over it. This toast must be served very hot.

The Recipe File

WHAT'S THE RECIPE?:
OUR HUNGER FOR COOKBOOKS

By Adam Gopnik

From *The New Yorker*

New Yorker cultural essayist Adam Gopnik is a wonderful
companion for armchair travels through the food world.
Something tickles his curiosity—a stack of cookbooks, say—
and before you know it, we're off on an enthusiast's joy ride.

A man and a woman lie in bed at night in the short hour
between kid sleep and parent sleep, turning down page
corners as they read. She is leafing through a fashion magazine, he
through a cookbook. Why they read these things mystifies even the
readers. The closet and the cupboard are both about as full as
they're going to get, and though we can credit the fashion reader
with at least wanting to know what is in fashion when she sees it,
what can the recipe reader possibly be reading for? The shelf of
cookbooks long ago overflowed, so that the sad relations and failed
hopes ("Monet's Table," "A Drizzle of Honey: The Lives and
Recipes of Spain's Secret Jews") now are stacked horizontally, high
up. The things he knows how to make that are actually in demand
are as fixed as any cocktail pianist's set list, and for a clientele of
children every bit as conservative as the barflies around that piano:
make Parmesan-crusted chicken—the "Feelings" of food—every
night and they would be delighted. Yet the new cookbooks show
up in bed, and the corners still go down.

Vicarious pleasure? More like deferred frustration. Anyone who
cooks knows that it is in following recipes that one first learns the
anticlimax of the actual, the perpetual disappointment of the thing

achieved. I learned it as I learned to bake. When I was in my early teens, the sick yearning for sweets that adolescents suffer drove me, in afternoons taken off from school, to bake, which, miraculously, meant just doing what the books said and hoping to get what they promised to yield. I followed the recipes as closely as I could: dense Boston cream pie, Rigó Jancsi slices, *Sacher Torte* with apricot jam between the layers. The potential miracle of the cookbook was immediately apparent: you start with a feeling of greed, find a list of rules, assemble a bunch of ingredients, and then you have something to be greedy about. You begin with the ache and end with the object, where in most of the life of appetites—courtship, marriage—you start with the object and end with the ache.

Yet, if the first thing a cadet cook learns is that words can become tastes, the second is that a space exists between what the rules promise and what the cook gets. It is partly that the steps between—the melted chocolate's gleam, the chastened, improved look of the egg yolks mixed with sugar—are often more satisfying than the finished cake. But the trouble also lies in the same good words that got you going. How do you know when a thing "just begins to boil"? How can you be sure that the milk has scorched but not burned? Or touch something too hot to touch, or tell firm peaks from stiff peaks? How do you define "chopped"? At the same time as I was illicitly baking in the afternoons, I was learning non-recipe main-course cooking at night from my mother, a scientist by day, who had long been off-book, as they say in the theatre, and she would show, not tell: how you softened the onions, made them golden, browned them. This practice got you deeper than the words ever could.

Handed-down wisdom and worked-up information remain the double piers of a cook's life. The recipe book always contains two things: news of how something is made, and assurance that there's a way to make it, with the implicit belief that if I know how it is done I can show you how to do it. The premise of the recipe book is that these two things are naturally balanced; the secret of the recipe book is that they're not. The space between learning the facts about how something is done and learning how to do it always turns out to be large, at times immense. What kids make depends on what moms know: skills, implicit knowledge, inherited craft, buried assumptions, finger know-how that no recipe can sum up. The recipe is a blueprint but also a red herring, a way to do something and a false summing up of a living process that can be handed on only by experience, a knack posing as a knowledge. We say "What's the recipe?" when we mean "How do you do it?" And though we want the answer to be "Like this!" the honest answer is "Be me!" "What's the recipe?" you ask the weary pro chef, and he gives you a weary-pro-chef look, since the recipe is the totality of the activity, the real work. The recipe is to spend your life cooking.

Yet the cookbooks keep coming, and we continue to turn down their pages: "The Asian Grandmothers Cookbook," "The Adaptable Feast," the ones with disingenuously plain names—"How to Roast a Lamb: New Greek Classic Cooking" (a good one, in fact)—and the ones with elaborately nostalgic premises, like "Dining on the B. & O.: Recipes and Sidelights from a By-gone Age." Once-familiar things depart from their pages silently, like Minerva's owls. "Yield," for instance, a word that appeared at the top of every recipe in every cookbook that my mother owned—"Yield: six portions," or twelve, or twenty—is gone. Maybe it seemed too cold, too technical. In any case, the recipe no longer yields; it merely serves. "Makes six servings" or "Serves four to six as part of an appetizer" is all you get.

Other good things go. Clarified butter (melted butter with the milk solids skimmed and strained) has vanished—Graham Kerr, the Galloping Gourmet, once used it like holy water—while emulsified butter (melted butter with a little water whisked in), thanks to Thomas Keller's sponsorship, plays an ever-larger role. The cult of the cooking vessel—the wok, the tagine, the Dutch oven, the smoker, the hibachi, the Tibetan kiln or the Inuit ice oven or whatever—seems to be over. Paula Wolfert has a new book devoted to clay-pot cooking, but it feels too ambitious in advance; we have tried too many other modish pots, and know that, like Elvis's and Michael Jackson's chimps, after their hour is done they will live out their years forgotten and alone, on the floor of the closet, alongside the fondue forks and the spice grinder and the George Foreman grill. Even the imagery of cooking has changed. Sometime in the past decade or so, the actual eating line was breached. Now the cooking magazines and the cookbooks are filled with half-devoured dishes and cut-open vegetables. Michael Psilakis's fine Greek cookbook devotes an entire page to a down-beat still-life of torn-off artichoke leaves lying in a pile; the point is not to entice the eater but to ennoble the effort.

WITH THEIR TORN LEAVES and unyielding pages, cookbooks have two overt passions right now: one is simplicity, the other is salt. The chef's cookbook from the fancy place has been superseded by the chef's cookbook from the fancy place without the fancy-place food. David Waltuck, of the ever to be mourned Chanterelle, started this trend with his "Staff Meals," and now we have Thomas Keller's "Ad Hoc at Home," and, from Mark Peel, of the Los Angeles hot spot Campanile, "New Classic Family Dinners." ("Every single recipe was tested in Peel's own home kitchen—where he has only one strainer, just like the rest of us, and no kitchen staff to clean up after him.") The simplicity is in part a reaction to the cult of complexity of Spain's Ferran Adrià school of molecular cooks, with their cucumber foam and powdered octopus. Reformations make counterreformations as surely as right makes left; every time someone whitewashes a church in Germany, someone else paints angels on a ceiling in Rome. But simplicity remains the most complicated of all concepts. I have in one month stumbled over six simple recipes for making ragù or Bolognese—plain spaghetti sauce, as it used to be known, when there was only one kind— with chicken livers or without, diced chuck roast or hamburger, white wine or red. Yet all movements in cooking believe themselves to be movements toward greater simplicity. (Even the molecular gastronomes believe that they are truly elemental, breaking things down to the atomic level.) Curnonsky, the greatest of the interwar gourmands, was famous for preferring the cooking of the provinces and of grandmothers to the cuisine of restaurant chefs, and the result was such monuments of simplicity as Tournedos Curnonsky: filet of beef with grilled tomatoes, poached bone marrow, and cognac-port-and-black-truffle sauce.

Simplicity is the style, but salt the ornamental element—the idea of tasting flights of salt being a self-satirizing notion that Swift couldn't have come up with. The insistence on the many kinds of salt—not merely sea salt and table salt but hand-harvested fleur de sel, Himalayan red salt, and Hawaiian pink salt—is everywhere, and touching, because, honestly, it all tastes like salt. And now everyone brines. Brining, the habit of dunking meat in salty water for a bath of a day or so, seems to have first reappeared out of the koshering past, in *Cook's Illustrated*, sometime in the early nineties, as a way of dealing with the dry flesh of the modern turkey, and then spread like, well, ocean water in a tsunami, until now both Keller and Peel are happy to brine everything: pork roasts, chicken breasts, shrimp, duck.

Although brining is defended with elaborate claims about tenderness, what it really does is make food taste salty, and all primates like the taste of salt. That's a feature, not a bug; we're doing what our peasant ancestors did, making meat into ham. Salted food demands a salty sweet, and we read that in Spain recently one connoisseur had "a chocolate ganache coated in bread floating in a small pool of olive oil with fleur de sel sprinkled on it," while we can now make pecan-and-salt caramel-cheesecake chocolate mousse with olive oil and flaky-salt sticky-peanut cookie bars for ourselves.

THE SALT FETISH HAS, I think, another and a deeper cause: we want to bond with the pro cooks. Most of what pro cooks have that home cooks don't is what plantation owners used to have: high heat and lots of willing slaves. (The slaves seem happy, anyway, until they escape and write that testimonial, or start that cooking blog.) But the pro cooks also *salt* a lot more than feels right to an amateur home cook; both the late Bernard Loiseau and the Boston cook Barbara Lynch have confessed that hyper-seasoning, and, in particular, high salting, is a big part of what makes pro cooks' food taste like pro cooks' food. But the poor home cook, without hope of an eight-hundred-degree brick oven, and lucky if he can press-gang a ten-year-old into peeling carrots, can still salt hard, and so salt, its varieties and use, becomes a luxury replacement, a sign of seriousness even when you don't have the real tools of seriousness at hand.

The urge to meld identities with the pros is tied to a desire to get something out of a cookbook besides another recipe. For beneath those conscious enthusiasms and trends lies a new and deeper uncertainty in the relation between the recipe book and its reader. In this the Great Age of Disaggregation, all the old forms are being smashed apart and their contents spilled out like piñatas at a birthday party. The cookbook isn't spared. The Internet has broken what once seemed a natural tie, between the recipe and the cookbook, as it has broken the tie between the news story and the newspaper. You can find pretty much any recipe you want online now. If you need a recipe for mustard-shallot sauce or boeuf à la mode, you enter a few search terms, and there it is.

So the old question "What's the recipe for?" gives way to "What's the cookbook for?," which turns it, like everything else these days, toward the memoir, the confessional, the recipe as self-revelation. Barbara Lynch begins her book "Stir" with a preface that sounds like the opening passages of "GoodFellas": "We were poor, fiercely Irish, and extremely loyal. The older boys I knew grew up to be policemen, politicians and criminals (often a mix of the three). . . . If I ever had thoughts at all as to what I might be when I grew up, they were modest ones. I might have pictured myself running a bar (in Southie) or opening a sub shop (in Southie). But having a restaurant of my own on Beacon Hill? No way. In fact, if a fortune teller had told me at fourteen what good things were in store for me, I would have laughed in her face and told her where she could shove such bullshit. . . . I marvel that any of us made it out of there without winding up in jail or the morgue." Michael Psilakis, in "How to Roast a Lamb," includes his own childhood traumas: "As I sat on top of the lamb, watching it struggle to free itself, as if in slow motion my father came up behind me, reached down over my right shoulder with a hunting knife, grabbed the lamb's head and ears, and, in one swift motion, slit the lamb's throat. . . . Blood shot out of the lamb like water from a high-pressure hose." You never had a moment like that with Julia Child or Joseph Wechsberg.

ANOTHER ANSWER TO THE QUESTION "What good is the cookbook?" lies in what might be called the grammatical turn: the idea that what the cookbook should supply is the rules, the deep structure—a fixed, underlying grammar that enables you to *use* all the recipes you find. This grammatical turn is available in the popular

"Best Recipe" series in *Cook's Illustrated*, and in the "Cook's Bible" of its editor, Christopher Kimball, in which recipes begin with a long disquisition on various approaches, ending with the best (and so brining was born); in Michael Ruhlman's "The Elements of Cooking," with its allusion to Strunk & White's usage guide; and, most of all, in Mark Bittman's indispensable new classic "How to Cook Everything," which, though claiming "minimalism" of style, is maximalist in purpose—not a collection of recipes for all occasions but a set of techniques for all time.

You see a progression if you compare the classics of the past century: Escoffier's culinary dictionary, Julia Child's "Mastering the Art of French Cooking," Julee Rosso and Sheila Lukins's "The New Basics," and Bittman's recently revised "Everything." The standard kitchen bible, the book you turn to most often, has evolved from dictionary to encyclopedia, and to anthology and then grammar. Escoffier's book was pure dictionary: quick reminders to clarify a point or make a variation eloquent. Escoffier lists every recipe for tournedos and all its variations. His recipes are summaries, aide-mémoires for cooks who know how to make it already but need to be reminded what's in it. (Is a béarnaise sauce tarragon leaves and stems, or just leaves?) This was the way all cooks cooked once. (In the B. & O. cookbook, one finds this recipe for short ribs: "Put short ribs in a saucepan with one quart of nice stock, with one onion cut fine, steam until nice and tender. Place in roasting pan and put in oven until they are nice and brown." That's it. Everything else is commentary.)

In "Mastering the Art of French Cooking," as in Waverley Root's "The Food of France," which came out at around the same time, the turn is encyclopedic: here's all you can find on a particular kind of cooking, which you will master by reading this book. Things are explained, but, as in an encyclopedia, what is assumed is the need for more and deeper information about material already taken to be essential. You get a list not of everything there is but of everything that matters. Julia gives you only the tournedos recipes that count.

You didn't want to master the art of French cooking unless you believed that it was an art uniquely worth mastering. When people did master it, they realized that it wasn't—that no one style of cooking really was adequate to our appetites. So the cookbook as anthology arrived, open to many sources, from American Thanksgiving and Jewish brisket through Italian pasta and French Stroganoff—most successfully in "The New Basics" cookbook, which was the standard for the past generation. The anthology cookbooks assumed curiosity about styles and certainty about methods. In "The New Basics," the tone is chatty, informal, taking for granted that the readers—women, mostly—know the old basics: what should be in the kitchen, what kinds of machines to use, how to handle a knife.

THE COOKBOOKS of the grammatical turn assume that you don't know how to do the simple things, but that the simple things, mastered, will enable you to do it all. Bittman assumes that you have no idea how to chop an onion, or boil a potato, much less how chopping differs from slicing or from dicing. Each basic step is tenderly detailed. How to Boil Water: "Put water in a pot (usually to about two-thirds full), and turn the heat to high." How to Slice with a Knife: "You still press down, just with a little more precision, and cut into thick or thin slices of fairly uniform size." To sauté: "Put a large skillet on the stove and add the butter or oil. Turn the heat to medium-high. When the butter bubbles or the oil shimmers, add the food you want to sauté." Measuring dry ingredients, you are told to "scoop them up or use a spoon to put them in the cup." And, "Much of cooking is about heat."

This all feels masculine in tone—no pretty side drawings, a systematic progression from recipe to recipe—and seems written mainly for male readers who are either starting to cook for friends or just married and learning that if you don't cook she's not about to. The old "New Basics," one recalls nostalgically, was exclamatory and feminine. "The celebration continues," reads the blurb, and inside the authors "indulge" and "savor" and "delight"; a warm chicken salad is "perfection when dressed in even more lemon," another chicken salad is "lush and abundant." The authors' perpetual "we" ("We like all our holidays accompanied with a bit of the bubbly"), though meant, in part, to suggest a merry partnership, was generous and inclusive, a "we" that honest-to-God extended to all of their readers.

Bittman never gushes but always gathers up: he has seven ways to vary a chicken kebab; eighteen ideas for pizza toppings; and, the best, an "infinite number of ways to customize" mashed potatoes. He is cautious, and even, post-Pollan, skeptical; while Rosso and Lukins "love" and "crave" their filet of beef, to all of animal flesh Bittman allows no more than "Meat is filling and requires little work to prepare. It's relatively inexpensive and an excellent source of many nutrients. And most people like it." *Most people like it!* Rosso and Lukins would have tossed out any recipe, much less an entire food group, of which no more than that could be said. Lamb is a thing they "fall in love with again every season of the year," and of pork they know that it is "divinely succulent." Bittman thinks that most people like it. His tone is that of Ed Harris in "Apollo 13": Let's work the problem, people. Want to thicken a sauce? Well, try Plan A: cook it down. Copy that, Houston. Plan A inadequate? Try Plan B: add roux. And so on, ever upward, until you get to the old one, which they knew on the B. & O.: add a little cornstarch. The progressive pattern appeals to men. The implication, slightly illusory, is that there's a neat set of steps from each point to the next, as in a Bill Walsh pass pattern: each pattern on the tree proceeds logically and the quarterback just has to look a little farther upfield.

GRAMMARS TEACH FOREIGN TONGUES, and the advantage of Bittman's approach is that it can teach you how to cook. But is learning how to cook from a grammar book—item by item, and by rote—really learning how to cook? Doesn't it miss the social context—the dialogue of generations, the commonality of the family recipe—that makes cooking something more than just assembling calories and nutrients? It's as if someone had written a book called "How to Play Catch." ("Open your glove so that it faces the person throwing you the ball. As the ball arrives, squeeze the glove shut.") What it would tell you is not that we have figured out how to play catch but that we must now live in a culture without dads. In a world denuded of living examples, we end up with the guy who insists on making Malaysian Shrimp one night and Penne all'Amatriciana the next; it isn't about anything except having learned how it's done. Your grandmother's pound cake may have been like concrete, but it was about a whole history and view of life; it got that tough for a reason.

The metaphor of the cookbook was long the pet metaphor of the conservative political philosopher Michael Oakeshott in his assault on the futility of thinking that something learned by rote was as good as what was learned by ritual. Oakeshott's much repeated point was that one could no more learn how to make good government from a set of rules than one could learn how to bake a cake by reading recipe books. The cookbook, like the constitution, was only the residue of a practice. Even the most grammatical of cookbooks dies without living cooks to illuminate its principles. The history of post-independence African republics exists to prove the first point; that Chocolate Nemesis cake that always fails but your friends keep serving anyway exists to prove the second. Unsupported by your mom, the cookbook is the model of empty knowledge.

All this is true, and yet the real surprise of the cookbook, as of the constitution, is that it sometimes makes something better in the space between what's promised and what's made. You can follow the recipe for the exotic thing—green curry or paella—and though what you end up with would shock the natives, it may be just as good as or even better than the thing intended. Before I learned that green curries were soupy, I made them creamy, which actually is nicer. In politics, too, where the unwritten British constitution has been turned into a recipe—as in the constitutions of Canada and Australia—the condensation of practices into rules can make for a rain of better practices; the Canadian constitution, for instance, wanting to keep the bicameral vibe of a House of Lords without having a landed gentry, turned it into a Senate of distinguished citizens by appointment, an idea that can rebound back as a model for the new House of Lords. Between the rule and the meal falls the ritual, and the real ritual of the recipe is like the ritual of the law; the reason the judge sits high up, in a robe, is not that it makes a difference to the case but that it makes a difference to the clients. The recipe is, in this way, our richest instance of the force and the power of abstract rules. All messages change as they're re-sent; but messages not sent never get received. Life is like green curry.

However we take cookbooks—grammatically or encyclopedically, as storehouses of craft or illusions of knowledge—one can't read them in bed for many years without feeling that there is a conspiracy between readers and writers to obscure the ultimate point. A kind of primal scene of eating hovers over every cookbook, just as a primal scene of sex lurks behind every love story. In cooking, the primal scene, or substance, is salt, sugar, and fat held in maximum solution with starch; add protein as necessary, and finish with caffeine (coffee or chocolate) as desired. That's what, suitably disguised in some decent dimension of dressup, we always end up making. We make béarnaise sauce by whisking a stick of melted butter into a couple of eggs, and, now that we no longer make béarnaise sauce, we make salsa verde by beating a cup of olive oil into a fistful of anchovies. The herbs change; the hope does not.

Mark Peel, in his Campanile cookbook, comes near to giving the game away: "We chefs all lie about our mashed potatoes," he admits. "We don't tell you we've used 1½ pounds of cream and butter with 1¾ pounds of potatoes. You don't need to know." (Joël Robuchon, the king of his generation of French cooks, first became famous for a purée that had an even higher proportion of butter beaten into starch.) After reading hundreds of cookbooks, you may have the feeling that every recipe, every cookbook, is an attempt to get you to attain this ideal sugar-salt-saturated-fat state without having to see it head on, just as every love poem is an attempt to maneuver a girl or a boy into bed by talking as fast, and as eloquently, as possible about something else. "Shall I compare thee to a summer's day? / Thou art more lovely and more temperate" is the poetic equivalent of simmering the garlic with ginger and Sauternes before you put the cream in; the end is the cream, but you carefully simmer the garlic.

ALL APPETITES HAVE THEIR ILLUSIONS, which are part of their pleasure. Going back to our own primal scene, that's why the husband turns those pages. The truth is that we don't passively look at the pictures and leap to the results; we actively read the lines and internally act out the jobs. The woman who reads the fashion magazines isn't passively imagining the act of having; she's actively imagining the act of shopping. (And distantly imagining the act of wearing.) She turns down pages not because she wants to look again but because, for that moment, she really intends to buy that—for a decisive imagined moment she did buy it, even if she knows she never will. Reading recipe books is an active practice, too, even if all the action takes place in your mind. We reanimate our passions by imagining the possibilities, and the act of wanting ends up mattering more than the fact of getting. It's not the false hope that it will turn out right that makes us go on with our reading but our being resigned to the knowledge that it won't ever, quite.

The desire to go on desiring, the wanting to want, is what makes you turn the pages—all the while aware that the next Boston cream pie, the sweet-salty-fatty-starchy thing you will turn out tomorrow, will be neither more nor less unsatisfying than last night's was. When you start to cook, as when you begin to live, you think that the point is to improve the technique until you end up with something perfect, and that the reason you haven't been able to break the cycle of desire and disillusion is that you haven't yet mastered the rules. Then you grow up, and you learn that that's the game.

MY INNER CHILD

By Charlotte Freeman

From culinate.com

Novelist Charlotte Freeman (*Place Last Seen*) blogs about the
quotidian joys and challenges of her scaled-back life in
Livingston, Montana, at http://livingsmallblog.com. Tragedy and
comedy are often intermingled—as in this essay, where
conquering a new recipe is one way to mourn her brother's death.

Last summer—nearly half a century after its initial publication—Julia Child's classic cookbook *Mastering the Art of French Cooking* hit the top of the national bestseller charts. The phenomenon was, of course, driven by the late-summer (and now video) release of the movie "Julie & Julia," which I confess I have not yet seen, although I was an early and ardent supporter of Julie Powell's blog, the Julie/Julia Project.

A flurry of articles immediately ensued: about how difficult it is to cook out of *Mastering*, and about the panic ensuing among ordinary cooks when confronted with the amounts of butter and cream called for in Child's classic French recipes.

On the one hand, Regina Schrambling warned *Slate* readers not to buy the book, because "you'll never cook from it."

On the other hand, the very *New York Times* article in which Child's bestseller status was announced also quoted a Florida woman who, horrified by the inclusion of salt pork in the famous boeuf bourguignonne recipe, decided that a can of cream of mushroom soup, a can of French onion soup, and a can of red wine were acceptable substitutes.

"Yes, Julia Child rolled over in her grave when I opened the cream of mushroom soup," Melissah Bruce-Weiner told the paper. "But you know what? That's our world."

Perhaps. But it's also a world in which everyone seems to be missing the point of both *Mastering the Art of French Cooking* and of the Julie/Julia Project. Both were about mastery, not about everyday ease.

Child set out to not only master the art of French cooking for herself, but to translate that precise tradition for an audience of "servantless American cooks" who had only the grim supermarkets of the 1950s from which to shop.

Two generations later, Powell set out to save herself from despair, not by inventing "30-Minute Meals" but by daring herself to cook each and every recipe in Child's exacting and daunting book.

These are not tasks taken on by women who are seeking to make their lives easier. These are tasks taken on by women seeking to test themselves, to see whether they can create something beautiful and delicious while hewing to a set of exacting standards.

Sometimes, the only way to save yourself is to take on a project, and for some of us, the projects by which we seek to do that involve cooking. I know, because it was four years ago that I set out to survive the first horrifyingly lonely Christmas after my brother died by cooking an enormous, elaborate croquembouche.

It was my first Christmas at home after Patrick was killed in a car wreck, and since I had no one to cook for any more, I decided I needed an elaborate cooking project to take with me to the several parties to which I'd been invited.

I needed something difficult. I needed something delicious. I needed something very, very festive. And a croquembouche—a tower of cream-filled puff pastries shellacked in hot caramel, traditionally served in France as a wedding cake—fit all those bills.

I think I must have seen a rerun of that hilarious Martha Stewart episode in which she and Child make dueling croquembouches. Stewart's is all tidy and neatly stacked, while Child's is sort of a festive pile.

"Ooh," says Child in her warbly voice, as she flings hot caramel strands in the direction of her dessert, "I like yours."

A croquembouche seemed right for Patrick. For several years running, he had made the Paris-Brest pastry out of a Jacques Pépin cookbook. The first time he'd piped out the *pâte à choux* for it, he thought it didn't look right, and so he threw it out. When he followed the recipe a second time, only to get the exact same result, he put it in the oven despite his doubts.

"I should have believed Jacques," he told me when I came home from Christmas shopping. "Look! It's gorgeous!"

And Patrick had loved Julia Child. As a very small child, her show was his favorite thing to watch on TV. He was so devoted to the original "The French Chef" that we used to tease him that he could make a perfect *bûche de Noël* by the time he was five.

It was Patrick who discovered that Pépin and Child would be in San Francisco, signing copies of their latest cookbook, and who insisted we go into town and get copies. There we were, the youngest people in the line by at least 15 years, and there Child was, pooh-poohing our hero worship, signing away while Pépin ushered clusters of star-struck ladies behind her for snapshots.

It was a lovely afternoon. Patrick's copy of that book was one of the things I made sure to keep when I had to clean out his things.

And so, the croquembouche. It took three days. On the first day, I made the cream puffs—dozens and dozens of cream puffs. Ninety-six, I believe. Then I made two flavors of pastry cream— Grand Marnier and chocolate. On the second day, I filled all the cream puffs. Finally, on the third day I made the caramel and started to assemble the thing.

The caramel was kind of scary; it's very hot and you need to keep a big bowl of ice water nearby in case of burns. And the directions said to dip the cream puffs in the caramel, which was also sort of daunting. But little by little, the thing started to set up.

I'd bought some of those pretty little silver balls to decorate it with, but the caramel set up so quickly that they mostly just skittered all over my kitchen. And I had a near-disaster toward the top. The first couple of caramel batches went pretty well, but as they started to thicken up, I thought I could lighten it by adding some of the sugar syrup that had melted but hadn't yet caramelized.

This was not a good idea. It looked like shiny brown caramel, but when it cooled on the cream puffs, it looked like the opaque, matte, dried sugar solution it was.

I was horrified. It was four o'clock, and the Christmas Eve open house was starting at six, and I hadn't made any plans for a backup dessert.

This is when I remembered Julia Child on Martha Stewart's show. What Would Julia Do? I cleaned out my saucepan and started a fresh batch of caramel. I was patient. I waited for that wonderful toasty smell, and then I carefully swirled the caramel until it was a clear medium-brown.

Then, still following the spirit of Julia Child, I dripped the new caramel all over the top of the croquembouche. As the caramel started to set up, I tried pulling strings of caramel out, so it'd get that nice spun-sugar kind of look.

It was still a little lumpy, and there weren't as many stringy glistening strands as I would have liked, but overall, it was beautiful. It was a beautiful croquembouche.

It was also nearly three feet tall and weighed close to 30 pounds. I had to get it out into the car, then drive across town, and then maneuver it past the sweets-loving, 125-pound golden retriever at the door.

All of which I managed. I'd finished my project. I hadn't cried all day. I had arrived at a party like a person who can survive disaster with aplomb. I'd called on my inner Julia Child, and she hadn't let me down.

That's what *Mastering the Art of French Cooking* is really all about. It's about poaching your salt pork for precisely the right amount of time it takes for American salt pork to resemble French lardons.

And that's what Julie Powell's project was about. It was about being determined enough to figure out how to split a marrow bone, or kill a lobster, or learn to make a perfect *pâte brisée*.

It's not about easy. Triumph never is.

I can only hope that all those new copies of *Mastering* will not go home and languish on cookbook shelves. But even if they do, there's another generation coming up, one who might, as my generation did, pull their mothers' copies off the shelf, start paging through, and discover the deep joy that comes from following Child's exacting directions in order to produce something delicious, and elegant, and—as the French would say—correct.

People of the Cake

By Diane Roberts

From *The Oxford American*

English professor, NPR commentator, BBC filmmaker, and
Oxford American contributor, Diane Roberts sketches her
family history in *Dream State: Eight Generations of Swamp
Lawyers, Conquistadors, Confederate Daughters, Banana
Republicans, and other Florida Wildlife*. Cake, she insists, is one
of their secret weapons.

I come from a family of cake fundamentalists.
We are people of the Cake. A baby is born and welcomed
with cake; there's cake for anniversaries, cake for graduating high
school or college; cake for passing the bar or the CPA exam, cake
for winning Second Runner-Up in the Miss Peanut pageant; cake
for getting out of prison, cake for visiting kinfolk, cake for Christmas and Easter and the Fourth of July; cake when you marry, when
you're sick, when you die.

Proust journeys back to the past via a madeleine (a small, scallop-
shaped cake, not a cookie); in *The Unvanquished*, Faulkner uses
cake—or the remembrance of cakes—to conjure the lost days of
peace and plenty before secession. Granny Millard asks Marengo
and Bayard what they'd like her to read to them. They want the
cook book: "Read about cake." Coconut cake, to be exact. Craig
Claiborne, the brilliant food writer and Delta gourmand, was also a
coconut cake man:

> One of my earliest recollections was watching my mother or one
> of the servants tediously grating coconut in large quantities,

sometimes for ice cream, sometimes for a curried dish, but more often than not for coconut cake, which was one of Kathleen Craig Claiborne's great specialties.

Indeed, one of my earliest recollections is watching my own grandmother whack a coconut with a machete. She'd hammer a sixteen-penny nail into the coconut's "eyes" and drain out the juice. Then she'd rive it in two and carve out the meat with an oyster knife. After only four or five hours of gouging, hacking, beating, boiling, and whipping, she would present the cake on a cut-glass stand that had been a wedding present to her own grandmother. It was as white and shining as a debutante's gown, covered in hand-shredded coconut, fuzzy as a French poodle.

I come from a family of cake fundamentalists. No mixes, no faux cream, no margarine, no imitation vanilla, no all-purpose flour. You should use Swans Down or some other cake flour: It's made of soft winter wheat with a low protein content, which makes the cake finer and airier. If the recipe says fresh coconut, don't you dare use that stuff in the bag. Suffering for your cake builds character. (We are Presbyterian, after all.) The first time I made Grandmama's fresh coconut cake, I grated the skin off my knuckles. People said it was delicious: You really didn't taste the blood at all.

After my fingers healed up, I moved on to making Old School cakes that didn't require hatchets, machetes, or other weaponry. Lady Baltimore cake is a luxurious pile of nuts, figs, cherries, and egg whites, soft as tulle and sweet as divinity. With that name, you'd think it was some old Maryland recipe dating from the days of the Calverts, but according to John and Ann Bleidt Egerton, it was invented by one Alicia Rhett Mayberry, a Charleston belle, sometime near the turn of the twentieth century. Owen Wister, author of *The Virginian*, named his 1906 novel after it:

> "I would like a slice, if you please, of Lady Baltimore," I said with extreme formality. I returned to the table and she brought me the cake, and I had my first felicitous meeting with Lady Baltimore. Oh, my goodness! Did you ever taste it? It's all soft, and it's in lay-

ers, and it has nuts—but I can't write any more about it; my mouth waters too much.

In 1898, Emma Rylander Lane of Barbour County, Alabama, published the recipe for what she called her "prize cake," a four-layer white sponge filled with an opulent mixture of egg yolks, raisins, and booze. This is the cake, remember, that got Scout tipsy in *To Kill a Mockingbird*. If you do it right, putting at least three-fourths of a cup of hooch (Emma Lane called for "one wine-glass of good whiskey or brandy") in the filling and drizzling another cup over the layers, letting it soak in, the Lane cake is a cocktail in baked form. I don't hold with lazy-ass modern versions that use boxed mix (I'm talking to you, *Southern Living*) or omit the bourbon. I realize there are people who insist that Jesus didn't turn water into wine at Cana, claiming it was actually Welch's grape juice. Please. Like Jesus would be so tacky.

Even foot-washing Baptists in dry counties know better than to make a Lane cake without alcohol. Celestine Sibley, the longtime columnist for the *Atlanta Journal-Constitution*, tells how her mother, not a drinker but a committed baker, drove down to Panama City, Florida, after church one day—hat, gloves, and all. She walked into a bar as "dark as the inside of a cow." A young woman "half naked and downright impudent" slinked over, saying, "Madam, this is a cocktail lounge." Evelyn Sibley drew herself up and replied, "My dear, I didn't think it was the Methodist parsonage! I'll have a half-pint of Early Times, please."

We cakeists value tradition. I've had the same kind of birthday cake (Angel Food), perched on the same cut-glass cake stand my grandmother used for her coconut cake, every single year of my life. At my first birthday, my mother made a magnificent pink cake decorated with spun-sugar daisies. The photographic evidence shows I smashed my fist into it. I'm told that I licked the thick, seven-minute icing off my arm and laughed. Now, I make sure there are no cameras around on my birthday.

For Christmas, it has to be fruitcake: a serious fruitcake, with muscovado sugar, candied pineapples, candied lemon and orange peel, citron, red and green cherries, raisins, cinnamon and nutmeg, cloves and ginger, dates and chopped pecans, baked slow and low. It's a treasure box of complex flavors, each one richer and more intoxicating, more seductive, than the last. Especially if you've kept the cake wrapped in rum-soaked cheesecloth for at least a month.

Fruitcake goes back to the Romans, maybe to Mesopotamia for all I know. The cookery book that Martha Washington worked on from the time of her wedding in 1749 to Daniel Custis until 1799, when her granddaughter Nelly Custis married Lawrence Lewis, contains four recipes for what she called "great cakes"—as opposed to small. Here's the one she made for Epiphany, or Twelfth Night, parties, original spelling preserved:

> Take 40 eggs and divide the whites from the yolks & beat them to a froth then work 4 pounds of butter to a cream & put the whites of eggs to it a Spoon full at a time till it is well work'd then put 4 pounds of sugar finely powdered to it in the same manner then put in the Youlks of eggs & 5 pounds of flower & 5 pounds of fruit. Add to it half an ounce of mace & nutmeg half a pint of wine & some frensh brandy. Two hours will bake it.

I'll tackle that monster after the recession cuts us loose and I can afford five pounds of candied fruit (which wasn't cheap even in Mistress Martha's day). In the meantime, there's pound cake. Don't scoff. It may seem like a plain Jane amongst cakes: no fillings, no icing, no cup of cognac, no grating or chopping. But once you bite into a piece of good pound cake, it's like when the librarian unpins her chignon and whips off her glasses: Oh my God! She's a total babe!

Pound cake is deceptively simple. Mary Randolph's 1824 cookbook *The Virginia Housewife* calls for a pound of butter, a pound of flour, a pound of powdered sugar, and twelve eggs. My mother's version is a little more complex, but not difficult. It's a beautiful cake, nut-brown on the outside, yellow as a daffodil inside. It's the cake she makes for people who do nice things, people with family in the hospital, and funerals. In spring, when we can get fresh, local strawberries, she makes it for shortcake. If there are leftover pieces, she makes trifle, soaking it in sherry, slathering it with blueberries or peaches, layering it with custard. She bakes it like Wynton Marsalis plays the horn—gracefully, improvisationally. She has a recipe, but never looks at it. Here is Betty Gilbert Roberts's Sour Cream Pound Cake.

Betty Gilbert Roberts's Sour Cream Pound Cake

1 cup (2 sticks) butter, softened
3 cups white sugar
8 eggs, separated
1 cup sour cream
3 cups cake flour
½ teaspoon salt
1 teaspoon baking soda
1½ teaspoons good vanilla extract

Preheat the oven to 325 degrees. Grease a tube pan and sugar the edges. Cream the butter and two cups of sugar until fluffy. While that's beating, use a hand-mixer to whip the egg whites. Add the third cup of sugar and continue whipping until they form stiff peaks.

Add egg yolks, one at a time, to the butter and sugar. Beat well. Sift the flour, salt, and soda together. Add, alternating wet and dry ingredients, the flour mix and the sour cream. Mix well. Add the vanilla, then fold in the egg whites. Try not to eat the batter (it's really good). Bake sixty to ninety minutes until a skewer comes out clean. Cool ten to fifteen minutes and turn out on a plate.

This cake is best savored with a glass of Kentucky whiskey or old Madeira or champagne, sitting in front of a bright fire, lying on the new grass in spring, or curled up on the sofa reading French ballads.

Yancey's Red Hots

By Wright Thompson

From *The Oxford American*

Though Wright Thompson's usual subject is sports—he's a
senior writer for *ESPN The Magazine* and espn.com—as a
Mississippian born and bred, musing about the finer points
of southern food is a natural sideline.

When people try to reassemble the broken pieces of
1950s Shelby, Mississippi, in their minds, they usually
start with Saturday afternoon. Families filled the streets, as impossible as that sounds now. Folks came to town to buy provisions for
the week, to get comics and floats for the kids, and maybe to bring
home a sack of burgers for supper. They caught a movie, a showing
of *High Noon* or *All About Eve*, and most of all, they heard the song
of the hot-tamale man. His name was Yancey, and he pushed a cart.
Even the kids playing in their backyards a few blocks away could
hear his voice.

"Red hots!" he'd yell, parked over by the train depot, which still
rattled with passengers and freight who thought the small town
was worth the coming and going. "Get your red hots!"

The tamales simmered in the big, steaming silver pots he kept
on the back of his cart. He only sold them on Saturday, and they
were the best damn red hots in Bolivar County, maybe even Coa-
homa, too. Yancey lived not far from the depot, in a shotgun over
at the Valley Gin Yard, where he worked for my family. He pushed
a broom around the gin, and he took care of my uncle's horses, and
he did odd jobs for my grandparents.

For extra money, he'd spend hours behind his house, tending to the big iron cauldron, boiling pork and beef, then grinding it all together with garlic, layering in salt, chili, and cayenne, smooth and easy, the way a man just knows how to throw a baseball, twenty-two pounds of meal giving him 567 red hots to hawk at the depot on Saturday.

Yancey was old, even then, and in the 1950s, he found himself sick. He didn't have any family, people remember, just people he'd worked for and people he'd fed. This is the story passed down in my family: One day, near the end, he called my grandmother over to his house. He wanted to give her something, he said. He didn't have money, or a watch to pass along, or even a photograph they could keep.

He wanted her to have his hot-tamale recipe.

He dictated the ingredients and the instructions, and she wrote them down, in her neat, rolling cursive. Not long after, Yancey died. No one yelled "red hots!" downtown anymore, then, eventually, no one went downtown at all. The gin shut down. My grandfather died. My grandmother got Alzheimer's and forgot everything, from her own children to the man with the cart. Then she died. Her friends died, too, and their children moved away. There aren't many people left in Shelby, and even fewer who remember Yancey. Even his last name is hazy. Is it Searcey? Or Searcy? "Everyone is gone," says eighty-five-year-old Jutta Ferretti, who was friends with my grandparents. "Everyone is gone."

It seems as if Yancey never really existed at all, but I know that he did. I'm holding a four-by-six recipe card. I turn it over, feel the thick card stock, run my fingers along my grandmother's blue script. Forgotten handwriting always gut-punches me; I can close my eyes and see a long-vanished hand moving over the page.

It's all there. Four pounds of pork and four pounds of beef. Four buttons of garlic, and the salt and chili and cayenne. One pound of meal—or maybe meat, the formal "l" could be a "t"—makes twenty-four tamales, she writes, and twenty-two pounds makes 567. I try to imagine the moment when this recipe first jumped from Yancey's mind to paper. What did he think would happen? Did he just want someone to know he'd been here?

I wonder what they must have tasted like, and I think about all the other little places in the Mississippi Delta that are gone, the tastes of my childhood, spots like Arnold's Fried Chicken in my hometown of Clarksdale, and the Rebel Roost in Drew, and Campbell's and Delta Kream in Tunica. Campbell's is a Chinese buffet now. I can still taste the fried chicken every time I drive through the intersection of Desoto and MLK. Who was Arnold? Where did he go? Maybe old restaurants aren't worth much thought, but they mean something to the people who look at the plywood windows and see a life turned to dust. Their loss does matter to the people who remember. Our food anchors us to a place.

My mother has never made Yancey's recipe, and neither have I. It's a lot of trouble, and we're all so busy, you know. But, determined to try at least once, on a chilly Saturday morning not long ago, I go down to the local butcher and have him boil and grind the meat—cheating already—and head home to soak the corn husks. I consult my mother. I consult one of my best friends, John Currence, a James Beard Award–winning chef, and Cesar Valdivia, a friend who owns a Mexican restaurant. It takes a village. My wife and I start making the paste and carefully spread it on the husks. We boil them, and the first two come apart, but the third holds its form.

"It's a tamale," my wife says, as shocked as I.

We keep trying, and the fourth is better than the third, and the fifth is better than the fourth. By the end, the things on the plate look like hot tamales and taste something like 'em, too. But they are not Yancey's tamales. The soul is missing, the little steps, his little tricks, the things that make food alive and not a list of bloodless steps that can be passed along via e-mail.

The secrets to the tamales are in between the lines on the recipe card. They're in the love, and in the expertise that comes only with practice. The recipe he passed down is vague, so vague it took a chef to fill in the blanks for me just to make it work, and I realize that the tamales lived in Yancey's heart more than in his head. There is a truth in them that cannot be taught in words, something only learned from years of standing over a black iron pot behind the Valley Gin and staring down into the darkness.

Once it's gone, the past cannot be preserved, even in faithful blue script, and once the man who yelled "red hots!" died, and the depot where he yelled it stopped seeing trains and eventually became a library, once the fryers went silent in Clarksdale and the griddle got cold in Drew, once the song of Saturday afternoon found itself living inside a recipe card on my kitchen island, well, it was gone, gone, gone.

Computers or Cookbooks in the Kitchen?

By David Leite and Renee Schettler

From leitesculinaria.com

Recipes are the lifeblood of this award-winning website, the
internet's closest thing to a glossy foodie mag. The site's
publisher/editor-in-chief David Leite and deputy editor
Renee Schettler spend their days poring over recipes—but,
apparently, in diametrically opposed formats.

He says: Come into our kitchen and you'll find cookbooks gracing it. About three dozen of them tucked
away on two shelves along one side of the cooking island, their
bindings perfectly even (thanks to a ruler I frequently nudge up
against them). But they're cooking eunuchs, nothing more than
decoration, as if we were selling the house and wanted to subtly
convey to potential buyers the domestic pleasures awaiting them in
those pages. The motherlode of books are found far away from the
UXBZ (unexploded bomb zone) of the kitchen: In CT, that
would be in my writing studio, and in NYC, the dining room.
Plainly put: No sauces, tomato stains, or grease smudges will deface
my books.

So it's curious that my laptop, which cost me three times my
monthly mortgage, is what I bring into the kitchen when I cook.

For me, comprehensiveness trumps logic. I know I should keep
the computer miles away from the stove and my preternatural
clumsiness. (I won't even eat near my computer during the day.)
But I just can't stay away from everything the Internet has to offer

while cooking. It's like having my own personal Schlesinger Library's Culinary Collection in my kitchen.

Whether you like it or not, just about any recipe you want to make from just about any cookbook is online, somewhere. (Me, I like it.) And I like having Portable Leite Brain—what I call my laptop—handy because I rarely cook from just one recipe. I pull from three or four at once, and the last thing I want is piles of books on the counter. Plus I oftentimes cook from this site but am curious how other sites and blogs whip up, say, gougères or bavette, so I browse. And soon enough, I'm lost in that great, wonderful, frustrating worm hole of cyberspace. Along the way I pick up a few tips from Michael Ruhlman here, a video from Mark Bittman there, and sometimes even a new idea for tomorrow's dinner.

Then comes the ritual of the printing of the recipes and the taping to the cabinets (something The One hates, because I once pulled off paint when ripping them down after a particularly frustrating dinner). After the kitchen is kitted out, the computer isn't out of reach—I never know when I might need more info, want to catch up on the latest episode of "Desperate Housewives" while onions sauté, or reply to Momma Leite, who likes to e-mail during the early evening.

What can I say—I have cooking ADD.

Of course, Portable Leite Brain's being in the line of fire (sometimes literally) has prompted me to jury-rig it for safety. First, I never have it next to the stove, anymore. We won't go there, but suffice it to say that I have a new laptop. I also cover the keyboard and screen with plastic wrap—kind of a giant computer condom, protecting it from all kinds of nasties.

Now, the one place I never hesitate to bring my beloved books is the bedroom. There I luxuriate in their words and pictures and sometimes even fall asleep with a pile at my feet. I don't know what that says about me or my relationship, but we're not going there, either. —*David Leite*

She says: If you could see the state of my cookbooks, you'd understand why I don't take my laptop into the kitchen.

It's not that I'm intentionally careless or that my cookbook collection is mistreated terribly. It's that I'm simply not the type of cook who can maintain the books in just-off-the-shelf condition. As my husband says, I really get into my cooking. I'm prone to what he describes as Seussian stacks of teetering pots and pans everywhere, and that's not all. Chopping boards balance over the kitchen sink. All four burners blast aflame. The narrow ledge outside our window doubles as a makeshift cooling rack. Guests have been known to duck and dive, but for me, there's a rhythm, albeit an occasionally discordant one. In the midst of this juggling act, there just isn't a lot of time to be prissy about things like splashes and drips and splotches. If there's a lull in the cooking, fine. Otherwise, it's just too distracting.

Even when I try, really try, to be careful, I just can't seem to pull it off. Just ask David. The last time—and I do mean the last time— he loaned me a cookbook, I set it safely outside the kitchen. One stray, damp thumbprint was all it took to give my habits away. *

I wouldn't dare take my electronics into that fray. Nor would I want to, practicality aside. You know how they say to use your bedroom only for sleep and, um, other bed-centric pursuits? I feel the same about my kitchen. I don't want to read emails that other people feel are urgent while my eggs perfectly sunnyside up—soft, please—slip tragically into mediocrity. And I don't want to interrupt everything to tweet 137 self-deprecating characters about the incident. Laptop as resource? Without a doubt. But not when I'm in the throes of cooking. I already did my homework, sussing out an ingredient substitution or summoning a technique online before I decide to stand facing the stove. If something comes up, I'll deal with it on my own. When I'm in the kitchen, it's time to cook. Anything else just messes up my mojo.

So the closest my delicate, Meyer-lemon-averse Mac gets to the mess—and I to its distracting charms—is the wee wooden schoolhouse chair in the foyer, just outside our galley kitchen. With my laptop's volume cranked, I can ponder deep thoughts from "All Things Considered" or croon off-key to Ella while otherwise considering things cooking-related.

---

* Okay, let's be real. A single watery fingerprint would be fine. But I could tell which recipe she tested by looking at the side of the book. The page was so wavy, it looked like an EKG readout.—David

As far as I'm concerned, perhaps the best use of technology in the kitchen is to photocopy a recipe in order to keep a book out of harm's way. Yet I'm a sucker for the sentient pleasures related to cooking from a book, which explains why my cookbooks are a mess in the first place. I need the soothing white space around the edge of the page in order to dance a duet with the ingredients in my imagination. I spend those idle moments waiting for a stock to burble lost in the lyrical headnotes of Judy Rodgers. And I learn every time my husband leans over my shoulder to eye an open cookbook to make pithy comments about the writing style, urge me to take more liberties with the ingredients, or muse over recipes that may be more to his liking.

They're not just cookbooks. They're scrapbooks of sorts. Telltale translucent stains from melted butter both grease and grace my mom's binder of go-to recipes. I continue her legacy with a blemish here (a smear of cilantro that escaped my maiden molcajete run with a Peppercorn-Coriander Root Flavor Paste) and a batter-splattered page there (the incomparable Laurie Colwin channeling Katherine Hepburn's brownies in a decades-old issue of *Gourmet*). Though the perfectionist in me sometimes cringes, I don't mind the splotches that shout out those memories, moments that probably wouldn't exist had the recipes blinkered onscreen. I don't mind them at all.—*Renee Schettler*

Does a Recipe Need to Be Complicated to Be Good?

By Monica Bhide

From www.monicabhide.com

In her cookbooks, such as *Modern Spice*, Monica Bhide updates traditional Indian cooking for a modern kitchen—translations that usually involve simplifying multi-step, multi-ingredient recipes. After pushback from some readers, she reflects on her strategy for doing so.

I was so proud of my cookbook, *Modern Spice*. That is, until the moment a reader approached me at a fundraiser. "Your recipes are too simplistic," she blurted out. It threw me for a loop—too simplistic? I developed *Modern Spice* keeping contemporary peoples' busy schedules in mind. My focus was to create and share recipes that did not sacrifice on taste but delivered on the "ease of preparation" promise.

The reader who approached me said that she had prepared my pan-seared trout with mint-cilantro chutney, but feared it wasn't really cooking because it was so simple. At first, I felt I had failed her. I wondered if I should apologize. Had I been unworthy of my readers' trust? Had I let them down?

I probed her a little, and her response surprised me even more. She loved the dish, and so did everyone who ate it. But it did not fulfill her cooking aspirations. "Indian cooking is supposed to be hard," she said. "And this book made it seem easy. That isn't real Indian cooking, right?"

Wait—isn't being able to cook something that's pleasing the point of a good cookbook? Does a recipe need to be complicated to be good?

I think what isn't necessarily obvious to many who read and cook from cookbooks is that creating simple recipes is often more difficult than creating complex ones. Conjuring a recipe that relies on only a few ingredients yet sends your taste buds into an orgasmic frenzy takes a great deal of understanding of ingredients: how they work individually, how to make them work together in perfect harmony, and how to cook them just right. It takes years of experience to learn, and to be able to teach, "simplicity." And that is my goal as a cooking teacher and a cookbook author—to teach students to be able to cook on their own.

It takes a lot of experience to prepare "simple" just right. In simple recipes with just a few ingredients, there's no place to hide. It takes guts—and culinary prowess—to cook that way. Please be aware that when I refer to simplicity in recipes, I don't mean dumbing down recipes. Yes, there are plenty of people who promise that our lives will be easier if we follow their "simple" plan to combine the contents of five tin cans for a meal. To me, that's a false economy of time and money, not to mention flavor.

My parents taught me how to cook—how to smell a melon, peel an onion, sear a fish, sizzle cumin. But most importantly, it was with them that I learned why freshness in ingredients matters so much and how a perfectly ripe tomato needs nothing more than a sharp knife to bring out its best. I grew up without a can opener in the house. My parents bought all their ingredients fresh. The only time I remember there being canned anything on the table was when my father fell in love with British baked beans and brought home several cans each time he traveled to London.

Instead, I grew up with spices and herbs—our recipes would be considered incomplete without them—and yet I never remember my mother using ten different spices in a dish. A few in the right combination always did the trick. I once received an e-mail from a reader who was really angry that one of my recipes for tea included only one spice. "Are you afraid of spices?" he demanded. On the contrary: If you know how much flavor a single good-quality spice—say, cardamom—can add, why would you add flavors that muck it up?

So what exactly constitutes a simple recipe? To me, it is a recipe that requires just a few ingredients, is smart in the way it uses those ingredients, doesn't require my entire paycheck, and teaches me something. *New York Times* food reporter Kim Severson wrote a piece a year or so ago on "deal-breakers" in recipes, in which she decried a particular recipe for requiring fresh pig's blood and another for demanding fleur de sel from buckets of seawater. Not happening in my kitchen.

Ask someone what their favorite dish is to make at home and rarely will they announce foie grais with bacon air, mint puree, and pine nut confit. Most times you will hear squash soup, light-as-air buttermilk pancakes, mom's recipe for lasagna. Yes, there is great joy in going to a restaurant and enjoying a complicated meal cooked by a legend like Daniel Boulud. But cooking at that level at home each and every day is neither possible nor desirable for most of us. I have kids, and as the *Boston Globe* so kindly put it, my recipes are "clearly the work of a mother cooking on weeknights." Even so, I bet Chef Boulud would agree with me that good recipes come from learning how to use ingredients wisely.

A chef who masters this art of simplicity is José Andrés. I recently prepared a recipe of his for slender stalks of asparagus bound together with thinly sliced Spanish ham and pan-fried. That was it: Asparagus. Ham. Pan-fry. Why is this notable? Those of you who know Andrés will know. Those of you who aren't familiar with him, let me tell you. José Andrés is an understudy of Ferran Adria, and he is a chef who regularly thrills at culinary innovation, who can desconstruct a glass of wine on a plate and who can wrap a drop of olive oil in sugar. But he is also a husband and a father who clearly understands the role of a home cook as well as his role as a cookbook author and teacher. He demonstrates this with an ability to show readers what they can make at home WITHOUT a nitrogen tank handy.

Should José's great-tasting asparagus recipe have made me feel like I wasn't cooking?

Cooking teacher and great TV chef Sanjeev Kapoor, who has sold millions of books, once told me that true culinary genius lies in knowing how to teach people to master dishes that they can easily create at home. It does not, he continued, lie in showing off what the chef knows. The scale of complexity in recipes is in no way a litmus test of how good or bad a recipe is.

So I leave you with this recipe for pan-fried trout with mint-cilantro chutney. And I say with great pride—simplicity is its charm.

Pan-Seared Trout with Mint-Cilantro Chutney

If you are reading this recipe and thinking, "Really, can it be that simple?"—yes, it is, and it is simply delicious. Don't take my word for it, though. Get a pan out and start searing! Julie's notes: Good substitutes for the trout are cod, snapper and tilapia.

Serve the trout with a drizzle of the Mint-Cilantro Chutney.

Serves 4
Prep/Cook time: 15 minutes

4 skin-on trout fillets, about 6 ounces each, halved lengthwise
Table salt
Freshly ground black pepper
1 tablespoon vegetable oil
¼ cup Mint-Cilantro Chutney

1. Season the trout fillets with salt and pepper.
2. Heat the oil in a large skillet over medium heat. When the oil begins to shimmer, add the trout, skin side down. Cook for 2 to 3 minutes. Flip over and cook for another 3 to 4 minutes, until the trout is cooked through.
3. Transfer to a plate lined with paper towels, skin side down.
4. Place each fillet on a serving plate and drizzle each with up to a tablespoon of chutney. Serve immediately.

Mint-Cilantro Chutney

This is the most popular chutney in India, hands down. It can be found in many Indian-American homes, in restaurants, and now in jars on grocery store shelves. Its charm lies in how simple it is to prepare. My father always adds a little yogurt to his chutney to make it creamy and then pairs it with lamb kebabs. My mom-in-law adds a hearty dose of roasted peanuts and serves it with savory snacks; Mom adds pomegranate seeds—you get the idea—to each his own. This versatile chutney has so many uses. Thin it a little and use it as a salad dressing for a crisp green salad; use it in the consistency provided here as a spread on a baguette topped with fresh cucumber slices; or simply drizzle it on some freshly grilled fish for a fresh flavor. One word of advice here: Green chutneys have a short shelf life. Make them in small batches and make them often—they only take a few minutes but the rewards are well worth the effort (which really isn't much). Julie's notes: I did use the optional serrano chile with some of the seeds, but I did not use the optional dried pomegranate.

Makes 1 cup
Prep time: 5 minutes

1 cup packed cilantro (leaves and stems)
1 cup packed mint (leaves only, please)
1 green serrano chile (optional; if you don't like too much heat, remove the seeds)
¼ small red onion, peeled and sliced
1 tablespoon dried pomegranate seeds (optional)
2 tablespoons fresh lemon juice
½ teaspoon table salt
Up to 2 tablespoons water

1. Blend the cilantro, mint, chile, onion, pomegranate seeds (if using), lemon juice, and salt in a blender to a smooth paste. To aid in the blending process, you can add up to 2 tablespoons of water, if needed. Taste and add more salt if needed.

2. Transfer to a covered container and chill for about 30 minutes.

3. Serve cool. This chutney will keep, refrigerated, for 4 days.

Personal Tastes

Farm City

By Novella Carpenter

From *Farm City: The Education of an Urban Farmer*

Carpenter's memoir of her urban farmsteading experiences
in a gritty section of Oakland, California, makes for
entertaining reading—funny, poignant, passionate, and
(literally) down to earth.

A pledge to eat exclusively from a July garden in the Bay Area, I reasoned, is a little like a mute person taking the vow of silence at a Vipasana-meditation retreat. I wasn't worried. The rules were simple:

1. Only food from the garden and the farm animals.

2. Foraged fruit from neighborhood trees OK.

3. No food from Dumpsters (except to feed the animals).

4. Items previously grown and preserved allowed.

5. Bartering allowed, but only for crops grown by other farmers.

In mid-June, I told all my friends about my approaching escapade in eating. This, I felt, was critical to its success—and commencement, for that matter. We giggled about my bravado, my moxie, my mad urban-farming skills. While I knew they would be cheering for me, they would also be keeping tabs. Back in March, when I had conceived of this harebrained idea, July had seemed so far away. Now that it was right around the corner, I was starting to think that my experiment in self-sufficiency wouldn't be much fun.

The week before it began, I ate everything in sight. In my excess, I pretended that I was A. J. Liebling in Paris. But I was in America, so I gorged from the buffet of cultures this country hosts. Chinese food, relishing that tarlike sweet-and-sour sauce, the pillowlike dumplings. Sushi. Small chili verde tacos from a roach coach in East Oakland, the perfect blend of pork simmered with green chiles. Falafel, creamy baba ghanoush, tabouli. Every morning I had a huge mug of coffee (sometimes two), brimming with half-and-half. I popped vats of popcorn, scoffed at greens (plenty of time for those later), inhaled chocolate bars, and drank lapsong souchong, a smoky tea whose flavor would be impossible to recreate. This weeklong binge left me a little heavier than my usual fighting weight. In a thrift store, I stood on a scale: 142 pounds.

The evening before June turned into July, I walked out into the garden to survey my future. In *Walden*, Henry David Thoreau wrote, "I was determined to know beans." I too was determined to know beans. I admired their sturdy leaves emerging from the black earth, their raspy stems that wound around whatever kind of pole I could find (currently, a curtain rod), the succulent flowers, and then the emergence of small beans, which could be plucked, blanched, and served plain—because the 100-yard diet didn't allow olive oil or balsamic vinegar.

While Thoreau, no food snob, was happy to cultivate a monotonous crop of beans on his three acres, I was determined to know other vegetables during my month of self-sufficiency on my tenth of an acre. And so I had planted sweet corn, Stowell's Evergreen, which was now about four feet tall and just coming into flower. I hoped some tasty niblets would be mine toward the end of the month. Brandywine tomatoes, too, and the green ones on the vine seemed like a good sign. Prodigious amounts of lettuce, collard, kale, and cabbage had sprouted up all over the garden. I had made a second planting of fava beans. More beans. Henry, did you know these lovelies, brought by Italians to this country? The onions were swelling, as were the beets. Potato vines were peeking out from under a mat of straw. The squash plants had a few young fruits, as did the cucumbers. Herbs like marjoram, oregano, rosemary, and thyme were flourishing.

The domesticated-animal kingdom was a realm in which Thoreau never dabbled. He scoffed that farms are "a great grease spot, redolent of buttermilk!" In my beloved grease spot, one of the chickens was laying an egg in what she thought was a clandestine nest under the bougainvillea. Seven ducks and two geese that I had ordered from Murray McMurray that spring were fattening in an open-air pen in the lot. Since they couldn't be trapped in a pen by an opossum or some other predator, I wagered that they would be safe, and a good source of protein. The young rabbits on the deck had gotten plump.

In my larder, I had jars of jam, stewed peaches, honey from last year's harvest, and pickles galore. My food-security future was bright. But as I assessed the food growing and thriving on the farm, a dark word crossed my mind, and I couldn't shake it. I walked upstairs and tried to forget. It felt like a gun to my head.

Carbohydrates.

I would have to ration the potatoes. Another potential problem crossed my mind, then another. Crop failure. Pests that kill plants and animals. Someone could steal all my food, an expansion on the great watermelon theft from the previous year. I peered out at the garden from my window. It was dark, and a wind had picked up. I could make out the cornstalks waving and the plum and apple trees rocking in the breeze. I felt a little queasy. As June evaporated at the stroke of midnight, suddenly my bold experiment, my attempt to prove myself as a farmer, seemed like the mission of an imbecile.

THE NEXT MORNING, as I picked a few apples to eat for breakfast, my first caffeine-withdrawal headache flashed across my temple. I had to go lie down.

Lying on my bed, with the morning sun filtering in and a breeze swirling the curtains into the sickroom, I wondered: How can I get out of this? It felt as if a monster had grabbed me and was going to hold me here for thirty—oh, no, why did I pick July?—thirty-one days. Why hadn't I weaned myself off coffee? Then another dreadful question: What's for lunch?

That afternoon Bill and I went to a friend's barbecue. Though I had eaten a jar of stewed peaches, a green salad, and at least ten ounces of honey, the smell of the grilling meat nearly knocked me down. Two yoga teachers I vaguely knew beckoned me over.

"I have the worst headache," I explained before they had the chance to read my aura.

"Give me your hand," Baxter said.

He pinched the area between my thumb and index finger. My headache went away. It was replaced by a growling stomach.

"I'm off coffee," I said with a sigh.

"You didn't do it gradually?" Raven asked.

I shook my head. Yoga people have been telling me for years that I should give up coffee, that it's full of toxins and other bad things. But when they suggest that I should stop drinking coffee, I want to tell them maybe they should saw off their legs.

Baxter gave me back my hand. The headache returned.

I looked around the party. There they were, my friends, standing next to the grill, dishing up salads, drinking beer. I had the sinking realization that social activities all revolve around sharing food. The act of setting up my 100-yard diet had turned me into an alien visiting from planet Weird in the solar system Healthy.

But then again, everyone at the party was on some kind of Bay Area diet kick anyway. The gluten-intolerant munched on ears of corn in the corner. The vegans had their own grill set up with toasting tofu. The raw-food vegans were sipping on freshly macheted green coconuts. The pescatarians were shoving ceviche into their faces. Defining ourselves by what we eat—that's what we do for fun around here.

I was sure that I could find a freshairian or a locavore to share my pain with but instead decided to leave early. I found Bill, an unapologetic omnivore, moving from grill to grill, stuffing sausages and ribs and veggie burgers into his mouth. I ripped a piece of watermelon out of his hand and insisted that, really, we couldn't stay another moment.

Later that day, I ordered three tea plants—*Camellia sinensis*—over the phone.

"I want the gallon size," I gritted out as the perky woman took my order. I needed a quick harvest.

"We'll include recipes for how to make tea," she assured me. The rest of the day passed in a painful haze.

ON DAY TWO, I made several unfortunate discoveries.

With dreams of latkes dancing in my slow-moving, uncaffeinated brain, I made my way out to the garden with a shovel and a bucket. I have a half dozen potato zones in the veggie garden. One sprawled out of a neglected compost pile. I imagined the fat little crusters down below mixing with the dried-up leaves and stalks that had been breaking down over the years. A carbohydrate dream.

In February I had nestled the potatoes, organic blues, bought at the grocery store, at the bottom of the compost bin. Over their round shoulders I dumped fava bean leftovers, hay cleaned out from the chicken area, spent pea vines. As the green potato stalks emerged I bundled them with more straw and green matter. In Matthew Biggs's *Complete Book of Vegetables*, the British garden writer advised, "New potatoes are harvested when the flowers are blooming; larger ones once the foliage dies back." (He also mentioned that Marie Antoinette wore potato blossoms in her hair.)

I knew it was early, my potatoes hadn't yet blossomed, but Mr. Biggs had no idea how carb starved I was. A plate of mashed potatoes. If I could eat that, I would be happy for the rest of the day.

But now that I was digging, the plant, I had to admit, didn't look very healthy. I peered closer. Oh, no. Potato bugs, hundreds of them, were gnawing on the leaves and stalk. I plunged the shovel into the dirt and brought up a generous scoop. Grappling through the dirt, I found exactly two purple potatoes. Small ones. The size of marbles. The mother potato was deflated from this effort, and a few pale shots slumped off of her girth.

I surveyed the rest of the potato plants tucked here and there around the garden. Instead of seeing bountiful plants whose secret underground parts would get me through this experiment, I saw only unproductive freeloaders. What I had hoped was an iceberg of carbohydrates, with plenty down below, was reduced to an ice cube bobbing in a swimming pool. It would be a very small crop indeed. I carefully placed the marbles in my bucket and went upstairs to prepare my feast.

While the spuds fried in a dry cast-iron pan, I paced the living room, wondering what the hell I was supposed to eat for the rest of the month. During the Irish potato boom, people had plenty of food because potatoes grow easily—and, more than that, they make you feel full. Without carbs, satiety would be a distant memory.

Then I noticed our mantel. For the past two years, some corncobs I grew my first year of squat farming had lingered up there, along with a set of deer antlers and a white orchid plant. Indian corn, grown and saved for decorations. Once mere objects—now, as I gazed up at the multicolored cobs, I saw food. Carb food.

And so I did something I'd never done before, I ate an item of home decor. From a yellow-and-blue-checked ear of corn, I carefully pried out the individual kernels from their cobby home and piled them onto the table. As I loosened each kernel I felt like a prairie woman or an Indian squaw. I whispered thanks to my past self, the carbohydrate provider, who had thought to save those ears. One cob yielded a handful of corn. I deeply wanted cornmeal pancakes. But I didn't have a metate, the traditional stone grinder that Native Americans used, and I wasn't about to destroy my electric coffee grinder.

But I did have a Spong hand-cranked coffee grinder I'd bought a long time ago, out of nostalgia. It's made of metal painted black and red, with a little removable pan that catches the grounds. My mom's artsy friend Barb always hand-ground her coffee. Barb wore bohemian outfits (men's clothes, flowing dresses with skeleton patterns), had red hair down to her butt, and once had a pet crow. I remember visiting her kitchen in Idaho as a child. Barb and my mom flitted around the kitchen, laughing and glad to see each other again. My sister and I, standing on a chair, took turns grinding the dark beans for their morning coffee.

When, a few years ago, I spotted a similar grinder at a basement sale of an Italian imported-foods shop, I couldn't resist. And of course, I hadn't used it since. Who wants to labor, precaffeinated, over a hand-grinder for ten minutes in the morning? Yet now this grinder would be my salvation.

I carefully placed the kernels into the Spong. It was as if I were a kid again, standing on a chair and grinding. Only this time, I had my full weight propped up against the table so it wouldn't shake as

I watched the kernels mill around in the hopper. But instead of the fetching aroma of fresh-ground coffee, I had the powdery residue of almost pure starch.

I've made cornmeal pancakes before, a family recipe adapted from *Joy of Cooking*. Add boiling water to cornmeal and let it rest. Add baking powder, salt, milk, an egg, and some melted butter, then mix. Of those ingredients, I had only the hot water and the egg. After letting an eighth of a cup of boiling water soak the yellow grain, I cracked an egg in, whipped it about, and poured the mixture into three blobs on a cast-iron pan.

I couldn't believe that the cakes actually puffed up like real pancakes. I ate them with a drizzle of honey and some stewed peaches on the side, with the blackened dwarf potatoes. They were the best pancakes I've ever eaten. I licked the plate. I counted the remaining corn cobs. Twelve.

A Glutton for Gluten

By Jess Thomson

From leitesculinaria.com

Amid this year's craze for gluten-free diets, Jess Thomson
faced a strict new eating regimen—hard enough for a normal
eater, even harder for a professional food writer, recipe
developer, and blogger, living in foodcentric Seattle. Before
the axe fell, she needed one last splurge.

I felt like I'd been punched in the gut. But in contrast to the
previous few weeks of feeling generally crummy, this time,
the wind was literally knocked out of me. By my doctor.

A few days earlier, she'd tested me for celiac disease, an auto-
immune disorder that prevents a person from properly digesting
gluten, a protein found in wheat, rye, barley, and, let's be honest,
just about everything good in this world. Now she'd just called
with the results, informing me that some of the tests were positive, some were negative. This wasn't normal. "Everything may still
be OK," she explained. "But we'll have to do more bloodwork to
be sure."

What my doctor didn't have to say was that if the second round
of tests came back positive, all of my relationships and habits surrounding cooking and eating would be annihilated. Even before
I'd gone to the doctor, I was shaken by the events of the previous
few weeks. Without my habitual food cravings, I feared the food
writer's equivalent of a divorce: loss of appetite.

Now, with the looming loss of gluten, it wasn't just the potential
forfeiture of bread that made me feel sick. It was the whole shebang: No more soy sauce. No more good, thick chowders. No

more bedtime bowl of Cheerios. It seemed that my entire relationship with food—and, by extension, my entire sense of self—might fall apart. I struggled to breathe, mentally catastrophizing my career in a matter of seconds. My doctor said she'd call Monday with the results.

It was Friday.

Friday, as it turns out, is a very long time from Monday. So I did what any self-respecting lover of all things food-related would do: I decided to spend the entire weekend having fabulous, unprotected sex with gluten.

I slammed two sticks of butter onto the counter to soften for chocolate-chunk cookies. Feeling stubborn and suddenly hungry for the first time in a month, I grabbed a pen and started scribbling down what I creatively titled "Things To Eat This Weekend." I concentrated my efforts outside of my own kitchen, desiring those things that weren't exactly practical to pull off at home. When I stopped to read what I'd written, I realized that these were the foods I lived to eat—foods that I could avoid only if I stripped my tongue of taste buds and invested in a considerable amount of hypnosis. If I was facing abandonment, I wanted a final fling. I'd savor a good, greasy kiss from the double-bacon deluxe with cheese at Red Mill Burgers. I'd lick a hundred translucent shards of impossibly flaky croissants from my fingers, eyes closed, thanks to Café Besalu. I'd slurp ramen at Samurai Noodle, memorizing how it felt as the noodles slithered in my mouth, my lips slippery with pork fat-flavored ChapStick. It would be a long, slow, tortuous dance through my culinary Eden.

As I pondered my list, it occurred to me that it's perhaps not a coincidence that "glutinous" and "gluttonous" are spelled so similarly. Nothing without gluten would pass my lips until Monday. I'd eat my way through the pain of pending rejection, savoring every detail, every quirk, every crumb.

That night, I gorged on an immodest number of cookies. I went to bed early but spent a couple of hours tossing, distracted, comparing my potential split with gluten to a very real separation. I pondered whether to call a friend of mine who'd just been dumped, thinking he might be able to help me feel less forsaken. After all, our situations seemed pretty identical, save for the minor detail that my break-up, should gluten and I permanently part ways, wouldn't leave me searching for a new apartment. I decided that at least I had that going for me, which calmed me slightly. I took a Xanax and passed out.

I spent the next day edibly etching the word "last" across my renewed appetite. My husband and I started our Saturday here in Seattle as we always do during ski season: with sausage-and-egg breakfast sandwiches. The last time I'll dig English muffin crumbs out of my ski boots, I thought. A full 20 minutes later, we stopped for a Frisbee-sized cinnamon roll slathered in orange-tinged icing. The last time I'll buy pastry that could double as a Princess Leia headdress. I had a BLT for lunch before polishing off the rest of the cinnamon roll. My last sandwich. We met friends for a drink later in the afternoon and I downed a hefeweizen. My last beer. Dinner was at Tavolata, my favorite Seattle pasta joint, where I swooned over my spaghetti studded with anchovies, chilies, and garlic, committing its flavor to memory. My last meal here. (OK, maybe that was a little dramatic. I could always go back and order something without gluten. But why subject myself to the hauntings of a hundred happier moments?) Afterward, I still had room for doughnuts.

Sunday morning. Before the newspaper had even hit the porch, I'd torn into a ham-and-Gruyère croissant. My husband and I cruised the farmers' market while munching on a crusty baguette. Then I ordered a slice of thin-crust pizza from the market's mobile wood-fired oven. I forced a vegetarian pal to come to Red Mill with me, where I picked the burger bun apart and obsessively rolled it into little balls before eating it. She just stared at me, not knowing what to say. We'd invited friends over for dinner that evening, so I made spelt risotto and, after licking my plate, gorged on pain de campagne dipped in olive oil.

All the while, something deep inside my brain, a little nagging whisper—or was it my husband's voice?—reminded me that there's more than one way to make a cinnamon roll, a slice of bread, or a strand of spaghetti. That, in fact, there's more to eat in the world than wheat. But, like a bitter divorcée-to-be, I had no interest in reason. I couldn't see a way forward without what I couldn't have.

With each bite that weekend, celiac disease seemed more and more probable. You know how sometimes something happens—or doesn't happen—and you make up a completely irrational explanation and then convince yourself that it's true? That's how I was with gluten. By bedtime Sunday, I was taking it personally. Gluten hates me, I thought. Then suddenly—OK, finally—it registered. No one had ever really broken up with me. I was being dumped for the first time. By a protein. Or not. I wasn't sure. And that was the problem.

I spent most of Monday staring at my phone, realizing that the last time I'd willed someone to call like this was when I was still wearing braces. Now, like then, I wanted validation. I needed resolution. I thought about sending gluten a handwritten note with two boxes: Check here if you like me. Check here if you don't like me. To distract myself, I made pizza with nettle pesto, kale, and semi-dried tomatoes, ate a panini while it was still too hot, and rattled around the house looking for other foods to cry over.

Late Tuesday afternoon, I got my call. The test results were all normal—except that stubborn antigliadin antibody, which some believe is the leading indicator of celiac disease. "You probably don't have celiac," were my doctor's opening words. "But we can't say for sure without a biopsy. You could try not eating gluten for a while. . . . Although, that might not be the solution, either."

I should've been elated. It seemed that gluten wanted me back. Mostly, anyway. So what now? Make-up sex, I decided halfheartedly. Spaghetti bolognese. And the next day, I'd go for that ramen I'd missed over the weekend. No protein dumps this girl.

But when I opened the pantry, I saw a bunch of needy, noncommital pastas and flours staring back at me, daring me to prove to them—and to myself—that I needed gluten. Now that gluten had decided to crawl back to me, head hanging, it looked rather pathetic.

One of my friends is Shauna James Ahern, a.k.a. Gluten-Free Girl, who's quite possibly the only person on the planet who makes eating gluten-free sound downright sexy. Maybe if I called her, she'd do break-up duty, commiserating with me. Reassuring me that no, I didn't need gluten. I tried for a moment to pretend that going gluten-free could be an adventure. Character building, even. I'll admit, I was curious to learn about all those flours I'd marveled over but never actually used in baking. I was sure Shauna would show me The Way. So I called her.

Some of her tests had come back negative the first time, too. Yet when gluten rejected her, she turned her back on it, defiantly and irrevocably, head held high.

I decided that mostly wasn't good enough. I didn't want to be the girl who was lucky enough to maybe get a second chance. No woman wants to be loved conditionally.

I was going to give eating gluten-free a try. It wouldn't be easy. I'd miss the burger joint. But what if I actually started feeling better?

I had my answer.

"It's not you," I said, staring into the pantry. "It's me. I just need some time to myself. Some time to think."

And with that, I packed up all of gluten's things and tossed him out.

The Doughnut Gatherer

By Dara Moskowitz Grumdahl

From *Minnesota Monthly*

Having children is a life-changing experience—but
Minneapolis/St. Paul food writer Dara Moskowitz Grumdahl
never anticipated how her oldest child would radically alter
her approach to food.

There such a thing as a bad doughnut? Until very recently I would have said: "Yes. Most of them." The gas-station doughnut. The grocery-store doughnut. The big-box store doughnut. These are mere vehicles for sugar and grease, and Americans would be better off if we ate carrot sticks until we could purchase superior artisan-made doughnuts.

I would have said this because I say it about every kind of junk food: nachos, pizza, chilidogs, cheese steaks, and so on. In fact, I've based most of my professional identity on this idea, that if you want to know what the best doughnut in town is, you simply go to 12 or 20 of the likeliest places and find the best. And you want the best, don't you? That's self-evident, right? Everyone wants the best.

I do. Or I did. Before I got pregnant, before I had kids. Now I've got a one-year-old who will eat anything—shabu shabu, red curry, sand—and a three-and-a-half-year-old who will eat almost nothing. Consequently, this food critic has learned a few things about food.

I'll call him Beans. That's not his real name. But I used to sing him a lullaby about bumblebees when he was a baby, and over time, bee turned to beans.

Beans was born colicky and beset by acid-reflux. Tilt him off an upright axis and his stomach acid would bubble past a little poorly functioning valve and make him scream. Until he was eight months old, he had to be held upright at all times. My husband would stay up walking and holding him until 3 a.m., at which point the alarm clock would ring and I would wake to hold him.

Things have gotten better, though not much. His stomach still hurts all the time, and he doesn't like food. He eats about a dozen things, all white, all things you'd want if you were recovering from stomach flu: pears, apples, Saltines, white bread, pretzels, Cheerios, string cheese, poached chicken meatballs, butter, and ice cream (rarely). That about wraps it up.

If you read the foodie press, you'll know it's a point of pride among today's parents to brag about what arcane foods their child delights in: Japanese nori paper, capers, Roquefort cheese. Ideally, the sentence you want to drop at the playground runs something like this: "Little Gabriel is such a snob, he won't eat cassoulet with truffle oil—only real truffles. I'm going to go bankrupt!"

Not us.

This is painful. As a food critic, it destroys the dream I had when I first got pregnant, that of running around to obscure taco holes and barbecue dives with my little sidekick. More urgently, as a parent, it means I have no way to bribe him.

Other children consider being sent to bed without supper punishment. Being sent to bed without supper would be Beans's preferred evening. (My husband and I have twice taken our pediatrician's advice to simply offer food, without insisting Beans eat it. Both times, after two days, when not a single morsel of food had crossed his lips, we buckled.) Other children can be coerced into all sorts of activities by offering or withholding dessert. We're as likely to get Beans to eat a cupcake as we are to get him to eat a block of soap. A few weeks ago, I got a bag of jelly beans in the mail as part of some promotion. I brought them home. We got Beans an egg carton, into which he happily sorted the jelly beans by color. Over the next week, he did this several more times—and not one jelly bean went missing. He has a bag full of Dum-Dum lollipops from which he has removed all the wrappers. He sticks them into modeling clay to make sculptures. Child-rearing experts tell us that one of the chief predictors of a child's future success is the ability to delay gratification, to choose two cookies in 15 minutes rather than just one cookie now. There are no studies on children who want no cookies ever.

Now, you may be thinking: Why don't you just cut the kid some slack and let him not eat? Isn't the ultimate state of enlightenment to live without desire? Hasn't Beans achieved this at the tender age of three?

If you are thinking this, it is probably because you are an idealistic 14-year-old without kids. I know this because I was once an idealistic 14-year-old without kids, and that idealistic voice still echoes in my head. I find myself incredulous how deep and dark my desire is to lure or coerce my kid into eating. This uneasy part of me, however, has been pummeled into submission by the panic-stricken part of me, the part of me that can't shake the memory of being at a friend's vacation house in Wisconsin where we met another family with a child beset by the same cluster of acid-reflux symptoms. This child's family didn't force her to eat. She was five years old, but she was the size of a slight two-year-old. Her family explained that her teeth were so soft, from lack of nutrients and vomiting, that she would probably soon get child-sized dentures.

So we force him to eat. Here's how: We turn on the television. There have been studies showing that sugar is more appealing to rats then cocaine. In my experience, television, to a curious toddler, is more powerful than either. We turn on a screen, and sit behind him popping bites of meatball and cheese in his mouth. It's a terrible option, except for all the other ones. I've heard other parents call television "the zombie machine." Exactly.

Then there's YouTube. For a while Beans was obsessed with church bells, and we would watch videos of ringing church bells, as well as glockenspiels, carillons, and hand bells. Later it was marble-runs and domino constructions falling down. Then he discovered a show that airs on the Discovery Channel called "How It's Made." The show consists of five-minute segments explaining the construction of crayons, novelty ice-cream treats, push brooms, and everything else. Beans' favorite was about doughnuts.

At first, I didn't think too much about it. It's not atypical for Beans to watch a two-minute YouTube clip hundreds of times. There's a 1979 Sesame Street abstract animation, set to a piece by Philip Glass, called "Geometry of Circles" that he must have watched a thousand times. But one night, I found him in his bath, shoving bath toys through the water, reciting: "A high-speed mixer works the yeast dough, then workers pull it off the machine into bins. From there, it goes into a hopper that extrudes the dough as a sheet. . . ." Not long after that, I found him shoving his favorite blanket into a drawer, slamming the drawer shut, then extracting the blanket and transferring it to a space beneath a footstool, all while providing this commentary: "Doughnuts used to be called 'oily-cakes' because they were deep-fried in pork fat. They were ball-shaped when Dutch pilgrims brought them to America. . . ."

"Beans, are you making doughnuts?" I asked.

"I am," he said. "I am making doughnuts. . . . A high speed mixer works the yeast dough. . . ."

Was this the thin end of a wedge?

I thought so—if doughnuts could somehow become more than a mechanical process to Beans, that is. I ordered some books.

Children's picture-book literature involving doughnuts is limited, but uniformly excellent. There's *Arnie the Doughnut*, by Laurie Keller, about a young ring of dough "chocolate-covered with bright-colored candy sprinkles," who is made through a series of numbered steps. Beans particularly enjoys step two: "Deep-fried," which involves Arnie swimming in oil and saying, "I'm soaking in boiling grease but I LOVE IT!"

After Arnie meets his fellow doughnuts in a pastry case, a rude doughnut hole points at a jelly doughnut and shrieks, "Eeeooo! His brains are leaking out!" To which the doughnut replies, "It's not brains, silly. It's jelly!"

Arnie is nearly eaten by his purchaser, Mr. Bing, which horrifies Arnie, and so he phones his baker to warn him, at which point he is informed that doughnuts are, in fact, made to be eaten. Arnie can't believe him.

"Are the other doughnuts aware of this arrangement?" he gasps.

There's also *The Donut Chef*, by Bob Staake, which details the war between "two donut shops on one small street! For customers they did compete!" This competition first involves discounts and extra frosting, but it soon devolves into something else: "Some were square and some were starry, some looked just like calamari!"

Eventually, after all the peculiar shapes have been mastered, bizarre flavorings are brought to bear, until the day a small girl named Debbie Sue ventures in, looking for a plain glazed doughnut. There is none. "We've donuts laced with kiwi jam/And served inside an open clam!" Staake writes. "Donuts made with huckleberry/(Don't be scared; they're kind of hairy)/And donuts made from spiced rum pears/So popular with millionaires!"

I bristled the first time I read *The Donut Chef*. (Were children's picture books really going to criticize molecular gastronomy? Really?) But over time it's grown on me, especially when I hear Beans reciting the doughnut-positive messages in the book: "Then all the people sang in praise/Of simple donuts dipped in glaze!"

But my favorite doughnut book is a recent re-issue of 1973's *Who Needs Donuts?* It's an odd, psychedelic-looking pen-and-ink drawn book by Mark Alan Stamaty, a famous illustrator whose work has appeared in the likes of the *Village Voice*, *Slate*, and *New York Review of Books*. The book tells the story of a boy who can never get enough doughnuts, and so one day he rides his tricycle to the city to get his fill. He pairs up with a professional doughnut-gatherer. As he and his pal roam the city, they often cross paths with a bereft-looking woman.

"Who needs donuts when you've got love?" she asks.

The answer? The bereft old woman herself, of course. After an escaped bull pierces a giant vat of coffee that sits above her basement home, she risks drowning until the boy uses his many, many doughnuts to rescue her—by soaking up all the coffee.

Perhaps what I like so much about *Who Needs Donuts* is that, aside from imagining a world in which children are unafraid of the city, it features the only professional doughnut-gatherer I've ever run across—besides myself.

In many years of restaurant criticism, I've written about doughnuts repeatedly. I actually have a sort of road map in my mind of what I consider the best doughnuts in town: There's Mel-O-Glaze, in south Minneapolis, home to the city's best raised-glazed doughnuts, as well as the cake doughnuts that I prefer above all others.

Sweet and rich, they're almost like pound cake. Even if I've been to six other doughnut places first, I can always eat a whole doughnut when I get to Mel-O-Glaze, which is saying something.

Then there's the Baker's Wife's, a mere 10 blocks north of Mel-O-Glaze. A lot of people argue that they make the best cake doughnuts in town, and I see that as a respectable opinion. They're less sweet, crisper, and they seem even more old-fashioned than most plain cake doughnuts.

I also really like Wuollet's, which has the area's best selection of the usual suspects: Long Johns, bear claws, and the like. Then there are our other lovable local doughnut places: Sara Jane in Northeast, Rosemark in St. Paul, Granny Donut in West St. Paul, Denny's Fifth Avenue Bakery in Bloomington, the Old Fashioned Donut Shoppe in New Hope.

On the way to Denny's Fifth Avenue Bakery in Bloomington, I fed Beans lines from all the books: "'Scuse me, Mister,' said the tyke, 'But where's the donut that I like? It isn't here, it isn't there—You think it's under that éclair?'"

We zipped down the construction canyon of I-35, between the dinosaur-sized diggers, oblivious to their dusty menace, for the topic of doughnuts was just that riveting. Denny's Fifth Avenue feels like it has been lifted whole from the 1970s; it's all Jimmy Carter bicentennial blue and naugahyde brown, slick, vinyl-touched, and awkward. Beans stood in front of the pastry case like a pro. There they all were, the Long Johns, the cream-filled, the jelly. Arnie had prepared him well for this moment.

"Is that brains leaking out?" Beans asked, rhetorically. "Nah, it's just jelly."

I got a dozen, and he got one just like Arnie, chocolate-covered, with bright-colored candy sprinkles. I placed it on a piece of wax paper and set it on his lap as he sat in his car seat. There it rested for the drive home. I fed him lines from the books all the way home: "Do you doughnuts know you're going to be eaten?" I asked. "Yes, we're delicious!" he replied. "Try us for yourself!"

When we arrived at home, I looked at the doughnut carefully. To the untrained eye, it might have seemed untouched. But there was one small blemish on the icing's surface, as if a thumb had smudged it, or a little mouse had, perhaps, taken a lick.

A few days later, we went to Wuollet's. The one on Hennepin Avenue that always has a pleasant mix of dog-walkers from Lake of the Isles, anti-coffeeshop rebel teens doing homework, and construction workers and tradesmen. We got a box of the assorted doughnuts. I particularly enjoyed the raised yeast one frosted with chocolate. It had a deep real-cocoa taste. However, even to my wishful eye, I knew that the sprinkle-topped doughnut I got for Beans was completely untouched. I coined a name for such perfectly lovely doughnuts that went unsampled: They were Holders. Beans liked holding them. In fact, he liked them so much that he would spend 24 hours holding on to them, moving them from plate to bag repeatedly. But if any icing got on his hands, he'd demand: "Mom, can you clean it up?"

We made a trip to Mel-O-Glaze. Sun twinkled from the wide parkway outside and into the vintage bakery. I thought the doughnuts were great. The raised glazed was light and dewy within, the cake doughnut was sweet and buoyant in just the right way. But, it, too, was a Holder.

We went to A Baker's Wife's, a tiny bakery cluttered as a church sale with baked goods, but the crisp little gem there was also a Holder. We even made the trip to Granny Donuts a nowhere-looking chain in West St. Paul. The doughnuts there were, at best, average, cold, and greasy tasting. I wished I had made mine a Holder, instead of a Taster.

Doughnuts, it turned out, were not the thin end of the wedge. In fact, doughnuts were starting to become a lot like parenting itself, which in my experience is a series of minute, constant, intolerable failures, interleaved with exhaustion, and punctuated by moments of heart-rending cuteness that somehow add up to general success. The success, of course, comes not from anything one does, but because of nature's plan: The kids grow. Before I had kids I'd hear things like, "Parenting is humbling," and I'd put that in the same basket as, "Life is sweet," and "Happiness is worth pursuing." Whatever. Now I know that parenting is humbling because you can put all the mighty force of your heart and mind into it and you will still be failing. Where'd I put that remote control?

Still, while doughnuts were looking to be a series of failures they also had become a habit, and when I picked Beans up from preschool one day, he asked for a doughnut. It was the end of the day when we stopped at Wuollet's, and they were cleaned out. So we crossed the street to SuperAmerica. I hoisted him up so he could peer inside the plastic doors at the plastic-looking donuts on their plastic trays, and Beans chose a raised-glazed and a vanilla-iced with bright candy sprinkles. Such doughnuts are the heroes, respectively, of *The Donut Chef* and *Arnie the Doughnut*. Beans put them in a plastic bag, and carried them around like carnival goldfish all evening. The doughnuts even came with us when we walked the neighbor's dog to the neighborhood garden. And as we sat in this garden, next to an old wishing well, Beans turned a handle.

Ka-thunk, ka-thunk.

"Mom," Beans said, "Mom I want to make a wish in the wishing well."

"Yes," I said. "You can make a wish. What do you want to wish for?"

"I wish for doughnuts," he said. He looked at me intensely, a little smile tickling his mouth with its little baby teeth slightly too far apart. "I wish for doughnuts," he said again.

I took the doughnut out of the bag and, to my astonishment, Beans actually tried eating it. Of course, he didn't know how, and went in icing-first, from the top. In the process, he gave himself a clown nose of white icing, and a matching goatee and moustache, too.

All I could think was: Really? A SuperAmerica doughnut?

I re-direct your attention to the central tenet of my professional existence, namely, that good food is better than bad food. This could not stand.

We went back to Mel-O-Glaze. Those doughnuts were still Holders. Back to Baker's Wife's. Holders. But then one day we were heading back to the house from the playground when Beans requested a doughnut. We stopped at a coffee shop with baked goods straight from some warehouse store. Beans got a pink doughnut with candy sprinkles—and began eating it straight-away, spinning it until he ate all the sprinkles and icing off the top. His one-year-old sister, sitting next to him in a double stroller finished her doughnut, then lunged for his. Amid the tussle, his doughnut cracked in half.

"Mom!" Beans shrieked, preparing to cry. Until he realized the breaking had revealed a secret inner-nugget of icing and sprinkles. Which he ate.

And now Beans eats doughnuts. I feel pride, because eating more, and not less, is an enormous triumph in our little world, and somehow we got from eating less to eating more. But more than that I feel painfully amused, because as per usual, triumph comes at the end of a chain of near total failure. And this chain of failures has even forced me to come to terms with something that readers have been telling me for years, an idea that I have so hotly resisted—that good enough is indeed good enough, that any port in a storm is better than none, and that there may well be no such thing as a bad doughnut. Sometimes.

Home Run: My Journey Back to Korean Food

By Roy Ahn

From *Gastronomica*

Though he now lives in Cambridge, Massachusetts, Roy Ahn
has had many hometowns—Seoul, South Korea; the Detroit
suburbs; the San Fernando Valley in Southern California. His
evolving sense of "Korean-ness"—epitomized by Korean
food—is still a work in progress.

L
ast winter, I dined with my then-pregnant wife, Amy, at a
Korean restaurant in a suburban strip mall, where all
good Korean food establishments seem to be. This hole-in-the-
wall, located on a stretch of highway outside Boston flanked by retail plazas and ranch houses, was filled with Koreans like myself,
plus a Caucasian or two, Amy being one. The proprietor sat us in a
spot away from the section with barbecue-grill tabletops, but the
smell of seared beef mixed with garlic, soy sauce, and brown sugar
still permeated our clothing. (Pop quiz: How long does the smell
of beef *bulgogi* linger in a pair of blue jeans? Answer: Until it gets
thrown into a washing machine.)

The waitresses spun like dervishes from table to kitchen to
table, bringing out vegetable and fish *banchan* dishes in one pass
and clearing them away in another, with little respite between customers to wipe their beads of sweat. I took particular notice of the
diners' white bowls, which reminded me of outsized pieces from
Go, my late father's favorite board game.

After a cup of tea and our own *banchan*, we awaited the main
courses. Mine would be *galbi-chim*—braised short ribs—served

with rice. I imagined pulling the meat off the bone and the flecks of burnt sesame seeds staining the white rice a deep brown, so I was understandably shocked when the waitress placed before me a bowl of oxtail soup. Had she misunderstood? No, I quickly realized. I had ordered the wrong dish.

On the surface, confusing *galbi-tang* with *galbi-chim* would seem an innocuous lapse. Both are beef dishes whose names share the same Korean-language prefix. But the two couldn't be more different. Imagine a Bavarian confusing knockwurst with bratwurst! As I lowered pieces of *kimchi* into the beef broth to give it a spice kick, and as Amy sipped her way through her bowl of bean-curd-and-vegetable stew, I wondered whether my slipup was an omen: could I be losing my ethnic bearings? If so, there could hardly be a worse time.

I was harboring all sorts of yuppie anxieties about first-time fatherhood—the unit cost of diapers and 529 College Savings Plans chief among them. But as a Korean-American, I was also worrying about our son's cultural identity. I especially looked forward to introducing him to my culinary heritage. That task would be solely up to me—Amy is from a multiple-generation Wisconsin family with European roots, and our culinary union is best described as Land of Rice meets Land of Cheese. Consider some of the foods you might see in her parents' house near Madison: pepper Jack, butterkasse, and Limberger cheeses, along with sauerkraut, pickled Brussels sprouts, and wursts of all kinds.

As for my parents, they won't be around to introduce my son to their native foods, teach him how to bow properly to his elders, sing Korean nursery rhymes, or explain to him that the number four represents bad luck for Koreans. Both of them died in a car accident when I was twenty-four.

I was born in Seoul in 1972. My parents, a physician and an elementary school teacher, were concerned about raising children in South Korea at a time when military conflict with North Korea seemed imminent, so they immigrated to the United States with my older sister and me when I was four. My official, stamped Korean passport noted that I was "90 cm" tall and weighed "11 kg"—about the equivalent of a twenty-five-pound bag of rice. But soon enough I began to grow, my chubbiness a testament to my success-ful American acculturation.

As a kid living in suburban Detroit, I loved two things above all else: Baskin-Robbins and the Detroit Tigers. (I still think the ice-cream-inside-miniature-batting-helmet remains one of the indus-try's greatest inventions.) Inside our apartment I would mark out my own baseball diamond, sprinkle the floor with talcum powder, and, using my father's thick medical textbooks as bases, slide my way across the room as though I were Lou Brock. Like many American boys, I dreamed of becoming a professional baseball player but lacked the athleticism to play beyond high school. My dream of pro ball quashed, I once told my mother that I wanted to become president of a Fortune 500 company. She laughed. A Cau-casian businessman would never allow a Korean to have that job, she said, steering me into the sciences instead.

My childhood love of ice cream notwithstanding, my favorite Korean dish was a bowl of rice drizzled with soy sauce and topped with a raw egg. I learned to crack the egg over the rice while it was still piping hot, so the egg would cook a little. Sometimes my mother would add some sliced *daikon* to this silky porridge that glided so easily down my throat. Over time, I began to add my own flourishes—a handful of cooked ground beef and a pinch of dried red-pepper flakes.

During my teenage years, after we moved to Los Angeles, I chose to downplay my ethnic roots. I was a Ralph Lauren–clad American teenager living in "The Valley," and my Korean heritage was an in-convenience. This applied to my culinary traditions, too. When I went out, I ate all the things my friends did—pizza, hot dogs, enchiladas, and fries with greasy chili that turned the paper wrapper orange. It's worth noting that two Korean-American boys were among my cir-cle, but we rarely went out for food from the homeland. Whatever the reason, they were much more comfortable than I was with being Korean-American. Still, when my circle of guy friends went out, we'd usually opt for fried zucchini with ranch dressing at Carl's Jr., chicken burritos at a Mexican food chain on Ventura Boulevard, or pasta at the Cheesecake Factory in Beverly Hills, all the while rock-ing out in our cars to the Beastie Boys and Run-DMC.

When I got home, I chased down all that American food with Korean fare. My mother, who spoke to me almost exclusively in her native tongue, cooked it herself or stocked up on prepared foods from our local Korean supermarkets. Variations of *kimchi* abounded: red-pepper-flecked radish cubes, cucumber slices, bell-flower root, and cabbage. Occasionally, too, there was yellow daikon, which paired well with ground beef, spinach, and rice. Or she would make ginseng chicken stew and *japchae*, a stir-fry of glass noodles, sliced carrot and onion, slivers of beef, and pink-and-white fishcake in a soy and sesame-oil sauce. Food to fuel the brain for studying deep into the night: a mother's loving manifesto for her son. I never had the heart to tell her that the food had the opposite effect—the sugar crash put me to sleep atop my school papers.

I should mention that our house in California had two refrigerators: one in the kitchen for American food, and one in the garage for the Korean food. I'm not sure why my mother was willing to go dual-fridge. I imagine she'd had enough bellyaching from me about the garlicky stench of "Mom and Dad's food" and complaints of how embarrassing it would be if my friends ever got a whiff of the real stuff we ate. She must have decided it wasn't worth the aggravation.

My father, for his part, took my resistance to Korean food poorly. He'd wanted me to be proud of his homeland. "Italian food smells, too," he once told me. But Korean dishes flavored with garlic smell different than Italian ones, and I imagined the odor exuding from my every pore. Leftover Korean food was even worse, announcing itself like a flatulent guest at a wedding. Never mind that a diet of smelly fermented vegetables, stews, noodles, and meats has nourished Koreans for generations.

You may imagine that my father disapproved of American ways. On the contrary, he immersed himself in the culture of his adopted country. Interstate road trips to amusement parks, Kentucky Fried Chicken, bowling. While he loved being Korean, he was fascinated by cultures other than his own and especially enjoyed commingling them. To this day, I can't picture a bucket of KFC extra-crispy without adjacent bowls of white rice and *kimchi*. My father's stacks of Japanese novels were piled right alongside Westerns by Louis L'Amour, and he listened to instructional language tapes on Spanish and Mandarin in his spare time. He often serenaded us on road trips with his rendition of "Tears on My Pillow," a number he'd learned from the soundtrack of *Grease*. Once, I watched him eat a bowl of white rice with ketchup, straight up. Another time, he used chopsticks to pluck Vienna sausages out of their tin. He was so pleased with his concoctions, so original in his wackiness, that I believe I inherited my own willingness to improvise from him.

My mother, by contrast, was never comfortable in the States. She struggled to pick up English and didn't make many friends outside her Korean church. A short woman with permed black hair, large brown eyes, and caramel-colored skin, darker than that of most Korean women I knew, she watched a lot of Korean soap operas on the VCR and seemed content to have a vicarious American experience through her children.

Little Korean boys do not take formal cooking lessons from their mothers; the kitchen is considered a woman's domain. Nonetheless, I made excuses to spend time with her there. Cooking Korean dishes means a lot of sautéing, boiling, grilling, and frying. She rarely baked. I considered my mother a great cook, although she always told me she was only so-so, modestly claiming there were other women at church who possessed skills far superior to her own.

I don't recall that we did a lot of talking while I watched her cook. She did not share with me the latest in church gossip, nor did she try to impart wisdom in the form of hackneyed analogies about food and life. Such things are better left for movies involving white people and karate. Instead, I recall marveling at the way she so deftly used a paring knife to peel fruit, her thumb applying pressure until the skin unfurled in a continuous ribbon. She had good hands for peeling, with strong fingers, neither long nor stubby. I watched her make simple dishes that, later on, when my parents both went to work, became my latchkey-kid staples.

There was one American experience my entire family did enjoy: eating steamed crabs at the Redondo Beach Pier. The dining experience was far from formal. We'd place our order, lay several pages of the *Los Angeles Times* atop one of the many communal tables, and wait for the crabs to steam. I remember how excited I was to buy lemons (for cleaning our hands afterward) and rent crab mallets. I'd crack my crab with authority, as though I were a judge lowering a gavel. Using my hands to eat, I tried my best to avoid touching the mustard-colored crab guts. Afterward, I played Skee-Ball until I drained my parents of ones and fives. As a family, we walked off our meals along the beach, sometimes until the sun set. My parents seemed so contented there. My mother was at ease at the beach, less concerned about fitting in, and she laughed a lot.

For a few years after my parents' deaths, I lived in a weird fog, unable to focus on my future or reconcile my past. I lost interest in all things Korean, including food. When my mother was alive, she would ask me questions in Korean and I would respond in English. After she was gone, my grip on the language loosened.

I began to work summers as a cook at an artists' colony café in a resort town in the Rocky Mountains. There, under the best of all possible circumstances—cooking for, and being inspired by, the master printmakers, woodworkers, painters, and ceramic artists who came through the colony—I learned to make crème brûlée, venison stroganoff, and other European dishes. In that nurturing atmosphere, as my confidence in cooking grew, so did my expressiveness through food. (Within limits, of course: my idea for a "healthful" sugar cookie made with lemon Ricola cough drops never made it onto diners' plates.) But something even more unexpected occurred: latent Korean influences began to insinuate themselves into the food I prepared. I fried rectangles of tofu in vegetable oil. I tenderized flank steak in garlicky *kalbi* marinades. I slipped scallions into whatever dishes I could. Sesame oil found its way into my sauces.

I can't say that I channeled my parents by cooking Korean food, or that food reinvigorated my innate sense of Korean-ness. I'm not at all certain about the synapses that get fired when human beings experience emotions from cooking and eating the foods of their childhoods. All I can say for sure is that something sublime happened in that mecca of Korean cuisine—the Rockies—where I rediscovered my native food heritage. My mother left behind no recipe cards. Instead, I created dishes based on my recollections of watching her cook, imagining her in that café kitchen with me, telling me to add a few more red-pepper flakes or dial down the sesame oil.

I still harbor mixed feelings about my parents' move to the United States. Would they still be alive today if we had stayed in Korea? It is, of course, a fool's errand to speculate about something like that. What I do know is that, because of their sacrifice, I have had terrific experiences and opportunities, and that our son, Charlie, will inevitably have the same. One day, if he so chooses, he may even become a corporate CEO—a Fortune 500 one at that. Or a professional baseball player, if I have any say in the matter.

As I write this, Charlie is just three months old. He has my mother's skin tone and big eyes, but otherwise no physical features that specifically remind me of either of my parents. He has my faint black eyebrows and Amy's broad smile. And because he does not cry when I play songs—well, not as much as usual, anyway—I've come to believe that Charlie likes music, especially party music, as much I do. Just last week, he and I danced in our living room to the Commodores' "Brick House."

Meanwhile, food remains a primary conduit through which I hope to instill in him the lessons of one half of his ethnic roots. I'm sad that my parents aren't around to help indoctrinate him into their culture. Even though it might be naive to think that by teaching him to eat and cook Korean he'll also learn about who they were, my gut tells me this is so.

Amy and I live near a Korean supermarket that sells a lot of foods from my youth: perfectly circular Shingo pears, each one cradled in its own Styrofoam nest, and too-sweet candies made from sweet bean, jelly, and agar-agar. I think how cool it will be to have these foods at Charlie's first birthday party. For that celebration I can imagine cooking dishes that capitalize on my knowledge of Korean and non-Korean cuisines. I will sauté fiddleheads with leeks and reserve the leek fronds for garnish. I will make potstickers, doing my best, just as my mother did, to get that even seal on the wrappers, which is so critical to keeping the ground pork and vegetable filling moist. I will put creative spins on Korean classics. I will wrap *bibimbap* ingredients—sliced beef, spinach, carrot slivers, bean sprouts, fried egg, rice—in *nori* straightjackets, drizzle them with wasabi aioli, and present these oversized, funnel-shaped hand rolls in metal Belgian *frites* stands. For dessert, I will experiment by baking sweet red beans *en croûte*.

Of course, I am getting ahead of myself. At the moment, Charlie's diet is limited to two options—fresh breast milk, or thawed-and-warmed breast milk.

Another way Charlie will learn is through language. At the peak of one of his nighttime crying fits last week, I found myself soothing him with calming words—"It's okay, it's okay"—but in Korean, the way my mother might have. Amy is learning the language, too. She has taken classes in Korean through an adult-education center. In fact, she can read and write Korean far better than I can. I intend to join her in these classes, or at least sit in front of a laptop with Charlie and complete our Rosetta Stone exercises together. I mean, who wouldn't benefit from learning the Korean word for elephant (*koo-kee-ree*)? Perhaps this way I will register even farther east on the Korea-meter.

Recently, we had a family dinner at a Korean restaurant in Cambridge. It was a more formal, or, at any rate, more urbane place than the one where I had made my ordering mistake. The host put us in a private room where we had to take our shoes off. During dinner, as Amy nursed Charlie beneath a cotton shawl, I dissected the ingredients in the *banchan* I ate, the proper method of constructing our *ssam* (lettuce wraps), using rice and meat and red kochujang paste. I pronounced aloud the Korean names of as many dishes as I could. And this time I remembered most of them accurately.

Amy fears that our son won't get a sufficient dose of Korean culture. It's a familiar refrain. But I will make sure to offer Charlie Korean food and, as my parents did with me, exercise patience if he doesn't want any. We will stick to one fridge in our house.

GOD LOVES YOU AND
YOU CAN'T DO A THING ABOUT IT

By Kim Severson

From *Spoon Fed: How Eight Cooks Saved My Life*

As *New York Times* food reporter Severson traces her career
(so far) in this revealing memoir, the chapters are strung—
like a connect-the-dots puzzle—along encounters with eight
different cooks, each of whom taught her a different life
lesson.

The first time I stood in front of Dooky Chase, it was still
slimy with flood water and looked for all the world like
another bowl of gumbo would never come from its kitchen.

A day earlier, I'd found one of the last seats on a plane full of
volunteers and evacuated flood victims heading from New York to
Louisiana. It had been three weeks since Katrina, and no one except rescue workers, soldiers and a handful of reporters were allowed inside the city limits. My friend Pableaux Johnson, who calls
himself "your Cajun grandma with a beard," told me he would
borrow a truck and help me work my way into the city. He was
born and raised in Louisiana. He's also a good, enthusiastic cook
and a food writer who is always up for an adventure. But mostly,
Pableaux is a lover of his people. And his people, especially right
after the storm, expanded almost daily to include those of us who
fell into his orbit.

When Katrina hit, he had been living in a rambling apartment
in Uptown, one of the few slivers of New Orleans proper that
stayed dry. He evacuated to St. Martinville, a little town that sits
nearly in the center of Louisiana Cajun country on Bayou Teche.

Pableaux owns a small wooden church there. He converted it into a house and put in a big kitchen where the altar used to be. A couple of months before the hurricanes of 2005, Pableaux published *Eating New Orleans*, an intensely detailed guide on how to work your way through the city's tables.

"Basically, I wrote the guidebook for eating in Atlantis," he told me as we climbed into his truck.

The city had been closed since the levees failed, and Pableaux had been scrambling to take care of his own big, extended family and all the hurricane refugees who ended up at his church. But he was aching to check on his New Orleans apartment and his friends' places, so when I told him I was heading down to cover the culinary aftermath of Hurricane Katrina, he offered to be my Sacagawea. We headed out from the church just a little past three A.M., hoping to make the drive in a couple of hours and get to work before it got light.

We came up on New Orleans from the backside, slipping into a city that was closed along a road we could barely find in the dark. As we crept along, the headlights hit a young man with his hand up. We slowed to a stop. He stepped over broken tree branches and walked toward the pickup. For a split second, he looked like a teenager lost in the dark of a New Orleans night, except he was holding a rifle. When he got close enough, I made out his National Guard uniform. His unit was one of dozens that set up checkpoints around the city. His job was to keep people out until it was safe. I handed over my *Times* identification card and a letter from my newspaper that stated I was there on bona fide news-reporting business. He waved us on, and Pableaux drove into the dark city, navigating around abandoned buses and fallen trees and trying not to hit the stray, hungry dogs that roamed the street.

We spent the morning checking on his friends' homes and his own apartment. Every house we saw had fresh spray-painted circles bisected with Xs. In each quadrant, there was a number or a letter. One indicated the date the house was searched, another the organization that did the search, and yet another the number of bodies found inside. Animal rescuers had roamed the city with cans of paint, too. They were much less discreet, sometimes covering a good portion of the front of a house with entirely unhelpful messages like, "Cute brown dog found here. Was hungry." In the weeks after the city reopened, pet owners were left to puzzle out where their animals ended up with only those cryptic notes for clues.

The flooded, empty city had been baking for almost three weeks in 90-degree heat. Each time we got out of the truck, a stench would hit us so hard we pulled our T-shirts up over our noses. It was the airborne muck from maggoty food and leathery patches of mud and algae mixed with gasoline and an untraceable stink that was not unlike a rotting sneaker filled with Époisses. After a day or two saturated with that smell, you had to throw out your boots and clothes.

We got to Mrs. Chase's restaurant by mid-morning. The streets were so quiet it made us jumpy. About five feet up from the wall, a water line circled the building like a sad halo. It was deep green at the top and faded to brown closer to the sidewalk, marking the water level as the floodwater slowly receded from the neighborhood. The mix of seawater and wind had stripped the leaves from trees and sucked the green from the grass, so everything looked like a black-and-white movie. A rusting fryer basket was on its side just near the front door. Not too far away a paperback copy of the Dooky Chase cookbook, its pages swollen open and splattered with mud, lay on the sidewalk.

When the storm came, Mrs. Chase had a freezer full of gumbo and crab, the same way she had forty years earlier, when Hurricane Betsy killed eighty-one people and injured more than 17,000. Back then, with no electricity, she knew it would all go bad. But she still had gas, so she cooked up everything she had and worked with the police so she could deliver her food to people stranded in their homes. Hurricane Katrina was different. Water breached the levees and flooded her restaurant before she could blink an eye.

As we stood in front of Dooky Chase, the smell from the rotting food in her walk-in coolers mixed with the swampy, stenchy floodwater that still pooled here and there. Little flies hovered around the restaurant, swarming out of grass so gray and dry it crunched when you stepped on it. Someone had broken in and made off with the liquor and the cash register, but her precious collection of African American art had been spared, hung too high on the walls for the water to get to it and not immediately important to people looking for food, booze or cash.

"Damn," Pableaux kept saying. "Damn."

I bowed my head and said a little prayer.

OF ALL THE potentially embarrassing things I've told you so far in this book, the fact that I pray every day is the one I used to be the most sheepish about. All that drinking until I passed out? No problem. Pull up a chair and let me tell you some war stories! But confessing that I believe in God? That's much harder for me to talk about.

I'm not a big Jesus freak or anything. My prayers are pretty simple. In the morning, I might say, "OK, God, here we go." And at night, especially after a bad day, I just say, "Oh well." I ask for some direction and the power to do the next right thing. I try to open my heart up a little more so the next day will be better. I don't tell many people I do this, especially the food people who make up the bulk of my professional life. Most of the food people I've known tend to get uncomfortable if you start talking about God and prayer unless you do it with irony or nostalgia. I know I used to. You might even be getting itchy right now.

Since I started making a living writing about people who grow and cook food, I've been invited to say grace—or even just pause for a minute to thank something bigger than us—maybe a dozen times before we all started eating. That's out of thousands of professional meals, and not counting Thanksgiving or Seder or dinner at my mother's house. But if you think about it, cooking and eating require the most consistent daily acts of faith of any activity, short of going to sleep and believing you'll wake up in the morning.

Each meal contains a thousand little divine mysteries. Who figured out that some beets should be golden, some red and others colored like candy canes? What blessed entity invented sugar and cacao pods and vanilla beans or figured out that salt can preserve and brighten anything? What are we to make of a hundred little lettuces and gnarled apples with so many names you can't remember them all? Who created melons and pork fat and peanuts, for crying out loud? And what of the miracle that is cheese?

Things get more mysteriously divine if you start to think about baking. Or how oil and garlic and egg yolk can make a glimmering, thick aioli. Mixing hot stock into a cold roux so it won't make lumps or mixing cake ingredients in the right order—butter and sugar together first, then eggs, then an alternating mix of flour and milk—are but two of the grand mysteries of the kitchen we blindly believe in. And we believe because someone told us the recipes would work. And so, on faith, we tried them. And once we tried them, and we saw that they worked, we became believers even though we had no idea how they worked. We spread the word to others who then tried them on faith, too. They became believers. Entire culinary cultures have been built on this kind of faith and trust.

Maybe you want to argue that all of the magic of the kitchen can be explained away in the cold scientific light of day. It isn't God but yeast that makes bread rise. A properly braised short rib is the result of a predictable release of collagen in heated connective tissue, not some deity that believes a sticky, glistening sauce can teach us about the beauty of the human condition.

Fine. So let's move to something you can't use science to argue about. Can the cold facts of the natural world explain that magic moment that comes when everyone at the table has just settled in to eat? Or the one that comes just when the delirious rush of sharing a good meal has ended? We sit around like grinning, milk-drunk babies who've just pulled away from the breast. Laughing comes easy. People glow. Out of nowhere, you have compassion for the jerk who was bugging you before dinner, so you ask if he'd like seconds on the braised artichokes. You belong to everyone else at the table and they belong to you.

You can't create that kind of communion alone, and you can't create it without food. That one moment ought to be proof to anyone that something greater than us is at work. It's a big part of why I have faith, but it doesn't explain why I pray my ass off every day. That's because it is the only way I have figured out not to have another drink. And trust me, no one wants me to have another drink.

Still, ever since that day in Alaska when I started praying, I have fought the complete embarrassment that comes when I talk about it outside of a circle of people who feel the same way I do. I felt like it made me weak, somehow. The big intellectuals I knew would surely scoff. Opiate of the masses and all that. It didn't help that I had grown up feeling the brunt of prejudice from people who use God to argue that I and my millions of gay and lesbian brothers and sisters should have no children, no civil rights and no happy eternity. In our household, Katia is the skeptical one. She knows that my believing in God keeps me sober, and she doesn't argue with that. And sometimes, she suspects there's even more to it. Like maybe there is a higher power. "Well, I hope you're right," she'll say.

But why was I so gun-shy about talking about it openly? Why couldn't I be more like Mrs. Chase, who will tell you without a blink that God is behind her every move. In the year after Katrina, I would check in on her by phone, keeping track of how she was getting along. In every conversation, she told me straight up front and center that she prayed every day, and that she had a lot of work to do. But it would get done, she said. God would see to it.

Mrs. Chase believes in a God who has all the answers, and really wants what's best for her. This is a bold statement coming from a woman who grew up in a segregated country that would not allow her to vote or mix too much with white people. She is a woman who watched her city and Dooky Chase, the restaurant where she had been cooking for more than sixty years, drown mostly due to a greedy and corrupt government. But still she has faith. And she has the kind of faith I longed for: one that had been tested. In the ten years since my last drink, I had faced a lot of internal demons and few external ones. Maybe that was test enough. Maybe I just had to stop doubting my own experience regarding faith.

ONE STICKY MORNING nearly a year after Katrina, I went looking for Mrs. Chase. I wanted to see how the restaurant was coming along, if she thought she might reopen soon. But I was also hoping to learn more about God. I found her in her FEMA trailer, which had been set up on a side street across from Dooky Chase. The trailer was so small that her husband had to stand outside when she cooked. Mrs. Chase had an infected sore on her leg, and she had to ease herself slowly along a path made out of plywood to get from the trailer to the curb. It would have made sense for her to retire, to move into one of the refurbished houses her children owned in the neighborhood. The mold, the gouging by the contractors, the impossibility of getting her infected leg properly treated in a city where the health care system had all but collapsed—any one of those things would have made lesser women walk away.

I wanted to understand why she stuck it out, and how her faith got her through the devastation of Katrina. I wanted to see if through her story, I could find the strength to believe in my own. I asked her how she found the stamina to get back up when it all seemed so impossible. How did she not just crumble?

"The strong have feelings just like the weak, but they just don't show it," she said. Besides, she said, Katrina wasn't the worst thing that ever happened to her. She had lost a child.

Her beloved eldest daughter, Emily, her right hand and the woman most likely to carry on all the traditions and knowledge Mrs. Chase had accumulated, died giving birth to her eighth child in 1990. That child died a short time later after complications from the birth. The day after her daughter died, Mrs. Chase was scheduled to open the restaurant at eleven A.M. So she did. "I lost myself in the pots," she wrote in her memoirs. That day, I asked her why. "I could not put my sorrow on the whole world," she told me. "Life goes on, and that's what we have to understand with Katrina."

I pushed her for a better explanation. You don't come across eighty years' worth of courage very often. I needed to understand where her strength—her faith—came from. She didn't mind elaborating, using a baseball analogy.

"I tell people all the time, I think God is just like a pitcher," she said. And He apparently favors the low, slow curveball.

"It's a fun thing to see. It's a hard thing to hit," she explained. "But if you work on hitting this low, slow curve, it's going over the fence. It's going out of here. So I just think that God pitches us a low, slow curve. But He doesn't want us to strike out. I think everything he throws at you is testing your strength."

But Katrina?

"I tell you, I think I had more tears in the gumbo pot than I had gumbo," she said. "But you just cry and you just keep moving. It's not fair to put your hurt on somebody else." And then she said something remarkable. Maybe God flooded New Orleans to show man his mistakes.

"When you saw those people floating around in water, you saw every mistake you made. You had too many people in this city who couldn't fend for themselves. Where were we? Why were we not directing these people?" she said. "The levees broke on us, but we had many warnings, many times before. Why were we not checking those levees out after each warning?"

Like anyone who was there, the images from those first few days still fill her head. She says she has heard people—her own neighbors, even—say God brought his wrath down on poor black people because they weren't living right. Or, they said, God just doesn't like people of color. After all, the rich white folks in the Garden District didn't get flooded out and didn't lose their family members and their homes. But Mrs. Chase sees it differently.

"Look at it this way," she told me as we sat in a back room at Dooky Chase. "If we would have been saved on this end, and the French Quarter and all the big, beautiful homes Uptown would have been destroyed, look what a predicament we would be in. We couldn't help them up."

Maybe the rich people were saved, she said, because they had the resources to help the poor people get back on their feet. If all the rich people had been washed away, no one would have been left to help the poor.

"Don't you see how good things work? No matter how bad it is, good things work."

Even now, when I'm on the floor, feeling scraped down to bare metal, I think about what she told me. And I try to follow her prescription: "Figure out what you have to do in life and then just go to work and do it. Look at your world as a beautiful world. And it is a beautiful world. It's just your job to make it a little bit better."

I figure I can do that. I can make the world a little bit better. They say religion is for people who are afraid of hell and spirituality is for people who have been through it. Even though I haven't been through a hurricane or lost a daughter, I have had my own little trip to hell. And I know I will have more trials. When I do, like Leah Chase and millions of other people on this earth, I will pray. Without shame and with an open heart.

ON HOLY THURSDAY, I made Mrs. Chase's gumbo z'herbes. It is a dish that requires faith. All recipes do, really. You have to trust the people who came before you, who burned a few things and threw out a few bowls of bad stuff in pursuit of a perfect dish. But in my interpretation of faith, whether recipe-based or soul-based, you have to have enough inner strength to change things up if you need to. God will send the directions, but you have to take the right steps.

The dish is served on Holy Thursday because for Catholics, that's the last day you get to eat a big meal before Easter. Catholics, my mother included, wouldn't eat meat on Good Friday. Those who hewed even closer to the faith would fast altogether. So you needed a good, meaty meal on Thursday to get you through to Saturday noon, when people would start eating normally again. Some food historians tie gumbo z'herbes to the African-Caribbean dish callaloo, but there is some indication it really has its roots in the Lutherans who settled in southern Louisiana in the 1800s and made a green vegetable soup for Holy Thursdays.

There is often a point when I'm cooking a new recipe that I panic. Sometimes it's just for a second, when a sauce isn't thickening or a batter seems suspiciously thin. I often start by blaming the person who wrote the recipe, assuming they didn't tell me that I need to whisk something for an extra few minutes or they left out an essential half cup of flour. Then, quickly, I turn the blame on myself for either hurrying through a step or doing something boneheaded like adding cayenne instead of paprika. I can be easily distracted, burning toast if the breakfast conversation is just too engaging. But I am also the kind of cook who can pull herself out of the culinary shame spiral pretty quickly, bravely plowing forward and hoping that some combination of good ingredients, strong kitchen fundamentals and a well-written recipe will allow me to pull off almost any dish.

Still, it was all I could do a few days before Easter to believe the thin, murky green swamp that filled my two biggest pots was going to taste any good at all.

My kitchen in Brooklyn is kind of a puffed-up galley, with a nice back door that opens to a patio. There is enough counter space to make my friends in their tiny Chelsea apartments jealous of the setup, although those same counters elicit pity from my friends in the suburbs out West. I had plowed through Mrs. Chase's recipe, and my small kitchen told the tale. It was as if a chlorophyll bomb had gone off. The sink was covered with trimmings from nine different greens, including carrot tops, collards and kale and a half head of lettuce I had in the fridge. Cutting boards held the remnants of ham, chopped brisket and andouille, smoked dark with pecan wood. In the two big pots, water seasoned with raw garlic and onions boiled. I had made a soft, brown roux in the grease from the hot sausage, and I had simmered a ham hock to make stock. I had pureed and pureed and pureed until everything was covered in green splatters, and the pots that once held ham stock now were filled with what smelled like a swamp with hints of forest fire.

Sara Roahen, an excellent cook and writer I met in New Orleans, spent some time cooking gumbo with Mrs. Chase. She recounts the experience in her fine, sweet book *Gumbo Tales: Finding My Place at the New Orleans Table*, which she wrote before and after Katrina. I called her when I was panicked over Mrs. Chase's gumbo recipe. There are several versions floating around, in Mrs. Chase's books and others. Sara's version begins with the warning that your kitchen will be a disaster. And she was right.

There I was, with two huge pots filled with muck. The thyme and salt and cayenne tasted raw and out of balance. It was too hot, maybe, or too bitter. I hadn't used Our Holy Mother of Lowry's Seasoning Salt, one of the great saints of the New Orleans spice rack. Maybe I used the wrong greens or should have added the chicken, like Sara advised.

"I think you just have to go with it," Sara said.

She was right. I said a little prayer and called people to the table. I had faith. Turns out the gumbo was awesome. It just needed time to come together.

THIS RECIPE IS my slightly tweaked version of Sara's recipe, which is a tweaked version of Mrs. Chase's. I have tasted both Mrs. Chase's and Sara's. They are both delicious, but different. Yours will be, too. This is cooking, not an assembly line. Just have a little faith in your own skill and in the experience of the cooks who went before you. Sara says that in every cookbook where the gumbo appears, the recipe requires an odd number of greens, say five or seven or nine, for luck. Don't get too worried about that. Mrs. Chase told Sara that the connection between the kinds of greens and luck isn't really that big a deal. Just select at least seven of the greens listed, although you can use what you have. But make sure the pile of greens seems like way too much to start.

Gumbo z'Herbes

Yield: Enough for a dozen or so people to have dinner, and maybe a little left over for the freezer.

1 large or 2 small ham shanks or hocks
At least 7 varieties of the following greens:
    1 bunch greens, either mustard, collard or turnip or a combination of all three
    1 bag fresh spinach or a box of frozen
    1 small head cabbage
    1 bunch carrot tops
    1 bunch beet tops
    1 bunch arugula
    1 bunch parsley
    1 bunch green onions
    1 bunch watercress
    1 head romaine or other lettuce
    1 head curly endive
    1 bunch kale
    1 bunch radish tops
3 medium yellow onions, roughly chopped
½ head garlic, peeled, cloves kept whole
2 pounds fresh hot sausage (a local sausage called chaurice is best, but hot Italian without fennel works well)
1 pound andouille sausage
1 pound smoked pork sausage
½ pound ham
1 pound beef stew meat
1 cup flour
Vegetable oil as needed

3 teaspoons dried thyme

2 teaspoons cayenne pepper

3 bay leaves

Salt to taste

2 cups cooked white rice

½ teaspoon filé powder (optional)

1. Place ham shanks or hocks in a large, heavy stockpot. Fill the pot with water and bring to a boil; reduce heat and simmer while you prepare the other ingredients.

2. Wash all greens thoroughly in salt water, making sure to remove any grit, discolored outer leaves, and tough stems. Rinse in a bath of unsalted water (a clean double sink works well for this).

3. Place half the greens, half the onions, and half the garlic in a heavy-bottomed stockpot or 3 to 4 gallon saucepan. Cover greens and vegetables with water and bring to a boil over high heat; reduce heat to a simmer and cook for 20 to 30 minutes, until greens are very tender. When they finish cooking, transfer them to a large bowl, using a slotted spoon, to cool. Repeat the process with the remaining greens, onions and garlic, doing it in two or three batches if necessary.

4. When all the greens have finished cooking, reserve the cooking liquid.

5. Place the fresh hot sausage in a skillet or medium-size saucepan and set over medium heat. Cook until rendered of fat and moisture. Remove the hot sausage with a slotted spoon and set aside. Reserve the fat.

6. While the hot sausage is cooking, cut the andouille and smoked sausage into ½-inch rounds and set aside. Cut the ham and the beef stew meat into ½-inch pieces and set aside.

7. In a meat grinder or a food processor, grind the greens, onion and garlic into a puree, adding cooking liquid to prevent the greens from getting too thick. Do this in batches.

8. Remove the ham shanks from their cooking liquid, reserving the liquid for stock. Once the shanks cool, pick and chop the meat and set it aside; discard the bones and the fat.

9. Pour the greens cooking liquid and ham stock into separate bowls. Using your largest pot, or the two stockpots in which you simmered the greens and the ham, mix everything together. (Divide the pureed greens, the sausages, the beef and the chopped ham equally between the two pots, if using two pots.)

10. Fill the pot or pots with equal parts ham stock and greens cooking liquid and bring to a simmer over medium-high heat.

11. Heat the skillet containing the hot sausage drippings over medium-high heat. With a wooden spoon, slowly but intently stir in the flour until well combined. If the mixture is very dry, add vegetable oil until it loosens some, making a tight paste that's still able to be stirred.

12. Continue to cook until the flour mixture begins to darken, stirring constantly. As Sara notes, you aren't going for a dark roux, but you do want the flour to cook. Courage is the key here. Don't be afraid to let it get dark.

13. When darkened and cooked, divide the roux between the two stockpots or put it into the single pot, dropping it in by spoonfuls and whisking to make sure that each is well incorporated.

14. Add thyme, cayenne, bay leaves and salt to taste.

15. Simmer for about an hour, or until the stew meat is tender, stirring quite often. Add more stock or water if it appears too thick.

16. Serve over white rice.

NOTE: *Filé in its pure form is a bright green powder made from pounded sassafras leaves. The Creoles and Cajuns picked it up from the Choctaw Indians, and used it as a spice and a thickener in the winter when okra wasn't available. If you like it, add it slowly at the end of cooking or even stir it into your own bowl at the table. Sara reports that Mrs. Chase told her, "It'll lump up on you" if you're not careful. Mrs. Chase's father used to grind sassafras leaves for her, and she told Sara that Creoles always add filé to their gumbo z'herbes, even if few cookbook recipes call for it.*

The Last Gourmet Supper

By Marisa Robertson-Textor

From fastertimes.com

Last fall, the sudden demise of *Gourmet* magazine sent a
seismic shock throughout the food world. Of all the obituaries
written for this iconic food magazine, perhaps the most
poignant was this insider memory, written by one of the
magazine's newest staffers.

Here's a dilemma: How do you have your Thanksgiving
and eat it too? For me, the answer is to celebrate early,
then head for warmer climes over the holiday itself. Imagine it: all
your friends clamoring to join you at a family-style banquet without family-style irritations. There's no getting stuck at the kids'
table. No Cool Whip. And most definitely no football. It's Thanksgiving for the Thanksgiving-lover—in a word, bliss.

But that bliss, officially known as Gobble Gobble Night, never
would have been achieved without *Gourmet* magazine. When I
started fact-checking there five years ago, I was just another girl
who loved to cook and thought she was pretty darn good at it—
when she thought about it at all. During my first week, between
making phone calls to price-check hotels in Rome and sending
e-mails to establish the precise differences in aging techniques between tawny, ruby, and non-vintage Ports, I wandered the magazine's mazelike hallways feeling like the youngest ensign assigned
to the Starship Enterprise. "Yes, but do you really braise it?" I'd
hear a senior food editor ask with the sort of concern I'd always associated with questions along the lines of, "Okay, but was it be-

nign?" I had thought I loved food—thought I knew it—but clearly I didn't. Not at all.

To say that working at the magazine fed my culinary knowledge is like saying that going to elementary school endows you with a love of literature. In an ideal world, yes; but first you need to learn to read. There are disadvantages to being surrounded by professors when you're a fumbling fourth grader, but the advantages—like that particular brand of ferocious generosity one only encounters in chefs—more than compensate. And you never know where that generosity might lead you. Back in the fall of 2006, during a discussion of the best turkey roasting methods with my colleague Lillian, I told her about my vision for a best-of-all-possible-worlds Thanksgiving. "Come with me," she said promptly. "I have something for you." It turned out there was an extra Bell & Evans bird down in the test kitchen. Did I want it? I did. But that was only the beginning. "You need aromatics," Lillian announced firmly, passing me several freezer bags packed with vegetable parings. "Wait, where are you going? Don't forget the turkey stock." One grocery bag was filled, then another. What ensign wouldn't seize the helm?

That first Gobble night was too much of everything: food, labor, stress. Everything, that is, except space—my modest dining room couldn't accommodate fifteen guests. "Could. Not. Eat," says my brother, Alex, when he remembers that evening, gritting his teeth like a superhero whose powers are being taxed beyond measure. "No. Room. On. Table. For. Plate." But the food, oh, the food! People still reminisce over the butternut squash and creamed-spinach gratin. It should have taken me 1¼ hours to prepare—and as the person who fact-checked that recipe, you might say I had a moral obligation to clock in at under 75 minutes—but just slicing the squash into ribbons took me almost twice that long. Then again, what was two hours? Planning the menu, scouring a dozen Brooklyn markets for ingredients, set up, clean up, not to mention the cooking itself—a good week of my life went into that first dinner. Like any Herculean endeavor, it didn't seem worth it. But then, after the final guest departed and the final dish was put away, came the afterglow.

By the following year, I was proficient enough in the language of the recipes not simply to follow the instructions, but to anticipate them: which vegetable would enter the pot next, when a hot liquid needed to cool off slightly before being incorporated into the remaining ingredients. That increased facility, combined with a Greek chorus of admonishments from the food editors—"Trust me, you don't need five vegetable sides." "Don't bother flavoring the whipped cream." "Outsource!"—made the second dinner far less demanding than its predecessor. (Although I realized I might have taken the outsourcing thing too far when my friend Daniel and his pals from Stockholm heroically carted six chairs and two enormous pots of caramelized-garlic mashed potatoes all the way from the West Village.) But these tactical advances—including turning my bedroom, the largest room in the apartment, into a makeshift dining room—didn't preclude new errors. Reasoning that I'd have more prep time if I held the dinner on a Sunday night, it never occurred to me that at 4 am Monday morning I'd still be in the kitchen, grimly rinsing pans.

Last year the guest list reached 25 people, but by that point the ritual was so familiar that it didn't occur to me to panic. And, in fact, there was only one tiny snag. Picking up my pre-ordered foie gras from a local shop the morning of the dinner, I realized I'd procured exactly that: a naked lobe of foie gras requiring hours of deveining, prepping, and seasoning. (If any of my friends noticed that their toasts with Sauternes gelée were in fact topped with chicken-liver mousse, they were kind enough not to mention it. Of course, some of them might have been relieved.) In the eternal dinner party battle between the immovable object of logistics and the irresistible force of pleasure, pleasure had triumphed. As I looked at my friends, their faces limned in gold by the flickering candlelight, something settled inside me. I had this night. I had them. And the unspoken corollary—the thing I didn't bother thinking about, because by now it was as natural as breathing—was that I had *Gourmet*.

This September, when it came time to fact-check the Thanksgiving menus for the November issue, it took me just minutes to pick my favorites: roast turkey with cream gravy, bacon smashed potatoes, pumpkin gingerbread trifle. Perfect. What I didn't realize—what I still haven't quite realized—is that I was working on the last issue of Gourmet ever. Next Thanksgiving, as cooks across the country don their aprons, for the first time since before America entered World War II, the magazine won't be around to help.

How does one mourn the loss of a cultural institution? It is a death, to be sure, but the grief is more amorphous, less straightforward, than what you feel for a person. It's like passing by your childhood home, now in a strange family's hands; like finding out that the library where you whiled away your adolescence has been torn down. Something you loved dearly is gone forever, and it is beyond your power to get it back. Yesterday, you were part of 69 years of collective wisdom; today, you are meeting with HR; tomorrow, you are once again just another unemployed thirtysomething with a passion for food. Ensign, where's your ship?

The only possible answer to that question lies in action. You've lost *Gourmet*. What do you do? You cook, of course. You start small, with the dishes you've made so often you know them almost as well as their creators: Gina's seven-layer salmon bites, Paul's egg salad with fennel and lemon, Maggie's chocolate babka. Then, when you're ready, you slowly leaf through all your old issues, recalling not just the dishes you made but—more important—all the ones you had once planned to make. All the phantom culinary visions that, unlike Gobble Gobble Night, were never realized. Remember that snowy Sunday in February when you were too sleepy to bother with the coffee-glazed doughnuts? Or how you gave up on preparing the Danish menu from the March 2007 issue because you couldn't find five dinner guests who, like you, were part Danish? You didn't do it then, but dammit, you're doing it now. You're tackling all the things that frustrate you, the things you're still terrible at, like pastry dough and anything involving a mandoline. Because while it's true that, having lived with *Gourmet*, you're now in a better position to live without it, there's a more enduring truth. You just don't want to.

RECIPE INDEX

PERMISSIONS ACKNOWLEDGMENTS

Grateful acknowledgment is made to all those who gave permission for written material to appear in this book. Every effort has been made to trace and contact copyright holders. If an error or omission is brought to our notice, we will be pleased to remedy the situation in subsequent editions of this book. For further information, please contact the publisher.

"The FedEx Meal Plan" by Brett Martin. Copyright © 2009 by Brett Martin. Reprinted by permission of the author. Originally appeared in GQ, November, 2009.

"Forgotten Fruits" by Gary Paul Nabhan. Copyright © 2009 by Gary Paul Nabhan. Used by permission of the author. Originally appeared in *Saveur*, October, 2009.

"And You Will Know Us By the Trail of German Butterballs" by Jonathan Kauffman. Copyright © 2009 by Village Voice Media. Used by permission of Village Voice Media. Originally appeared in *Seattle Weekly* on July 1, 2009.

"Soul Food" by Amanda M. Faison. Copyright © 2010 by *5280: Denver's Magazine*. Used by permission of the author. Originally appeared in *5280: Denver's Magazine*, April, 2010.

"The Need for Custom Slaughter" by Barry Estabrook. Copyright © 2010 by Barry Estabrook. Used by permission of the author. Originally appeared on politicsoftheplate.com, January 20, 2010.

Excerpt from the book *Eating Animals* by Jonathan Safran-Foer. First published in *The New York Times Magazine*, copyright © 2009 by Jonathan Safran-Foer. Reprinted with permission of Little, Brown and Company. All rights reserved.

"Attack of the Anti-Meat Crusaders!" by Lessley Anderson. Copyright © 2010 by Lessley Anderson. Used by permission of the author. Originally appeared on chow.com on January 15, 2010.

"Dear Zagat: A Hearty Thanks for Your 30 Years of Service. Now Go Away." by Tim Carman. Copyright © 2009 by *Washington City Paper*. Used by permission of *Washington City Paper*. Originally appeared in *Washington City Paper*, September 18, 2009.

"El Bulli Gets Bested" by Carla Capalbo. Copyright © 2010 by Carla Capalbo. Reprinted by permission of the author. Originally appeared on zesterdaily.com, June 1, 2010.

peared in *The Daily Gullet*, the literary magazine of the eGullet Society of Culinary Arts & Letters at eGullet.org., May 17, 2010.

"The Juicy Secret to Seasoning Meat" by Oliver Strand. Copyright © 2009 by Oliver Strand. Used by permission of the author. Originally appeared in *Food & Wine*, July, 2009.

"Feed It or It Dies" from *52 Loaves* by William Alexander. © 2010 by William Alexander. Reprinted by permission of Algonquin Books of Chapel Hill. All rights reserved.

"How to Make Perfect Thin and Crisp French Fries" by J. Kenji Lopez-Alt. Copyright © 2010 by J. Kenji Lopez-Alt. Used by permission of the author. Originally appeared on seriouseats.com, May 28, 2010.

"Rather Special and Strangely Popular: A Milk Toast Exemplary" by John Thorne. Copyright © 2009 by John Thorne. Used by permission of the author.

"What's the Recipe" by Adam Gopnik. Copyright © 2009 by Adam Gopnik. Reprinted by permission of the author. Originally appeared in *The New Yorker*, November 23, 2009.

"My Inner Child" by Charlotte Freeman. Copyright © 2009 by Culinate, Inc.. Reprinted by permission of the Culinate, Inc. Originally appeared on culinate.com, December 29, 2009.

"People of the Cake" by Diane Roberts. Copyright © 2010 by Diane Roberts. Reprinted by permission of the author. Originally appeared in *The Oxford American*, April, 2010.

"Yancey's Red Hots" by Wright Thompson. Copyright © 2010 by Wright Thompson. Reprinted by permission of the author. Originally appeared in *The Oxford American*, April, 2010.

"Computers or Cookbooks in the Kitchen?" by David Leite and Renee Schettler. Copyright © 2010 by David Leite and Renee Schettler. Reprinted by permission of the authors. Originally appeared on leitesculinaria.com, March 15, 2010.

"Does a Recipe Need to Be Complicated to Be Good?" by Monica Bhide. Copyright © 2010 by Monica Bhide. Used by permission of the author. Originally appeared on monicabhide.com, March 28, 2010.

"Chapter 18" from *Farm City: The Education of an Urban Farmer* by Novella Carpenter and Willow Rosenthal, copyright © 2009 by Novella Carpenter and Willow Rosenthal. Used by permission of The Penguin Press, a division of Penguin Group (USA) Inc.

"A Glutton for Gluten" by Jess Thomson. Copyright © 2010 by Jess Thomsen. Reprinted by permission of the author. Originally appeared on leitesculinaria.com, April 5, 2010.

ABOUT THE EDITOR

HOLLY HUGHES is a writer, the former executive editor of Fodor's Travel Publications, and author of *Frommer's 500 Places to Take the Kids Before They Grow Up*, *Frommer's 500 Places to See Before They Disappear*, and *Frommer's 500 Places for Food and Wine Lovers*.

SUBMISSIONS FOR
BEST FOOD WRITING 2011

Submissions and nominations for *Best Food Writing 2011* should be forwarded no later than May 15, 2011, to Holly Hughes at *Best Food Writing 2011*, c/o Da Capo Press, 11 Cambridge Center, Cambridge, MA 02142, or emailed to best.food@perseusbooks.com. We regret that, due to volume, we cannot acknowledge receipt of all submissions.